A Conceptual Approach to Social Impact Assessment

Collection of Writings by Rabel J. Burdge and Colleagues

Rabel J. Burdge

Social Ecology Press
Middleton • Wisconsin

Burdge, Rabel J.
    A conceptual approach to social impact assessment : collection
of writings by Rabel J. Burdge and colleagues / by Rabel J. Burdge.
    p. cm.
    Includes bibliographical references.
    Preassigned LCCN: 93-087341.
    ISBN 0-941042-16-2

    1. Social indicators. 2. Technological innovations--Social
aspects--Evaluation. 3. Social prediction.   I. Title.

HN25.S57 1983   303.4'83
                                       QBI94-680

Social Ecology Press™
P.O. Box 620863
Middleton, Wisconsin 53562-0863

Printed in the United States of America

10 9 8 7 6 5 4 3 2 1

TABLE OF CONTENTS

INTRODUCTION

i

CASE STUDIES IN SOCIAL IMPACT ASSESSMENT

PUBLIC INVOLVEMENT AND SOCIAL IMPACT ASSESSMENT

SOCIAL IMPACT ASSESSMENT IN AN INTERNATIONAL CONTEXT

LIST OF FIGURES

LIST OF TABLES

PREFACE

Social impact assessment emerged in the early 1970s as an applied social science field in response to the need to understand the impacts on human populations of natural resource developments and environmental policy alternatives. The impetus was the passing of the 1970 National Environmental Policy Act (NEPA) by the U.S. Congress. The first meeting of practitioners and academics on social impact assessment was convened by C. P. Wolf, in the fall of 1973, at the annual meeting of Environmental Design Research Associates (EDRA) held in Milwaukee, Wisconsin. Sue Johnson and Rabel Burdge presented the paper; *Social Impact Assessment: A Tentative Approach* (Chapter 2) at that first meeting. Twenty years later, in the Spring of 1994, the Interorganizational Committee on Guidelines and Principals for Social Impact Assessment published *Guidelines and Principals for Social Impact Assessment* (Chapter 9). That committee included representatives from the Rural Sociological Society, the American Psychological Association, the American Sociological Association, the American Anthropological Association, the Society for Applied Anthropology, the American Agricultural Economics Association, and the International Association for Impact Assessment. The other eighteen (18) chapters in this book represent the contribution of the author and his colleagues to the development of social impact assessment in the intervening twenty years.

By the mid-1990s, social impact assessment was a recognized sub-field of the social science disciplines of sociology, geography, political science, anthropology, psychology and the planning arts. SIA is now an integral part of integrated environmental management and the importance of public involvement as a component of social impact assessment is recognized by planners and legislators alike.

Organization of the Book

Introduction—Chapter one traces the history of social impact assessment and how the field has developed as a research, planning and policy field — both independently and within the context of environmental impact assessment.

Development of a Social Impact Assessment Model—Chapters 2 through 5 describe the evolution of the social impact assessment model first outlined in the early 1970s by Sue Johnson and Rabel Burdge as a conceptual framework for studying the impacts of reservoir construction on human populations. This section begins with the introduction of the comparative diachronic model and ends with a discussion of 26 social impact assessment variables used to understand the social impacts of development and community change. Each chapter builds on the previous one as the author details the evolution of a comparative model of social impact assessment. The SIA framework may be used to organize research findings and as a guide for practitioners who want to understand and do SIAs in the context of the planning and environmental assessment process.

The Methodology of Social Impact Assessment—Chapters 6 through 10 outline the key concepts both for the study of and the practice of social impact assessment. Chapter six is a critical analysis of the place of the social scientist in doing interdisciplinary environmental impact assessment. Chapters 7 and 8 outline the conceptual and empirical components of a social impact assessment and a broader framework within which the social scientist finds theoretical direction for the study of impact assessment. Chapter 9 reports the work of the interorganizational committee which developed the monograph; *Guidelines and Principles for Social Impact Assessment.* The methodology section concludes with a suggested outline for a university level course on social impact assessment.

Case Studies in Social Impact Assessment—Chapter 10 is an historical analysis of how one remote Alaskan community adjusted to the boom-bust cycle of development over a period of 100 years. Chapter 11 summarizes key findings of an interdisciplinary study of the Lake Shelbyville reservoir. That investigation was an attempt to determine if the impacts predicted in the initial environmental impact statement—in fact happened. Chapter 13 reports on the successes and failures of an interdisciplinary environmental assessment research team charged with evaluating the social, economic and bio-physical impacts of reservoir construction.

Public Involvement and Social Impact Assessment—Public involvement is a central and continuing component of the EIA-SIA process. Chapter 14 defines public involvement (PI) in the context of social impact assessment and outlines procedures for incorporating PI into the NEPA process. Chapters 15 and 16 describe important needs assessment and public involvement techniques which may be used in the SIA process. This section concludes with an analysis of the public involvement program developed by the U.S. Bureau of Land Management to involve their diverse publics in the evaluation of land management alternatives.

Social Impact Assessment in an International Context—The last chapters apply the concepts and techniques of social impact assessment to areas outside of North America. Chapter 18 outlines the institutional and cultural constraints to the use of the EIA-SIA procedures in Third World settings. Chapter 19 points out the benefits of SIA and some suggestions which might lead to successful implementation in project evaluation. The last chapter outlines the importance of and methods for integrating social, environmental, risk, technology and health assessment into the planning process.

Acknowledgements

Those individuals listed as co-authors for the contributed chapters have devoted much of their career to the development and implementation of social impact assessment. The practice of social impact assessment and the social science community is indeed grateful for their efforts. Of those colleagues, four have been particularly important to my career. Sue Johnson, wherever she may be, originated the ideas behind the comparative diachronic model and first recognized the possibilities for the social scientist under the NEPA legislation. William R. Burch Jr., of Yale University, is a latter day Aldo Leopold. He understands and is able to articulate the historical participation of humans in the ecosystem. Roy Rickson is one of the few scholars who has successfully organized the findings of social impact assessment within the context of sociological theory. Donald R. Field, of the University of Wisconsin, is one environmental sociologist who recognized that to succeed an emerging discipline needs an infrastructure of publications, professional organizations as well as a following among practitioners. He has devoted his career to developing the scientific support for environmental and natural resource sociology.

Kathy Reeves of the Institute for Environmental Studies typed the many drafts of this book as well as the revisions of the monograph; *Guidelines and Principles for Social Impact Assessment*. I am truly appreciative of her dedication over the last three years. Tori Corkery did the formatting and layout for this book.

Rabel J. Burdge,
April 15, 1994
University of Illinois
Urbana, Illinois
USA

INTRODUCTION

Chapter 1

A BRIEF HISTORY AND MAJOR TRENDS IN THE FIELD OF IMPACT ASSESSMENT[1]

Rabel J. Burdge

A HISTORY OF IMPACT ASSESSMENT

The U.S. President, Richard Nixon, signed the National Environmental Policy Act of 1969 (NEPA) on December 31, 1969. Under that law, proponents of development projects and policies that involved U.S. federal land, federal tax dollars or federal jurisdictions were required to file an environmental impact statement (EIS) detailing the impacts of the proposal, as well as project alternatives, on the physical, cultural and human environments. The NEPA legislation also required mitigation measures for impacts and a monitoring program to ensure that mitigation was actually working (NEPA, 1970). Very few members of Congress, the industrial development community, the environmentalists, or indeed Nixon himself, foresaw how the new law would change the way the world community looked at environment issues and development projects. Henry "Scoop" Jackson, the late Senator from the State of Washington, was responsible for including the "triggering mechanism" in the NEPA legislation, which required an Environmental Impact Assessment (EIA) if Federal land, laws or monies were involved. The inclusion of the triggering mechanism was a unique legislative requirement and ensured that EIS statements would be written.

Figure 1-1 shows a chronology of the key events in the history of impact assessment, particularly in North America. In February, 1970, the Bureau of Land Management in the U.S. Department of the Interior submitted a eight-page EIS statement to accompany the application for the Trans-Alaska pipeline permit. Two days later the Wilderness Society, the Friends of the Earth and the Environmental Defense Fund filed suit contending that the EIS statement was inadequate because it did not consider what pumping hot oil through a pipe laying on the ground would do to the permafrost. In addition, no provision was made for a disruption of the annual migration of several caribou herds due to the pipeline and the road that was to be built beside it. Although not specifically mentioned in the litigation, some observers wondered where all those construction workers and their families would be housed who came North to work on the pipeline (Dixon 1978:3).

Three years later the permit to build the pipeline was issued. In the meantime, the EIS statement had grown from eight pages to eight feet. More importantly, most of the potential environmental problems had been addressed to the satisfaction of the

[1]Abridged from the original. Rabel J. Burdge. 1991. A Brief History and Major Trends in the Field of Impact Assessment. *Impact Assessment Bulletin*, 9(2): 93-104. Reproduced here with permission of the author and the publisher.

courts, the plaintiffs and the Alyeska Pipeline Company (a collection of U.S. and Canadian oil companies that owned leases on Prudhoe Bay). Anticipatory planning had worked and all sides agreed that the NEPA (National Environmental Policy Act) process had allowed project proponents to deal with issues that might otherwise have been overlooked. Until the Exxon Valdez set sail on Prince William Sound in 1990, no unforeseen environmental damage could be traced to pipeline activity. After the decision to build the pipeline was made, one of the Inuit Chiefs made the following comment ...now that we have dealt with the problem of the permafrost and the caribou and what to do with hot oil, what about changes in the customs and ways of my people...(Dixon 1978:4).

Unfortunately, as the Inuit chief pointed out, the social impacts on both the indigenous and other Alaskan populations were never addressed. Would the traditional cultures and way of life be changed by so massive of a construction project? What about the influx of construction workers that spoke a different dialectic (of English) and brought a distinctive life style with them? Obviously, with a total population of 300,000 (in 1973) the State of Alaska could provide only a fraction of the estimated 42,000 persons that would work on the pipeline during the periods of peak construction. Because of these and other related events the impacts of development on the human populations began to be discussed alongside bio-physical and economic alterations (Dixon 1978:8). The term social impact assessment (SIA) was first used in 1973 to refer to the changes in the indigenous Inuit culture due to the pipeline.

One of the key events in establishing the importance of social impact assessment in project appraisal was the inquiry regarding the Mackenzie Valley pipeline. Between 1974 and 1978, Justice T.R. Berger of the British Columbia Supreme Court, conducted an extensive inquiry into the proposed pipeline from Mackenzie Bay in the Beaufort Sea along the Richardson Mountains with connections to pipelines in British Columbia and Alberta (Gamble 1978 and Berger 1983). Although proposed by Canadian oil companies, the money to build it came from the U.S., because the gas and oil would end up in the Chicago market. The inquiry was important because social impacts on the native populations were considered in depth. Furthermore, native populations were provided money to present their views and the hearings were conducted in the native villages in the local dialect.

The founding of the International Association for Impact Assessment in 1981 provided an international forum for persons interested in research and the practice of EIS, SIA, technological assessment and other types of assessments. A year later, IAIA published a journal titled *Impact Assessment Bulletin*, which provides an outlet for academics and practitioners to review the state of the art of impact assessment and related fields.

By 1983, most U.S. federal agencies had formalized environmental and social impact assessment procedures in agency regulations. The social impact variables listed for assessment were included under the label of *socio-economic* impacts.

The European Economic Community began to recommend environmental impact statements for their members in 1985, and by 1989 the recommendation became a requirement. The event is significant, not only because of the diversity of language and culture involved, but because it was becoming apparent that the British approach to towne planning could not adequately deal with environmental problems.

An equally important event happened in 1986 when the World Bank made a public commitment to include environmental impact assessment in their project appraisal process. The event was important because the requirement represented a split with the Reagan Administration policy of minimizing environmental assessment. By now it was obvious that many Bank funded projects were failing due to environmental problems and a lack of fit with the social and cultural milieu of the project communities. Taking their cue from the World Bank, regional donor and lending institutions began to incorporate environmental and social impact assessment into their project appraisal procedures.

The decision of the World Bank was further reinforced by publication in 1987 of *Our Common Future* by the United Nations Committee on Environment and Development. Commonly known as the Brundtland Report, the recommendations on sustainability received wide acceptance outside the United States and further accelerated the interest in environmental and social impact assessment. The need for impact assessment was enhanced by a continued string of environmental disasters due primarily to the lack of prior planning. Decision makers within many governments and donor agencies were turning away from narrow economic criteria in project evaluation and instead opting for an emphasis on long-run ecosystem sustainability. Social and environmental impact assessment provided the framework with which to conduct such evaluations.

OBSERVATIONS ON TRENDS IN EIA AND SIA

Social and environmental impact assessment have permanently altered the way we look at and think about project planning and appraisal and development in general. The key to the NEPA legislation was anticipatory change. The major benefit was that many bad projects were never proposed or at least were stalled, because the consequences of the development on the human and bio-physical environment were not previously considered in the planning stage.

Important Consequences of EIA-SIA Legislation

The 70s was the decade in which the largest number of EIA statements were completed. By the end of that time, agreement had been reached on the components of the statements, and we began to observe the long run importance of the NEPA process.

1. The process changed policy makers thinking about the benefits of pre-planning (although in most cases only a little bit). This change was particularly true for engineers and others from technical backgrounds.

2. As environmental planning before the event became more accepted, officials in more development-oriented agencies and ministries saw the process as stopping or slowing economic development. However, the string of environmental disasters resulting from decisions made on narrow technical and economic data reinforced the need for environmental and social assessment in the very early stages of the planning process.

3. The NEPA process initiated a more general movement to examine other development and policy settings on an ex-ante basis. Knowledge gained in a variety of development settings made it possible to understand and predict future development

Figure 1.1
Key Events in The History of Environmental and Social Impact Assessment

1970	Passage of NEPA (last day of 1969)
1970	1st Earth Day, April 22nd
1970	Suit filed against Alyeska Pipeline Company and Department of the Interior over the EIS prepared for the permit allowing construction of the Trans-Alaska Pipeline
1971-1976	Expansion of NEPA style legislation into 23 U.S. States
1970-1973	Initial attempts to prepare Environmental Impact Statements by the U.S. Army Corps of Engineers
1970-1976	Courts clarify the requirements of EIA and SIA
1973	Council on Environmental Quality (CEQ) issues guidelines for the preparation of environmental impact statements
1973	Environmental Assessment and Review Process (EARP) established in Canada (amended in 1977)
1974	Beginning of Berger Inquiry regarding the proposed Mackenzie Valley Pipeline from the Beauford Sea to connections in British Columbia and Alberta
1974	EDRA-1 Environmental Design Research Associates meet in Milwaukee, Wisconsin-first professional meeting on EIA
1978	Final CEQ Guidelines issued for preparation of environmental impact statements
1980	*Environmental Impact Assessment Review* - first issue
1981	International Association for Impact Assessment founded in Toronto at the 1981 meeting of the American Association for the Advancement of Science (AAAS)
1981	Reagan Administration reduces funding for the Council on Environmental Quality which oversees the NEPA process
1982	First International Social Impact Assessment Conference in Vancouver, B.C.
1983	Most U.S. federal agencies develop regulations for environmental and social impact assessment
1986	World Bank requires social and environmental impact assessment for all development projects
1987	*Our Common Future* (the Brundtland Commission report published)
1989	European Economic Community requires environmental impact assessment for member countries
1991	International Association for Impact Assessment holds tenth annual meeting (IAIA '91)
1992	Earth Summit in Rio de Janeiro, Brazil
1993	U.S. Council on Environmental Quality considers Social Impact Assessment Guidelines and Principles
1994	Environmental Assessment Summit in Quebec City, Canada

events by looking at past events. It was found that planning based on previous social science research allowed for better prediction of future events.

4. Research on the types and frequency of exposure risks has made health effects an important part of the assessment process. The continued interest by the World Health Organization (WHO) in environmental assessment is an indication of this trend.

Tentative Agreement on Content of the Bio-Physical Impact Assessment Statement

1. By the early 80s, most researchers and practitioners had agreed upon the ecological, biological and physical components of an EIA. Federally subsidized water related research in the 60s provided a good theoretical and empirical basis for organizing impact statements because impoundments and diversion projects were large scale and resulted in massive alterations to the physical environment. By the late 70s and the 80s that research effort spread to health and human impacts.

2. Research funds for ex-post facto studies in the field of bio-physical impact assessment were reduced in the late 70s and 80s in the U.S. The result was a slowing of the accumulation of data that could have been added to the storehouse of knowledge about future impacts.

3. However, just as funding looked bleak, the emergence in the late 80s of bio-sustainability as a research topic provided an opportunity to extend impact assessment research to biological and conservation issues.

Lack of Integration of EIA-SIA into the Planning Process

The failure to include environmental assessment in the planning process is a classic case of *who's to blame*. The *Impact Assessment Bulletin* (1990) devoted two issues to analyzing the problem and suggesting some remedies.

1. The first problem, which is only now being overcome, is that EIS and SIA statements were seldom prepared by planners or those trained in the planning process. Because EIAs were generally completed by the project proponent, engineering and architectural consulting firms were the first to shape the content of the statements.

2. However, the engineers were not the only unprepared profession; the city and regional planners systematically ignored environmental issues and information in the planning process. Trained in land use allocation and aesthetics, the planning profession had little experience in incorporating environmental and social concerns into the planning process.

3. The traditional British Towne Planning System was very useful in land use allocation and preservation decisions and in allowing public comment during the decision period. However, the British approach does not specifically include an environmental component. The integration of EIA-SIA into the planning process has been slowed because many countries that used the British system assumed that environmental concerns would be accounted for through that process. The recent decision by the European Community to require EIA is an indication of dissatisfaction with the traditional planning process.

4. However, if the goal of integrating EIA-SIA into the planning process is achieved, another potential problem surfaces. How is a mitigation plan developed and who is responsible for implementing a long-term monitoring program?

Rediscovery of the EIA-SIA Process

The time worn phrase "reinventing the wheel," probably applies more to impact assessment than any other type of planning activity. Persons attending the annual meeting of IAIA have every range of experience—from new persons in agencies assigned to do impact assessment to those who have devoted their life to practicing and promoting the field.

1. The first problem is the continued shifting of ministries and agencies in both federal and provincial governments charged with implementation of impact assessment. For example, under the parliamentary form of government, ministerial portfolios often change with each new government, thereby creating confusion as to which ministry is responsible for environmental assessment.

2. Also, there appears to be a constant shift in personal actually responsible for administration and supervision of the EIA-SIA process. Rather than seeking people with experience, assessment responsibilities are given to the lowest paid and the most recent additions to the agency. In the U.S., the SIA positions are often used to fill affirmative action quotas.

3. Another problem is that the content of the impact statements, to include the findings and the procedures, seldom make there way into the scientific literature. Persons in consulting firms and government agencies who prepare EIA and SIA statements do not receive credit for writing up their findings and experiences for research publications. While EIA-SIA documents are not intended to be research, they do represent any important source of knowledge about the types of impacts that occur in different project settings. An *EIS Digest* first appeared in the early 70s, however, it ceased publication when the numbers of EIAs in the U.S. began to decline.

4. The field of impact assessment does not have a series of agreed upon concepts or list of variables around which to accumulate research knowledge. The problem is particularly acute for the field of social impact assessment and when EIA and SIA statements are used as the basis for environmental policy analysis. Academics and practitioners of social impact assessment need to reach some tentative agreement on concepts, procedure and content.

5. When planning departments begin to offer courses in EIA and SIA, the practitioners must be consulted. At present, these courses focus on either compliance with the letter of regulations or the spirit of the NEPA process and that environmental concerns should always be considered in the planning process.

Project or *Policy* Level?

Problems in establishing the boundaries of an impact assessment have made it difficult to generalize the findings and communicate the results to policy makers. The geo-political boundaries of the assessment delineate the range of data collection and the location to which impact events may be projected. In general, the bio-physical and social impacts are most observable and can be measured at the project or community level. The economic benefits of a project generally occur and can only be measured at the regional or national level. Research knowledge about bio-physical and social impacts has accumulated at the project level making it difficult to generalize these findings to a regional or national level.

Another boundary problem is how to attribute social impacts at the community or local level resulting from a decision made or an event occurring in a different part of the world. For example, what would be the social impacts of bringing 36-channel satellite television to the indigenous populations of Alaska and the Yukon and Northwest territories? If a worldwide embargo continues on elephant tusks, how will that policy influence game management practices in the southern countries of Africa?

The Role of an International Association (IAIA)
of Professionals in Integrated Environmental Management

The practitioners and bureaucrats in the fields of impact assessment must put more emphasis on monitoring, post-impact evaluation, mitigation procedures, and cumulative effects. More attention must be given to the question of how to weigh the significance of different environmental, social, and economic effects in the decision process? IAIA, as an organization of practitioners and professionals, can assist in addressing these issues.

1. First the organization must continue the networking function by expanding their publications to include items of immediate interest to the profession; continue to provide opportunities to purchase journals, bulletins and books which report the latest research in the field; officially sponsor and promote new titles in an EIA-SIA book series; in cooperation with interested organizations and offer professional training programs during the annual meeting; and finally to include the interest areas of members in the directory.

2. Encourage the formation of, provide support for and eventually affiliate with regional and national organizations in impact assessment. Examples of such organizations include the Environmental Institute of Australia, the Institute for Social Impact Assessment in Canada and the Association for Social Assessment in New Zealand. IAIA now has affiliated chapters in South Africa, Quebec, and Ontario, Brazil and Europe.

3. Encourage the formation of topical and content interest groups within IAIA. These interest groups would then be allocated program space at the annual meeting.

4. Develop, maintain and publish a worldwide directory of federal, provincial, state and municipal ministries and agencies responsible for and/or conduct all types of impact assessment.

5. Both Canada and New Zealand are attempting to implement legislation which would include the basic components of environmental and social impact assessment within the larger context of integrated environmental and project management. These proposals see impact assessment as but one component of an overall goal to achieve sustainability by including environmental concerns along with economic analysis in the decision process. Much of the impetus for integrated environmental management comes from the recommendations first detailed in *Our Common Future*. The International Association for Impact Assessment must provide leadership in promoting impact assessment as part of integrated environmental planning and management.

REFERENCES

Berger, Thomas R. 1983. Resources Development, and Human Values. *Impact Assessment Bulletin,* 2(2):129-147.

Council on Environmental Quality (CEQ) 1978, National Environmental Policy Act - Regulations, *Federal Register*, Vol. 43, (230): 55979-5600.7 Washington, D.C.: Government Printing Office.

Dixon, Mim. 1978. *What Happened to Fairbanks: The Effects of the Trans-Alaska Oil Pipeline on the Community of Fairbanks, Alaska* Boulder, CO: Westview Press.

Gamble, D.J. 1978. The Berger Inquiry: An Impact Assessment Process. *Science*, 199 (3 March): 946-952.

NEPA. *The National Environmental Policy Act of 1969*, Public Law 91-190:852-859.42, U.S.C.

United Nations Environmental Programme. 1987. *Our Common Future*. Toronto and London: Oxford Press.

DEVELOPMENT OF A SOCIAL IMPACT ASSESSMENT MODEL

Chapter 2

SOCIAL IMPACT STATEMENTS: A TENTATIVE METHODOLOGY[1]

Sue Johnson and Rabel J. Burdge

BACKGROUND

This chapter reports one of the first attempts to develop a methodology for Social Impact Assessment within the context of the Environmental Impact Assessment process. The general approach involves using ex-post facto analysis of a project similar in as many respects as possible to one being proposed to make social impact predictions. Consideration is given to the kinds of similarities needed to "match" projects; e.g. geographical location, size and scope of project and the social and economic characteristics of the affected community. The examples reported here deal with reservoir construction projects; however, the general methodology, with adaptations, can be used for other large-scale projects, to include highway construction, urban renewal, waste disposal, and watershed management, among others. Social impact assessment is here divided into two categories: the impact on persons who must be relocated and the impact of the project on the community and adjacent counties.

One of the more ambitious and laudable goals of an environmental impact statement is discovery and the possibility of preventing irreversible effects of physical development before all opportunity is lost. While planners and legislators often think of dirty air or a spoiled stream as impacts; most forget that irreparable damage can occur among the human population and in human communities. Part of this forgetfulness is due to beliefs in human capacity for adaptation. Undoubtedly, part of it is due to the reluctance of social scientists to make predictions about human behavior for public policy. However, we must point out that a lack of concern for prediction and long-range planning on the part of scientists and technicians has led us to our present environmental fix. In this chapter we propose a predictive methodology for use in the social component of environmental impact statements.

Irreversible effects on an individual can be horrifying, as when an old person dies while being relocated for a new highway, or alarming, as when a poor person is forced into debt to buy a "low income house" because rental property is scarce due to an urban renewal project. Other irreversible effects include the unseen erosion of self-confidence and psychological well-being of an aged widow deprived of her only home, that was in the family for generations, and who finds herself severed from personal relationships that have endured for decades, because her land is "needed" for development.

---

[1]Abridged from the original. Sue Johnson and Rabel J. Burdge. 1974. Social Impact Statement: a Tentative Methodology. in *Social Impact Assessment: Man-Environment Interactions*. C.P. Wolf ed. Dowden, Hutchinson and Ross: Stroudsburg, PA. pp 69-84. Reproduced here with permission of the authors and the publisher.

On the community level, we might find small villages served by county roads suddenly inundated with tourists who tear up the roads and wreak havoc with a pastoral routine. The traditionally-rural community may suddenly find its farmland more desired for the construction of second homes for distant urbanites than for agricultural use. Some effects of resource development are temporary, such as the usual decline in tax base or the influx of workers while a reservoir is in the construction phase. Others are irreversible, such as the loss of agricultural land, the disruption of a traditional rural community or the destruction of unique fauna and flora. Our attempt is not to distinguish reversible or temporary effects from irreversible ones; rather is it hoped that the suggested methodology will make it possible for planners to gauge the kinds of effects that are likely when natural resource developments are proposed.

While there are economic considerations in a social analysis, they are given less attention in this chapter. Examples of economics variables in reservoir construction include number of recreational visitor days, changes in the tax base, agricultural crops, markets and subsidies, changing demands for local services and alterations in the budgets of local government. (Goldman, McEvoy, and Richardson 1973: 173). Nor are institutions and their response to change the focus of this chapter. Attention is focused on quantitative and qualitative social considerations or impacts, which may or may not have economic dimensions, but which tend to be ignored in current economically-slanted impact studies. Examples include: social interaction patterns, number of old people in an affected community, psychological well-being, socio-economic status of potential migrants and community residents, and their changing quality of life. Attention is also focused on the varying degrees of validity and utility associated with data collected for a social assessment study. Our proposed methodology is possible because only recently have there been enough operating projects to begin a list of likely impacts.

COMPARATIVE DIACHRONIC STUDIES

The Comparative Diachronic Model

The major purpose of this chapter is to propose *comparative diachronic analysis* as a methodology for assessing the social impacts of a natural resource development project or policy change. In its simplest form, diachronic analysis means investigation of a phenomenon at two different points in time; such as before and after the construction of a reservoir. What we propose to add here is a comparative dimension: the post-construction analysis of a similar project or projects forms an empirical basis for making predictions in the pre-construction phase about the post-construction situation. In the remainder of this chapter, the social impact segment of the study will be called *social impact situation* and the comparative segment, *the comparison study*. Figure 2.1 graphically presents the comparative diachronic model to be used in researching the social impact situation. What we describe here is the optimum case for making an empirical study, knowing that real life situations are often subject to temporal and monetary constraints, and as such, may fall short of the ideal.

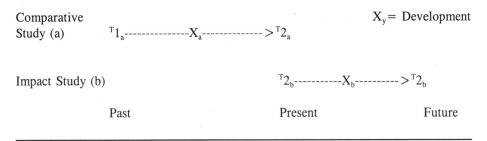

Figure 2.1
Time Dimensions of a Comparative Diachronic Study
to Predict Social Impacts of a Proposed Resource Development Project

Comparative X_y = Development
Study (a) ^T1_a--------------X_a------------->^T2_a

Impact Study (b) ^T2_b----------X_b----------->^T2_b

          Past   Present   Future

How the Time Dimension Influence Social Impacts

The nature and scope of a project helps define potential impacts, particularly if human populations must be relocated. These individuals and their families form a very special kind of sub-class of social impacts. Relocatees are among the first to be affected, and their lives are altered in major ways. Because of their special relationship to a development, they deserve study in and of themselves. The major social impacts on relocatees begins with the *news* that a reservoir will be built and often extends past relocation. Therefore, the time dimension for studying persons to be relocated may be long, depending on real estate transactions. Some projects remain in the pre-construction phase for decades. In the case of reservoir construction, the people who must move tend to relocate near their previous homes, which in turn leads to changes in the impacted community (Johnson and Burdge 1974a).

For our example of reservoir construction, lakes often take years to fill and reach their full range of recreation activities. However, given the kind of data available for measuring social impacts, we recommend a five-year period as minimal and ten years or more as desirable for studying the comparison project and for making predictions about the proposed project. Much of the data recommended for use is gathered at five- or ten-year intervals, and this forms part of the rationale for choice of time periods.

The Purpose of the Project

A reservoir designed primarily for flood control and recreation, with industrial development and water quality as secondary benefits, will have a different impact than a reservoir designed primarily to provide water for irrigation. The anticipated-benefits will influence the manner in which the reservoir facility is managed. Completed projects selected for comparative purposes should have basically the same hierarchy of benefits — e.g. recreation, flood control, industrial development, water quality or irrigation.

Before proceeding, we must note that industrial development is a very problematic aspect of the projection of future benefits from reservoir construction. As Hargrove found in a study of twenty reservoirs...if the area is otherwise desirable for industrial location and the reservoir project provides key factors which were previously missing, the area will experience rapid development. However, if the area is deficient in location factors that are not provided by reservoir development, the project will not stimulate the local economy (Hargrove 1971:4). Hargrove's generalization is somewhat limited, however, because recreational benefits were largely ignored. In keeping with the non-economic focus of this chapter, industrial development and recreational benefits will be mentioned as but two of the many variables that may be analyzed in a social impact study.

Criteria for Matching Projects

We recommend that *both* the relocated persons and the community or the counties involved be the focus of the study for a social impact statement. The general criteria for matching projects is shown in Figure 2.2. Generally speaking, with regard to rural development projects, the geographic and political unit that most reflects both community definition and identification is that of the County. It is also the most available source of data to compare changes (Korsching 1974). Therefore, except for relocation-type developments in large urban areas, we recommend the County as the unit of comparison.

Figure 2.2
Key Dimensions For Matching Present And Proposed Development Projects

---

---County as unit of analysis (rural areas)
---Similar project size and purpose
---Similar geographical and cultural region
---Similar data collection time frames
---Use of comparable data sources

Secondly, we recommend that projects with similar objects should be selected for comparative purposes. This will be simpler in the case of single purpose projects such as national recreational areas or waste disposal sites. In matching for locational similarities, comparative projects should be selected from within the State of proposed construction, although nearby states will do if there is geographical similarity. For instance, reservoirs constructed in Kentucky are often located in the Appalachian area with its mountainous terrain and distinct Appalachian subculture. Comparisons of Eastern Kentucky reservoirs with reservoirs in neighboring states within the Appalachian region might be more appropriate than with reservoirs in Western Kentucky.

The U. S. Censuses of Population Characteristics, Agriculture, Business and Industry all provide data for matching population characteristics. Assuming that the prediction period for the social impact study is ten years into the future, data need to be collected for the comparison county for the ten-year Census period that overlaps the development. For purposes of matching development areas we recommend the following types of information: the age/sex structure of the population, the size of community (counties), the labor force patterns and residence. Gross discrepancies in any of these basic dimensions between comparison and impact counties are likely to have a distorting effect on predictions.

The U.S. Census of Agriculture, conducted at five-year intervals, includes information on average farm size, average value of land and buildings, and the economic class of farms. If industrial development is already present or represents a large proportion of the benefits to be expected, the Census of Business and Industry, also conducted at five-year intervals, can be used to match retail, wholesale and service patterns of the areas under consideration. Data on the above listed variables are collected for the impact community and the comparison community for the most recent Census, and for the previous ten years on the comparison community. Since Agricultural and Business Censuses are published every five years, those years most closely approximating the comparison community before reservoir construction, are utilized.

A most important step in our procedure is to establish a reasonable similarity for the pre-construction periods in the comparison community and the impact community. Absolute magnitudes of difference naturally will change with time, and since one comparison may be ten years in the past, compared with the present, or recent past, no absolute standards for matching can be given. Therefore, we must look for similar patterns in the matching variables. Ideally, we also want a population that is similar in age structure, ten years ago, to the present comparison community, but such a goal may be difficult since rural areas have been losing population. However, if an age differential is present in one of several potential comparative communities, the age structure should assume high importance in the selection of a matching county since it is linked to income and employment levels of a community. Other patterns that should be similar include industrial mix and the economic class of farms.

If several reservoirs are operating near the proposed construction site, or in nearby states with geographical similarities, the available of data can be used to select a comparative reservoir for study. If the secondary data are carefully collected, the match on basic community characteristics, will increase the accuracy of impact predictions.

The Impact of Relocation on Families and Individuals

The affects of relocation are felt in the pre-migration period, during relocation, right after relocation, and in some cases for decades into the future (Johnson and Burdge 1974a). It is necessary to specify who is likely to be affected and in what way by relocation. This can only be predicted by studying a population which has been relocated in the past. In the matching process described previously, a recently-built reservoir will serve the best for making predictions about relocation. Field work, to include personal interviews, is a necessary component of this portion of an impact study unless data about forced migrant populations are readily available.

For example, residents in three Eastern Kentucky counties were to be relocated due to the construction of two reservoirs. The authors had previously interviewed a post-relocation population of rural Kentuckians in a nearby reservoir area very similar to the one being proposed (Burdge and Johnson 1973). The respondents were asked to reconstruct their relocation experience and to make comparisons between their pre- and post-migration situations. In addition to the usual background information, we collected data on changes in social interaction patterns with friends and family and change in levels of organizational involvement. The respondents were asked questions about what kinds of assistance the Army Corps of Engineers gave them prior to and during the move. We also asked for the history and description of their previous and present residence, what had been important considerations in having to move, and what kinds of living conditions they hoped to locate. They were asked about their satisfaction or dissatisfaction with their relocation and what financial aspects of their life had been most affected by the move. Finally, attitudes toward reservoir construction, as well as attitudes toward the federal government, were measured.

The population to be relocated has been surveyed with regard to basic background data, attitudes toward present residence and toward moving, present social interaction patterns, and information on employment and income levels. Respondents were then matched with those already relocated on basic demographic characteristics to predict how the post-relocation population was adjusting.

The basic patterns of social impacts will emerge from this diachronic comparison. The predictions for those about to be relocated are that older people and persons who were extremely attached to their place of residence or with little money will find relocation very painful and problematic. Many farmers will find they cannot buy land comparable to what has been taken and will settle for less acreage of lower quality if they remain in the area. For many relocatees, the disruption of social interaction patterns with friends and family will be the heaviest blow and will contribute to poor adjustment to relocation. In general, non-farmers, those who are younger and have a decent job and education will do better. Generally, the quality of housing for most relocatees will improve (Burdge and Johnson 1973).

Community Level Impacts

Social impacts also take place at the community or county level. Here the social changes may be less dramatic and less detectable on a daily basis, but the impacts on the lives of people in the community are no less dramatic. In Figure 2.3, we briefly outline seven categories of information which could be obtained for analysis and use in an environmental impact statement. These categories represent sources of information which have different levels of sensitivity to local impacts. We suggest that as one goes from census data, Category I, to survey data, Category VII, these data are more and more reflective of the local community which is being impacted.

Census data are collected periodically in a systematic manner and are extremely reliable. However, data are summarized on such an aggregate level that it is often difficult to know those changes due to the resource development and those due to other causes. In cases of highly aggregated data, we recommend choosing a *control* county, matched in the same fashion as the comparison county, but lacking a similar resource development project. Rates of change and absolute change in comparison, control, and impact counties can be analyzed to isolate changes due to resource development.

The order presented in Figure 2.4 provides an approximate indication of the cost required to get the social impact information. As one moves from secondary information to primary data the cost will rise — but they are collectable at more frequent time interval. Copying and correlating information from census data is much cheaper than searching out archive information or interviewing persons that are about to move.

Figure 2.3
Schematic Outline of the Relationship of Key Information Sources to Time Lines in a Comparative Diachronic Study[a]

Comparative Study:

^T1_a --- $> ^T2_a$
(1960)   (1970)

I. Census Data	I. Census Data
II. State Records	II. State Records
III. Business Statistics	III. Business Statistics
IV. County Records	IV. County Records
V. Selected Agency Information	V. Selected Agency Information
VI. Archive Information	VI. Achieve Information
	VII. Survey Data

Impact Study:

^T2_b --- $> ^T3_b$
(1970)   (1980)

I. Census Data	I. Census Data
II. State Records	II. State Records
III. Business Statistics	III. Business Statistics
IV. County Records	IV. County Records
V. Selected Agency Information	V. Selected Agency Information
VI. Archive Information	VI. Achieve Information
VII. Survey Data	VII. Survey Data

Control Study: (when necessary)

^T1_c --- $> ^T2_c$
(1960)   (1970)

I. Census Data	I. Census Data
II. State Records	II. State Records
III. County Records	III. County Records

[a] 10 Years Minimum Time Dimension (Hypothetical Dates)

DATA SOURCES FOR SOCIAL IMPACT ASSESSMENT

The remainder of this chapter outlines the kinds of data that should be obtained for each of the categories as shown in Figure 2.4 as well as key variables which reflect changes in the quality of life of the residents if reservoir development were to occur.

Census Information

The *Census of the Population* includes data on the age, gender, educational, occupational, racial, ethnic and residential composition of the population by city, county, and state aggregates. In addition, data are available on migration, size of family, ages of family members, previous residence and medium family income. Social impacts due to resource development might start with an analysis of the age and sex structure of the population and occupational composition of the county. Most other census variables would in some way be related to these variables. Age and sex structure, particularly if there is an improvement in the quality of life of rural residents, might show a decline in average age of the population if outmigration is slowed. The occupational opportunities in the community might show the addition of new occupations and increased services (increasing occupational diversity) due to resource development.

The *Decennial Housing Census* reports data on the condition of housing, number of persons per room, and the average value of houses—all indirect data on the quality of life of residents. If resource development brings an increase in general prosperity, these numbers might increase.

The *Agriculture Census*, taken every five years, includes data on farm size in acres, value of buildings, crops and livestock, plus social and demographic information on the operator and the farm family. Data are summarized by economic class of farm, which is an important indicator of the commercial level of agriculture in the study area. If a reservoir floods valuable bottomland, then changes in agricultural land use should be discernable in commodity composition, gross farm sales and the economic class of farms. A decline in commercial farming resulting from the subdivision of farms is a likely impact.

The *Census of Business and Industry* and the *Census of Manufactures* provides data on the kind or nature of businesses as well as the growth and decline of various industries. These censuses include items on retail and wholesale trade, employment figures, payrolls, taxes, general reserves and expenditures. Because it is taken every five years and supplemented by much county and state level data, it represents an important barometer for economic and social change. Expectations about likely changes in business and industrial patterns are similar to those listed under the population census increased, that is, diversity and perhaps the presence of new businesses will accompany development.

The *County and City Data Book*, published annually, is the best single source of population data if regular census publications are not available. Also, there are special reports on public employment, published annually, which can be used to monitor changes in public services since 1952, and on county business patterns, which gives detailed data on major industry groups, number of employees by employment class and number of reporting units, employees and taxable payrolls.

State Records

All states, by law, are required to keep current statistics on births, marriages and deaths. These data are accurate for persons born since 1910. The marriage rate is an index of potential household formation, an important component in economic growth. The age-specific fertility rate is a factor in population growth. In low-income areas with high fertility, if the general quality of life improves, one would look for a decline in fertility and an increase in middle-class patterns of childbearing.

The infant and maternal mortality rate is an index of general health care and the death rate by age an index of the general health of the population. Information on all forms of public assistance is available through State and County records. The tax assessment records are an index of the aggregate wealth of the community under study. The federal government publishes a bibliography of state reports on state and local government finances. Transportation data includes information on the condition and numbers of state and county roads and traffic counts. Often, if a community has a recreation-oriented resource development, roads and traffic patterns will show an increase (Drucker, 1973). Most state level data are available on an annual basis.

Figure 2.4
Outline of Information Sources for Social Impact Statements

I. Census Information a. Population b. Housing c. Agriculture d. Business, retail, services, and manufacturing e. Special inter-census reports	**IV. County Records** a. Transportation expenditures b. Natural resource expenditures c. Land transfer records
II. State Records a. Vital statistic b. Epidemiological data c. Public assistance d. Tax assessment records e. Transportation expenditures	**V. Selected Agency Information** **VI. Archive Information** a. Newspaper reports b. Transcripts of public hearings c. Agency meetings and logs
III. Business Statistics a. Family income b. Per capita income c. Personal disposable income	**VII. Survey Data** a. Interviews with community leaders b. Interviews with sample of general population c. Interviews with impacted persons and families

Private Records and Reports

Except for aggregated data on family income, little financial information is available from census data. Private record sources publish information on per capita income, disposable per capita income and measures of money flow on a county basis.

Sales Management is such a publication. Monthly sales tax records are an important indicator of changing economic activity.

County Records

The basic unit of analysis for our proposed impact study is the county. For example, deed transfer records give the value of property, the kind of property, and prior ownership information. From these data, the rate of property transfer over time and subdivision activity can be shown. Baseline data should be obtained before the project is proposed so that relative changes due to resource development can be measured. Annual or semi-annual monitoring of these records gives a continuous picture of the impact of reservoir development on land use practices.

Selected Agency Information

Agencies of both the state and federal government collect and report data for local units of government about a wide range of activities. These reports may be based on personal interviews as in the monthly survey of the labor force by the Department of Labor, or compiled from secondary sources such as health agency reports. The question here is which are the relevant state and federal agencies associated with a particular resource development. In the case of reservoir construction in the western U.S., it might be the Bureau of Land Management and the National Park Service. There are state agency counterparts active in most of these projects. These sources often have concrete data on several kinds of impacts.

Archive Information

By archival information we mean newspaper reports, public transcripts and historical accounts. These data need to be summarized by persons trained in content analysis and library research. The goal is to assemble opinions, attitudes and descriptions of situations in the community which have developed as a result of the project. Because each source of information is biased in that it represents agency, official, or editorial opinion, it must be evaluated from that standpoint. Other sources, like the transcript of hearings about projects, are located with the agency responsible for the hearings. Archive information is very important in developing social impact statements for it deals with the actual event under study. It also represents an important transition between the aggregate data discussed above and first person information on likely impacts.

Survey Data

Personal interviews from pretested questionnaires and collected by trained social scientists represent the most reliable form of information about the social impacts of a reservoir or other natural response development project. From interviews it is possible to understand the effects of a project on the community and the individuals that are relocated. Personal interviews have the disadvantage of being quite expensive, but this expense is more than out weighed by the timeliness and validity of these data.

Under the category of survey data, we include interviews with community leaders of civic, business and important voluntary and religious organizations. Information on the attitudes of these persons toward the proposed project is important, because they influence the opinions of many other persons. Also, the identification of community leaders allows us to establish the nature of power relationships in a community. Interviews with a sample of the general population of the county in which a reservoir has been constructed helps us to know the extent of social impacts.

A listing of sources of data alongside key variables makes trade-offs due to limitations of time and money possible. In one project, a twenty percent sub-sample of persons to be relocated was studied intensively (Johnson and Burdge 1974a). Generalizations were made to the entire relocated population about which only basic background data were available, much of it gathered from informants. Another kind of trade-off would be to use Categories I, II, and III, all easily available data sources for studying community impacts (using comparison and control counties) and then survey the population to be relocated, using past studies as a guide to what is likely to happen. However, when one does not collect data at the local level data, (Categories IV-VII), it would be difficult to understand the changes for those who live in the affected communities. Finally, we strongly suggest that detailed personal interviews be conducted with the individuals who must be relocated due to project development. These are the people who suffer the most and their story can only be told by communicating to decision-makers through an unbiased interviewer.

CONCLUSION

The purposes of this chapter have been threefold. First, we have suggested *comparative diachronic analysis* as a method for predicting the impacts of a proposed natural resource project. Secondly, we have outlined some elements that we think must be included in a social impact statement and finally we have suggested key social impact variables and the data sources that might measure them. Our proposal is preliminary and exploratory and the substance of this outline will be developed in future publications (Burdge and Johnson 1974; Johnson and Burdge 1974a).

There are four major problems to overcome before our model is fully operational. First, a statistical procedure must be developed to examine the changes that take place in qualitative variables between the various time frames. We must be able to establish whether or not the change has meaning and if it does what are the consequences for the individuals and the communities. Secondly, we have to relate the contents of this chapter to the guidelines for Environmental Impact Statements published by the Council on Environmental Quality. We have made the case that our variables should be some of the components of an Environmental Impact Statement. Thirdly, we must establish the actual measures that will fit under each of these broad categories. Finally, we have to translate our model into comprehensible terms that can be understood, not only by other scientists, but by planners who must make decisions as well as those persons likely to be impacted by the proposed development. We are careful to point out that in order to direct this task toward a useful purpose, social assessment indicators from primary and secondary data will have to be created. The collection of primary data and interpretation of the meaning of social impact on individuals will form the vital underpinnings of a social impact assessment methodology that relies primarily on secondary data sources, yet transmits a portrayal of the impacts on human populations.

REFERENCES

Burdge, Rabel J. and Sue Johnson. 1973. *Social Costs and Benefits of Water Resource Development*. Lexington, Kentucky: Kentucky Water Resources Research Institute, Research Report No. 64.

Burdge, Rabel J. and Sue Johnson. 1977. Socio-Cultural Aspects of the Effects of Resource Development. in *Handbook for Environmental Planning: The Social Consequences of Environmental Change*. James McEvoy III and Thomas Dietz eds. New York: John Wiley, pp 241-279.

Drucker, P. and J.E. Clark, L.D. Smith. 1973. *Sociocultural Impact of Reservoirs on Local Government Institutions*. Lexington, Kentucky: University of Kentucky Water Resources Research Institute. Research Report No. 65.

Goldman, C.R., J. McEvoy and P. J. Richardson. 1973. *Environmental Quality and water Development*. San Francisco: W.H. Freeman and Company.

Hargrove, M.B. 1971. *Economic Development of Areas Contiguous to Multi-purpose Reservoirs: The Kentucky-Tennessee Experience*. Lexington, Kentucky: University of Kentucky Water Resources Institute. Research Report No. 21.

Johnson, Sue and Rabel J. Burdge. 1974a. Analysis of Community and Individual Reactions to Forced Migration Due to Reservoir Construction. in *Water and the Community: Social and Economic Perspectives*. D.R. Field, J. Barron and B. Long, eds. Ann Arbor Science Publishers, Inc. pp. 169-188.

Johnson, Sue and Rabel J. Burdge. 1974b. A Methodology for Using Diachronic Studies to Predict the Social Impact of Resource Development. Presented at the Meeting of the Rural Sociological Society, McGill University, Montreal, August.

Johnson, Sue and Rabel J. Burdge. 1974c. Social Impact Statements: A Tentative Methodology. Presented at the Fifth Annual Conferences of the Environmental Design Research Associates, School of Architecture, University of Wisconsin, Milwaukee, May.

Korsching, P.F. 1974. *An Ecological Approach to Urban Dominance*. Lexington, Kentucky: University of Kentucky, Department of Sociology. Unpublished. Ph.D. Dissertation.

Chapter 3

SOCIOCULTURAL ASPECTS OF THE EFFECTS OF RESOURCE DEVELOPMENT[1]

Rabel J. Burdge and Sue Johnson

INTRODUCTION

Our approach to understanding how people and communities react to planned environmental change combines an anthropological model with sociological and social-psychological concepts and utilizes data from a wide array of sources collected, by and large, for purposes other than the study of social impacts. Our indicators measure attitudes and receptivity toward resource development and use quality-of-life measures derived from secondary sources. (Drucker, *et. al.* 1973; Smith 1970; Burdge and Ludtke 1972; Johnson 1974; and Burdge and Johnson 1973).

The approach here is a practical rather than theoretical one. In seeking to understand the behavior of people and communities affected by resource development, we also seek to predict what the probable impact of development will be. Using a comparative model, we study the course of events in a community where planned environmental change has occurred and extrapolate from that analysis what is likely to happen in another community where a similar developmental change is proposed. In other words, we wish to know if given similar pre-development conditions and similar resource development projects, the social impact of a completed development project in Community A can be generalized to and predictive of what will happen in Community B where development is planned.

Another goal of impact assessment is to discover irreversible and undesirable social effects of resource development before they occur rather than having cause to regret events after they happen. Simply to discover irreversible effects is not enough, however, because we must attempt to implement programs to avoid undesirable effects of the impacts. It is the planning agency or agencies that bear the responsibility for intervening in such matters.

Social scientists can also speak to the issues of alternative plans and alternative impacts of development proposals using our model. Moreover, if likely social impacts can be assessed, recommendations for mitigating actions can be made. This is an important reason for doing a social impact statement — for even reversible but undesirable effects can sometimes be avoided if we know what they are.

---

[1]Abridged from the original. Rabel J. Burdge and Sue Johnson. 1977. The Socio-Cultural Aspects of the Effects of Resource Development. in *Handbook for Environmental Planning: The Social Consequences of Environmental Change.* James McEvoy III and Thomas Dietz eds. New York: Wiley and Sons. pp. 241-279. Reproduced here with permission of the authors and the publisher.

Part of our goal is to provide a methodology for gathering basic data that can be used and generalized to other studies of social impacts. Moreover, it is hoped that our arguments will be persuasive enough that agencies which must do social impact statements will take the NEPA process seriously enough to provide the necessary time and money to support social science efforts.

Basic Concepts

Natural resource development brings changes to the local community whether the development is small, like a new city park or large, such as the construction of a new reservoir or the opening of a mine. The nature of social change will vary with the kind and size of a development project as well as the nature of community in which the project is located. To study social change sociologists must switch from their traditional focus on structure in social organizations to a more dynamic assessment of the social impacts of planned change.

Community is left undefined here because the definition will depend on the area of primary and secondary social impacts. It may be a neighborhood where a freeway is planned (primary impact) and the city which the freeway is to serve (secondary impact). In rural areas, it may be the entire County where development is proposed (primary) and possibly nearby counties (secondary). When we speak of a dynamic approach to community, we include past history which lies within it the capacity for adaptation and change. Also found in the history are certain unique features that will affect capacity for adjusting to planned change. Firey's classic study of land use in central Boston illustrates the importance of such unique factors (1947). What this means for the study of social change is that trends from similar developments and the unique features of the community must be balanced in making predictions about social impacts.

Large-scale planned change, which characterizes natural resource development, can have an effect on the entire fabric of a community; on its institutions such as government and schools; and on its size, due to in-or-out-migration. Its economic base may grow because of potential for industrial development and the creation of recreation-based revenues. The social interaction patterns of its members may change — for physical reasons if people must relocate because of development or for social reasons if there are dramatic changes in the social class levels of those who may profit from the development. Land use practices will change, if farmland is turned into lakes with adjoining marinas and vacation homes. In short, the entire matrix of community beliefs, values, attitudes, norms, and practices will be affected.

It is almost impossible to catalogue and study the true dimensions of social impacts for change has a way of creating other changes. Much as the proverbial rock thrown in a pond, the complexity increases with each ring. However, there are key sociological dimensions that can be measured which reflect, albeit imperfectly, fundamental and important characteristics of a community. Studied over time, these same dimensions can give us valid insight as to what are the basic processes of social change when natural resource development occurs. Faced with a proposal to undertake a natural resource development, the community and the agency proposing the change must look at other communities to gain a reasonably accurate expectation of how the project will affect their community.

The Comparative Diachronic Model

One way to capture the dynamic quality of social impacts is to metaphorically take a series of snapshots over time as development progresses and try to fill in what happened in between. This, in essence, is what a diachronic model represents; the study of the same phenomenon at two different points in time (Figure 3.1). In this case the time periods are usually before and after development occurs.

Figure 3.1
Time Dimensions of a Comparative Diachronic Study
Used to Predict Social Impacts of Proposed Resource Development

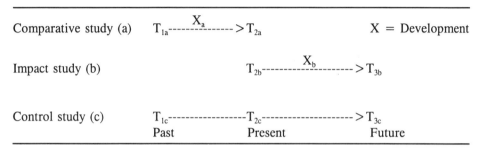

Our model is comparative in that after studying the social impact of a natural resource development in one community, it may be compared to a similar community where a similar type of development is proposed, to make that predictions about future social impacts. The model also permits a re-study of the impacted community to assess what the actual impact has been, so that the fit between predictions and outcomes can be measured. The basic comparative diachronic model is shown in Figure 3.1.

There are many data sources available to study changes between the pre- and post-development period due to resource development. To do the latter, one needs a control community so that ongoing changes can be isolated from developmental changes. The control community can also help predict the no-project alternative.

In addition to providing an empirical basis for predicting social impacts, the model allows for a more dynamic interpretation of events and can provide monitoring of short-term impacts. Moreover, this kind of frequent monitoring provides a continual check on the direction of predictions.

TIME DIMENSIONS INFLUENCING SOCIAL IMPACTS

Pre-development Period

Although the nature and scope of a natural resource development helps define the potential impact, the unfolding of impacts in time is an important consideration. Impact actually begins long before construction starts. As soon as people in a community hear that a project is planned, they begin reacting in different ways. Some will seek more information, others will be apathetic because it seems distant, and unrelated to their lives. A few will try to profit from the proposed project.

Moreover, there are a host of political considerations depending in part on who is initiating the project, what kind it is, whether it will require congressional approval or a local referendum. Generally, if the proposed project looks as if it will benefit the community, most local leaders will favor it. This, of course, raises the issue of who will benefit. There are costs, both monetary and personal, associated with every natural resource development, and a social impact study should specify who will benefit and who is likely to pay.

Knowing about a project in advance allows individuals and community to make plans to minimize costs of the project and to maximize benefits. Drucker's (1972) study of the preconstruction period of the Taylorville reservoir found that long before actual construction there was considerable land turnover, mostly on the fringe of a proposed reservoir and park. Much of this land was bought by non-residents. Of course, if there is no recreational component to resource development, this kind of land speculation may not occur.

If people are going to be relocated to make room for resource development, this opens an entire dimension of impact that is related both to the quality of life of individuals and to the impact of the project on the community as a whole. In a study of persons to be relocated for the Taylorville reservoir, Smith (1970) found many to be suffering from *pre-migration stress*, that is, they were mourning the loss of their homes and their interactions with friends and relatives before these events actually took place. In this case the psychological cost in long-term suffering was great because residents were told they were to be moved 13 years before the event happened.

The place of public participation in planning and as part of social impact assessment is subject to controversy. Nevertheless, the way communities respond to proposed projects can be categorized in general terms. A study in the Delaware Basin listed four factors to maintaining effective public participation for the development of water resources; real problems, concerned citizenry, dynamic leadership, and cooperative agencies (Felton 1968). Public participation is important, because an uniformed or misinformed public may fail to act on developmental issues or if ignored, may reject proposals (Conner and Bradley 1972). The process of obtaining and maintaining citizen participation takes a great deal of time in the planning stages. Unfortunately, plans about resource development are often created in a vacuum — with no public participation in the planning period. Rather, the public is confronted with a full-blown plan and asked to accept or reject it. This kind of planning reflects the agency's view that social impact assessment is a means of bureaucratic compliance with NEPA and not a new way of thinking about the planning process.

The lack of public involvement is seen as a negative social impact, as least in the beginning stages of resource development. Ignoring social impacts and not doing public involvement may be one reason why so many projects are subject to bad publicity which leads to lengthy and acrimonious litigation. This kind of public reaction is expensive in time and money for project proponents.

Wolf (1974) distinguishes between *project effects* and *planning effects*. The act of planning a project can and does have significant impact on a community regardless of whether the project ever comes to fruition. Negative reaction to a plan could promote at least temporary community cohesion where none existed before. Similarly, community cooperation in working to enhance project benefits can also increase cohesion.

During Construction of Resource Projects

This perception of benefits of proposed natural resource development is generally found among urban residents and those who see direct gain (Smith 1970; Andrews *et. al.* 1970; Burdge and Johnson 1973 and Drucker 1973). Some optimism diminishes during the construction phase when there is a loss in revenues due to land development and a strain on services as construction workers move into the community. One community in Oregon so overreacted to perceived economic benefits that they expanded to meet the temporary service demands of the construction phase and later found themselves without the anticipated economic benefits and straddled with additional costs of the maintenance of those expanded services (Smith *et. al.* 1971).

Short-term impact on the community's source of revenue depends on how much land is being taken by the development and if it is an agricultural community, how much ground will be taken out of farming. If the development agency, acquires the land at a slow but regular rate the community can adjust its property valuation rates and avoid the decline in revenues (Drucker 1973).

Stramn (1968) found that either very large towns or very small ones were usually less affected by the construction phase of natural resource development. Apparently, large communities are better able to absorb the impacts of more construction workers, while very small communities are not saddled with the temporary migration of construction workers who commute to the construction site. In a small isolated town where construction workers lived for several years during the construction phase, Peele found the short-term costs to the local community were devastating, even though the long-term benefits were surprisingly generous (1974).

After Construction

Most waste resource projects include a cost-benefit analysis that specify anticipated benefits in dollar terms for such elements as water quality, flood control, tourism and recreation, and industrial development. However, there have been few systematic empirical attempts to determine whether these benefits actually materialized. In a study of 20 reservoirs in Kentucky and Tennessee, where industrial development was the goal, Hargrove found that unless other favorable factors were present and unless water availability fulfilled a need, industrial development was not likely to occur at any greater rate than if there had been no reservoir. He also found substantial variation in the size and direction of anticipated economic benefits of water projects after their completion (Hargrove 1991).

Currently, social impact statements that fit NEPA requirements do not have an evaluative component, that is, there is no follow-up to see if predicted impacts actually occur. Most predictions are derived from a study of the host community and what can be found in the literature. The comparative diachronic model does have a systematic evaluative component built into it for monitoring both long- and short-term impacts. Moreover, the predictions are derived from a post-construction analysis of similar projects.

Projections about the social impacts of development are best if grounded in research and theory. This is why we argue both for post-construction analysis of water resource projects to specific social impacts and for more basic research on social assessment. Our model appears adaptable to both purposes. However, only valid data about communities that have been impacted and the collection of primary data about the community to be impacted can begin to provide a picture of what is really likely to happen.

Gardner and Hurtquist compared perceptions of benefits from a reservoir that had been in operation since 1959 to a recently constructed one. As a comparison they used persons still living on an uncontrolled river. They found that after the reservoir had been in operation, negative opinions about the management of the reservoir began to surface, even though the community as a whole had been in favor of its construction (Gardner and Hurtquist 1973).

It appears that people confuse flood control with the idea of no flooding rather than controlled flooding. Therefore, downstream farmers who began to cultivate floodplain land and those who leased easements from the Corps of Engineers were dismayed to find their land flooded more often and to greater depths than previously. The operators of the reservoir sought to keep the pool up to recreation-user specifications and to prevent additional flooding in a distant river drainage basin. This meant that farmers were experiencing controlled flooding that interfered with the normal planting/harvest cycle. However, those living downstream from the newly constructed reservoir were much more optimistic about being flood-proof.

Gardner and Hurtquist (1973) also found that over time weather and operation of the reservoir vary and some of these benefits, particularly agricultural ones, begin to be perceived as costs to the farmers. Many local people feel that if the reservoir were operated differently, some of these costs would disappear. They were particularly incensed at the idea that *their* dam was used to control flooding on another river miles and miles away and that they were paying the cost of protecting large cities downstream. It is unlikely, however, that operation of the reservoir will be changed to suit the farmers' interests at the risk of less flood protection downstream. Clearly, this is a case of conflicting interests and one not easily solved, if solvable at all.

These findings point to the complex role that time plays in social assessment. It may be that the impacts of reservoir projects never end but rather are lost in the *flood* of impacts from related projects. The order of impacts assessed depends in large part on the methodology used to collect the data, methods of analysis and the time dimension through which measurable impacts are to be traced.

APPLICATION OF THE COMPARATIVE DIACHRONIC MODEL

The work of testing the comparative diachronic model is just beginning, so the methodology must be considered as tentative and subject to change. Figure 3.2 gives general criteria for matching present and proposed reservoir development projects. The same criteria, with the exception of a similar resource development project, would hold for selecting control counties.

Unit of Analysis
The unit of analysis for which data are readily available in rural areas is the *county*. The county is the geographical and political unit that most reflects community definition and identification in rural areas (Drucker 1972). Since most resource development occurs in rural areas, we are focusing on that setting. Urban development may require different matching criteria and a different geographical unit of analysis.

In most social impact situations more than one county is affected by resource development, and in these cases all counties of potential impact should be included. Generally speaking, area of impact varies directly with the magnitude of the project. A comparison county containing an already completed and operating project is selected using the general matching criteria listed in Figure 3.2. Clusters of control counties (prediction of what would happen without the project) may be selected in a similar manner. This stage sets the scene for the selection of comparison and control counties. Using the dimensions discussed in the following sections.

Figure 3.2
Key dimensions for matching present
and proposed resource development projects

- County as unit of analysis (rural areas)
- Similar project size and purpose
- Similar geographical and cultural region
- Similar data time frames
- Comparable secondary data sources

Time Dimension

Future predictions must take project life into account which could range from 30 to 100 years. Realizing that choice of time frame is somewhat arbitrary and conditioned by type of project, we suggest a 10-year period or more for studying the comparison county and for making predictions about the impact county.

Much of the data recommended for use in the study of social impacts are gathered at 5- or 10-year intervals, and, therefore, provide a reason for choosing at least that long a period. Remembering that even well-collected social science data lose predictive utility with time, consideration is also given to periodic monitoring of other sources of information that appear more frequently. These data may be used to study the dynamics of impact on such factors as land use, recreational development, and fluctuations in tax revenue, as well as checking on the direction of predictions made about the impact county.

The Nature of the Project

Natural resource development projects include reservoirs, mines, parks, wildlife sanctuaries, and power plants, among others. The validity of any predictions of social impact rests first with choosing comparative projects similar as possible to the one proposed. For example, reservoir projects intended for flood control and recreation with industrial development, water supply and water quality as secondary benefits would have a different impact than one designed to provide water for irrigation. Most public projects have cost-benefits analyses that tell the researcher the size of the proposed project and the order of intended benefits. The choice is easier for single-purpose projects, such as national recreation areas or a coal-gasification plant.

Other Project Matching Criteria

Comparable projects should be selected from within the same state where construction is proposed, although nearby states will do if there is cultural and geographical similarity. The more projects there are for comparison and the greater their similarity with proposed projects, the more reliable will be the results of the social impact study.

Social and demographic characteristics of the counties are also among the general matching criteria. To compare the pre-development characteristics of the comparison county with those of the county of proposed development, an adjustment to a 10-year or more difference in time may be required. Since communities change with time, one must look for similarities in patterns of variables rather than search for complete homogeneity.

We suggest that five variables be chosen as final matching criteria. In Table 3.1 an example is given for locating comparison and control counties in Eastern Kentucky. However, we simply list and provide a rationale for the selection of each of the indicators. Most of these measures are available from the *County and City Data Book*. In Table 3.1 Johnson County is the site of the proposed reservoir. A control county could be chosen from the other four. With the exception of the percent employed in farming, Morgan County is the best match.

Population Size And Structure - Population size and area of the county are the most fundamental dimensions. Population size is related to ability to absorb impact as is the age/sex structure, particularly the age structure (dependency ratio), because it is linked to the income generating potential population (Bates 1970).

Area Of The County - This variable is important from the standpoint of the ability to absorb and adapt to social change. Another measure of potential to absorb change is the size of the project in acres as a percentage of county size.

Percent Urban - As the population of a county becomes more urban, it becomes more concentrated. A population that is closer together tends to have more community organization and a more cosmopolitan lifestyle. Social change of any kind is more easily accepted by urban persons.

Agriculture--Per Capita Value of Farm Products Sold - Per capita value of farm products sold is indicative of the degree to which the county is agricultural versus other rural industries. Although not available from the *County and City Data Book*, the amount of minerals produced may be an alternative indicator for rural industries. Forest products also are listed under agriculture.

Labor Force Patterns - The occupational categories of the census are particularly important if industrial development is projected as a benefit of the project. As an alternative, patterns of retail, manufacturing, and service businesses from the Business Census may be compared. The percentage of people employed in farming is an indicator of the importance of agriculture.

SOME CAUTIONS ABOUT USING THE COMPARATIVE MODEL

The real world will not always provide perfect matches for proposed natural resource development. The selection of projects for comparison is the most important step in the process, because claims for validity will be based on similarity and comparability. Therefore, we have recommended using several points of comparison, choosing what we consider key variables to be controlled (as much as possible) in a diachronic model. The reader should again refer to Figure 3.1.

Table 3.1
Matching Data for Johnson County (Reservoir Area)
and Surrounding Control Counties for 1970

	Johnson	Lawrence	Magoffin	Martin	Morgan
Population numbers	17,539	10,726	10,443	9,377	10,019
- Percent female	50.9	50.5	50.5	49.8	49.8
- Median age	31.4	31.7	23.9	22.2	29.5
Area (square miles)	264	425	303	231	369
Percent urban	22.1	0	0	0	26.6
Per capita value of farm[a] products sold (in dollars)	19.78	105.26	37.54	3.63	218.88
Percent employed in selected occupations:					
- Farmers and farm managers	.6	5.2	2.2	.4	12.5
- Professionals and managers	19.7	15.0	16.3	17.7	20.1
- Clerical and sales	16.5	7.0	22.2	10.9	14.2
- Craftsmen and foremen	14.8	20.2	17.7	15.3	12.6

[a]Off Farm sales of $2500 or more.

Many natural resource development projects are located in or have an effect on more than one county. This means the quantity of data to be collected is somewhat larger. It also means that making comparisons between impact, comparison, and control counties is a more difficult task. It is our recommendation that *best fit* be used although there may be considerable variation among potential comparison and control counties in terms of matching criteria. In Table 3.1, all are similar with the exception of medium age, population size and the value of farm products.

The attribution of changes due to natural resource development as opposed to changes that would have occurred anyway opens up the issue of causality. Comparison of rates of change and absolute change in the comparison, impact, and control counties provides the basis for assessing which changes may actually be attributed to resource development.

A distinction between short-term impacts such as loss of the tax base during the construction phase in reservoir development and long-term impacts, such as growth in tourism and second homes should be considered. The time for studying impact begins immediately in the pre-construction phase for baseline data and continues, systematically for as many as 10 or 15 years in the future. In addition, data may be utilized from 10 to as much as 30 or more years into the past for comparison and control counties.

SOURCES OF DATA AND KEY SOCIAL IMPACT VARIABLES

Table 3.2 lists sources of data that can be used for research into social impacts. A similar table was shown in the previous chapter. These data range from the decennial censuses to personal interviews. Also, as one goes down the list from census to personal interviews these data are available in shorter time periods, making possible the monitoring of short-term impacts and the updating of predictions. All levels of data need to be collected and analyzed for comparison, impact, and control counties to provide a truer picture of which social impacts occur as a result of project activity. The procedures for assembling data shown in Table 3.2 are covered in chapter two. In a social impact study our hypotheses are derived from the comparison community, past studies of impact, and from any unique features of the impact county.

Table 3.2 shows the list of variables for the proposed social impact analysis. Our goal is to move from vague concepts to concrete empirical indicators that can be used and understood by informed and educated lay and professional people interested in the SIA process. This is not a laundry list of social science variables; but rather variables that have been found through investigation to be related to the impacts of natural resource development. At a minimum, each paragraph describes the variable to include the label and, if appropriate, its conceptual indicator. Next, where the data is located and how the indicator is constructed. Finally, how the information is interpreted and how it might change with impact. This chapter discuss only State and Federal agency reports, archive information, and personal interviews.

State And Federal Agency Reports

The Congressional mandate to develop EISs extends, at least, to all federal agencies and most States. For example, the Army Corps of Engineers deals with reservoir development and river drainage, the National Park Service with recreational expansion, and the U.S. Forest Service with competing demands for forest resources. Each of the agencies issues periodic reports of its environmental activities. Included in this report are records of the interchange of these agencies with the institutions and the people in local communities. A proposed natural resource development could also bring about conflict among various federal and state agencies.

The following is a list of federal agencies that may operate on a county basis. The list is not applicable to all regions of the county — in the arid and forested West much of the land in a County is managed by either the Forest Service or the Bureau of Land Management.

1. The *Cooperative Extension Service* maintains a county agent and appropriate staff in most counties in the United States. These persons assume an active role in most forms of community development.

2. The *Soil Conservation Service*, operating through a state and regional staff, helps farmers adopt improved cropping and farm conservation practices. The interchange between the Soil Conservation Service and the farmer may have much to say about the environmental attitudes of U.S. farmers.

Table 3.2
Sources of Data and Key Social Impact Assessment[a]

I. **U.S. BUREAU OF CENSUS PUBLICATIONS**	IV. **COUNTY AND OTHER LOCAL RECORDS**
A. Census of Population	A. Improved local highways[b]
1. Area and Population Size	B. Record of deed transfers[b]
2. Urban population proportion	C. Value of real property
3. Labor force composition	D. Per capita local expenditure for education
4. Productivity of the population	E. Land-use patterns[b]
5. Extreme incomes	F. County relief expenditures
6. Educational attainment	G. Other Measures
7. In- and out-migration	
B. Census of housing	V. **STATE AND FEDERAL AGENCY REPORTS**
1. Dwelling	A. Cooperative extension service
2. Household modernity	B. Soil conservation service
3. Owner-occupied homes	C. Farmer's home administration
C. Census of agriculture	D. Department of Health, Education, and Welfare
1. Value of farm products sold	
2. Average farm size	VI. **ARCHIVE INFORMATION**
3. Agriculture tenure classes	A. Newspaper reports
D. Census of business and industry	B. Official transcripts of public hearings
1. Per capita retail sales	C. Cost benefits analysis of present and proposed projects
2. Economic complexity	
3. Unemployment rate	VII. **DATA FROM PERSONAL INTERVIEWS**
4. Government complexity	A. Personal and family background variables
II. **STATE RECORDS**	B. Socioeconomic status
A. Marriage rate	C. Attachment to place and ancestral ties
B. Birth rate	D. Identification with community
C. Death rate	E. Previous occupational and geographic mobility
D. School attendance records	
E. Public assistance payments	F. Attitudes toward and knowledge of resource development in general
F. Local educational expenditures	G. Quality of individual and family life
G. Permits for resource or mineral removal	H. Participation in public decision making
H. Reported criminal activity	I. Institutional variables
III. **PRIVATE RECORDS AND REPORTS**	
A. Per capita disposable income	
B. Median family income	
C. Bank receipts	

[a] Also shown in the previous chapter.
[b] Useful variables for monitoring short-term impacts and checking on the direction of predictions made about impact.

3. The *Farmers Home Administration* provides long-term low-interest loans to farmers for the purchase of land and buildings. Rural resource development could bring about a decline in Farmer Home Administration loans while, at the same time, the Federal Housing Administration and the Veterans Administration may be making more loans in the impact community. The local Rural Electrification Administration (REA) Cooperative provides rural people with electricity and telephone service.

4. Some branches of the *Department of Health, Education and Welfare* maintain offices at the county or regional level to administer the Social Security program. Certain health statistics gathered on a nationwide basis are also collected and channeled through the State Department of Health. Data on state and federal welfare expenditures for the County may be obtained from these agencies.

Archive Information

Archive information refers to newspaper accounts and transcripts of public hearings about a proposed project. The idea is to assemble opinions, attitudes, and descriptions of situations in the community related to the project. Assessors must remember that each source of information is biased because it represents agency, official, or editorial opinion. Archive information is very important in developing social impact statements, for it deals with the actual event under study.

1. Newspaper Reports outline the events leading to development of the project and editorial opinion about anticipated costs and benefits. Local news accounts provide only one source of information for, if a local editor or publisher favors a projects, s/he may not print information regarding the opposition. Newspaper accounts also provide a rallying point for local opinions and may be used as a reference point for personal interviews with local residents.

2. Official Transcripts of Public Hearings provide a composite opinion about a proposed development for those persons who actually attended the public hearings. As public hearings become institutionalized, these transcripts should provide insight regarding opposition and support forces for resource development.

3. Cost-Benefit Analysis is essentially a justification of a project based on engineering and economic analysis. The benefits of flood control reservoirs for example include improved water supply, flood control, and outdoor recreation . The benefits should equal the costs of developing and maintaining the project. These studies provide many project parameters around which to build the social impact study.

Data From Personal Interviews

Interviews with leaders in the comparison and impact counties will provide data on actual and perceived impact of resource development. In the comparison community we have the benefit of hindsight from leaders who have actually seen the impact of development. These results may be compared with what leaders in the impact county think will be the changes.

Surveys of residents in the comparison community will show the distribution of project impacts. The reconstruction of past events due to resource development is needed to assess impacts at the personal level. A similar survey conducted in the impact community can provide information on what people think is likely to happen, and a follow-up survey would tell us what the real impacts on the population were.

Instead of listing specific information sources, as was done previously, we list categories of variables that might be used in studying impacts related to resource development.

1. Personal and family background variables includes age, family life cycle, and residential history. As in most forms of social change, the older, long-term, less mobile population experiences more adverse effects from resource development (Burdge and Johnson 1973).

2. Socioeconomic status is the composite of education, occupation, and income and is calculated for the household head. Generally, persons in the lower socio-economic groups benefit the least by projects, although agencies are supposed to help these people.

3. Attachment to place and ancestral ties refers to the degree to which persons are willing to move from their present place of residence. Two factors appear to be important here, one is the attachment to a particular place and the other is the degree to which the family history is associated with the land. Research has shown that the greater the attachment to place, the more difficulty a person or an individual is likely to have in adjusting to a new location (Burdge and Ludtke 1972).

4. Identification with community emphasizes association with the wider neighborhood, town, or county. Community is undefined in the sense of geographical size. Community ties could be factors in resisting or encouraging the social change initiated by a reservoir or other development in a community.

5. Previous occupational and geographical mobility refers to the number of changes in occupational classification and changes in location that the individual has experienced. Research has shown that upwardly mobile occupational and geographically groups are more receptive to social change and are more likely to see the benefits of such change. Conversely, persons who experience little occupational mobility or who seldom change residence are less likely to perceive and receive the benefits of resource development.

6. Attitudes and knowledge toward resource development and development in general refers to the attitude and knowledge on the part of the population regarding the development under investigation. Attitude scales are helpful not only to locate persons holding positive and negative attitudes toward the development but also identifies those people who have no attitudes toward the project. Knowledge of project development reflects a general awareness regarding areas affected, dates, potential benefits or costs, and sponsoring agencies.

7. Quality of individual and family life refers to the degree to which community members have adequate housing, a good job, adequate diet, educational opportunity and medical care. Most federal developments have the expressed goal of improving the quality of life of the impacted population.

8. Participation in public decision making refers to the degree to which community members were able to participate in any decisions that may effect their future. It is assumed that under a democratic system each individual or family should have a say in their future and that no outside agency or group has the right to impose unilateral change.

9. Institutional variables include such community institutions as law enforcement, local government, transportation, health and sanitation, religion and even family stability.

Objective data may sometimes be gathered from personnel files for turnover and growth in local government employees or from school records. Additional data on institutions and their role in and reaction to natural resource development can be gained through personal interviews with local officials. A rationale for these kinds of measures is found in Webb, *et.al.* 1968. At a more local level, impacts on such features of community life as home-owned grocery and retail stores also may be determined by personal interviews.

Much can be gained through simple observation of the community and how it functions. What is to be observed and for what reasons is a research decision contingent on the kind and size of the community and the type of natural resource development under study. (Gold 1974 provides examples of ethnographic techniques).

CONCLUSIONS

In this chapter we have outlined an approach to studying social impacts. The model presented here provides direction for basic research on the issue of natural resource development and as a guide for use by practitioners in the field.

By outlining a comparative conceptual scheme, we challenge our peers to think in more dynamic, comparative, and holistic terms about natural resource development (see Figure 3.1). We feel the community profiles that appear in many EISs are lacking in perspective. The current state of the art is often times analogous to looking at a snapshot of a family and trying to reconstruct its history, present status, and future. However, the fields of sociology, anthropology, geography, political science, economics, ecology, and psychology - all have theories, findings, and methodologies that have relevance to the study of resource development (Cottrell 1951).

We have purposefully limited ourselves to citing studies of water resource development because it is our area of interest and because we feel much from this field can be generalized to other forms of rural development. A major drawback of our model is that it calls for specific research at some future point in time. However, there are creative compromises that can be made with the model. We may be able to reconstruct past events through analyzing secondary data sources if we are called in during the construction phase of a project. Or we can use data sources from within the community of impact if we have a good literature review to provide the comparative dimension.

We have attempted to move beyond enumerating the hundreds of social variables that have some potential bearing on the study of social change to isolate what we feel are major variables which, if studied, monitored, and interpreted, will yield a fairly accurate view of the dynamics of social impacts due to natural resource development.

REFERENCES

Andrews, Wade C. and Dennis C. Geersten. 1970. *The Function of Social Behavior in Water Resource Development.* Logan, Utah State University: Institute for Social Science Research on Natural Resources and Center for Water Resources Research, Research Report No. 1.

Bates, Clyde T. 1970. *The Effects of a Large Reservoir on Local Government Revenue and Expenditure,* Lexington, University of Kentucky: Water Resources Institute, Research Report No. 23.

Burdge, Rabel J. and Richard Ludtke. 1972. Social Separation Among Displaced Rural Families: The Case of Flood Control Reservoirs. in *Social Behavior, Natural Resources and the Environment.* William R. Burch, Jr. *et.al.* eds., New York: Harper and Row, pp 85-108.

Burdge, Rabel J. and K.Sue Johnson. 1973. *Social Costs and Benefits of Water Resource Construction.* Lexington, University of Kentucky: Water Resource Research Institute, Research Report No. 64.

Conner, Desmond M. and Keith T. Bradley. 1972. Public Participation in the St. John River Basin. Proceedings of the American Society of Civil Engineers, Washington, D.C., August.

Cottrell, W.F. 1951. Death by Dieselization: A Case Study in the Reaction to Technological Change. *American Sociological Review.* 16 (June) 358-365.

Drucker, Phillip. 1972. *Impact of a Proposed Reservoir on Local Land Values.* Lexington, University of Kentucky: Water Resources Institute, Research Report No. 51.

Drucker, Phillip, J.E. Clark, and L.D. Smith. 1973. *Sociocultural Impact of Reservoirs on Local Government Institutes.* Lexington, Kentucky: University of Kentucky Water Resources Research Institute, Research Report No. 65.

Felton, Paul M. 1968. Citizen Action in Water--Asset or Liability? in *Proceedings of the Fourth American Water Resource Conference.* Phillip Cohen and Martha Francisco, eds. Urbana, Illinois: American Water Resources Association.

Fiery, Walter. 1947. *Land Use in Central Boston.* Cambridge: Harvard University Press.

Gardner, James S. and Nancy B. Hurtquist. 1973. *The Human Ecological Impact of Structural Flood Control on the Iowa River, Iowa.* Ames, Iowa: Iowa State Water Resources Research Institute, Completion Report.

Gold, Raymond L. 1974. Social Impacts of Strip Mining and Other Industrializations of Coal Resources, in *Social Impact Assessment.* C.P. Wolf, ed. Stroudsburg, PA: Hutchinson, Dowden and Ross, pp. 73-90.

Hargrove, Michael B. 1971. *Economic Development of Areas Contiguous to Multi-Purpose Reservoir: The Kentucky-Tennessee Experience.* Lexington, Kentucky: University of Kentucky Water Resources Research Institute.

Hogg, Thomas C. 1968. Social and Cultural Impacts of Water Development in *People and Water*. Emery N. Castle, ed. Corvallis: Oregon State University Water Resource Institute.

Johnson, Sue. 1974. Recent Sociological Contributions to Water Resources Management and Development in *Man and Water*, L. Douglas James, ed. Lexington, Kentucky: University of Kentucky, University Press of Kentucky.

Peele, Elizabeth. 1974. Social Impacts of a Remote Coastal Nuclear Power Plant: A Case Study of the Mendocino Proposal. Oak Ridge, Tennessee: Oak Ridge National Laboratory.

Smith, Charles R. 1970. *Anticipation of Change, A Socioeconomic Description of a Kentucky County Before Reservoir Construction.* Lexington, Kentucky: University of Kentucky: Water Resource Research Institute.

Smith, Courtland L., Thomas C. Hogg and Michael J. Reagan. 1971. Economic Development: Panacea or Perplexity in Rural Areas. *Rural Sociology*, 36(2): 173-186.

Stramn, Gilbert G. 1968. Water Development and Society in *Sociological Aspects of Water Resources Research*. Wade H. Andrews, ed. Logan, Utah State University: Social Science Institute Series, Report No. 1.

Webb, Eugene I. *et.al.* 1968. *Unobtrusive Measure: Nonreactive Research in the Social Sciences*. Chicago: Rand McNally.

Wolf, Charles P. 1974. Social Impact Assessment: The State of the Art. in *Social Impact Assessment*. C. P. Wolf, ed. Stroudsburg, PA: Hutchinson, Dowden and Ross. p. 1-41.

Chapter 4

THE SOCIAL IMPACT ASSESSMENT MODEL AND THE PLANNING PROCESS[1]

Rabel J. Burdge

INTRODUCTION

Elected officials, local community leaders, and urban and regional planners must approve or disapprove proposals for public and private development projects as well as changes in local, state, and federal government programs and policies. These people need a better way to anticipate the possible social consequences of proposed actions on human populations and communities. Social impact assessment (SIA) offers an effective means of anticipating and planning for social impacts prior to project development or program implementation.

By *social impact assessment* we mean the systematic advance of appraisal of the impacts on the day-to-day quality of life of persons and communities when the environment is affected by development or a policy change (Bowles 1981, Burdge 1985). Examples of social impact settings that fall within the jurisdiction of local officials include school and plant closings; major construction and resource development projects, and the siting of hazardous and sanitary waste facilities.

The SIA process alerts the community, community leaders, planners, and project proponents to the likely benefits and costs of social impacts (Finsterbusch 1980). In addition, each participant receives a realistic appraisal of possible ramifications and suggestions for project alternatives and possible mitigation measures before the decision to go ahead has been made. SIA information provides useful criteria for interpreting and evaluating the proposals of outside agents seeking to promote change in local communities (Finsterbusch 1985). Despite the obvious usefulness of SIA, research findings from the variety of social impact settings have not been consolidated and codified into materials suitable to guide local decision making, although some progress has been made (Finsterbusch 1980; Branch *et al*. 1984; Carley and Bustelo 1985).

The purpose of this chapter is to briefly outline the barriers to the consideration of social impacts in the planning process, explain the SIA model, delineate the SIA variables, outline the sources of data to measure them and comment on the connections between SIA and the planning process.

---

[1]Abridged from the original. Rabel J. Burdge. 1987. The Social Impact Assessment Model and The Planning Process. *Environmental Impact Assessment Review*, 7 (2) 141-150. Reproduced here with permission of the author and the publisher.

Background

SIA in the United States developed out of a need to apply the knowledge of sociology and other social sciences in an attempt to predict the social effects of environmental alteration for development projects subject to the National Environmental Policy Act (NEPA) legislation of 1969. These legal and regulatory mandates require project proponents to assess the social effects of a development in a variety of environmental impact settings before the decision to proceed is made.

The NEPA process was intended for large projects that had obvious environmental consequences. However, as community leaders and local planners know, even the smallest projects may have serious social implications for more restricted geographical locations. The community approach to understanding SIA assumes that a new project or policy change alters the normal flow of social change. Furthermore, the impact event will vary in specificity, intensity, and duration. Hence, local leaders and decision makers need to understand better the social impacts of a given development rather than just being aware that general social impacts of a given development rather than just being aware that general social change may take place. The practical goal of SIA is to anticipate likely areas of impact, to utilize the information in the planning-decision process, and to implement appropriate ways to mitigate anticipated negative impacts.

The SIA process assumes that both the direct and indirect effects of social impacts are more easily observed, measured, and interpreted at the community or county level. The more restricted the area of study, the easier it is to identify the sequence and duration of social impacts. For example, the rapid influx or outflow of construction workers is easily observed, but the shift of the power structure from long-term residents to an outside agency is less obvious.

The goal of SIA is to identify and understand the consequences of change for human populations and communities, given different impact events. When that research information is available it will sensitize people to the social impacts likely to occur at the community level. Unfortunately, the use of SIA in the planning-decision process has been inconsistent.

Barriers to Public Consideration of Social Impacts in the Planning Process

Following are the major reasons why decision makers, project proponents, and, for the matter, local community leaders and planners often ignore SIA:

• **Many people feel that understanding social impacts requires only common sense, everybody should know what social impacts are.** Knowledge about social affects comes from the study of past development events. One purpose of SIA is to make knowledge about social impacts available to planners and decision makers.

• **Social impacts cannot be measured and, therefore, should be ignored.** <u>In truth, many social effects are easily understood, and ways of measuring the outcomes can be demonstrated in a variety of settings</u>. SIA measurements are quite reliable because data may be collected and evaluated at the community and county levels. The SIA model proposed here represents a step towards demonstrating how the magnitude, duration, and sequence of a social effects might be assessed.

• **Social impacts seldom occur; therefore, it is a waste of time to consider them.** Social impacts always occur, but like other impacts (economic, biological, and physical) they may not always be significant. Participation in the SIA process allows community leaders to understand those significant social effects that are likely to occur as a consequence of a project proposed in their community.

• **Social impacts always deal with costs, not benefits, and are, therefore, always used to slow up or stop development projects.** Change of any kind brings social costs to some and social benefits to others. The analogy is similar to the ideas behind cost-benefits analyses used in economics. The costs of building a reservoir project to include land acquisition and relocation expense are weighed against benefits such as reduced flooding and improved water quality. If the benefits come out on top, the decision generally is to go ahead. However, the social costs are almost always borne at the community or local level. Economic benefits tend to be justified on a regional or statewide level. Thus, an aspect of the planning process is to know which groups and individuals will benefit from the proposed development or policy change. In the case of a plant closing, social costs may be quite devastating to community residents, while the economic benefits of a cheaper or better product accrue at the aggregate level.

• **Social impact assessment generally increases the price of the project.** In the long run, SIA almost always saves money. The SIA process allows the social concerns of the population to be considered during the initial phases of planning, not after the decision has been made. The SIA process alerts local leaders to the variety of impacts and changes that might occur as a result of project development and/or policy change. Rather than become embroiled in controversy stemming from a decision based on inadequate information, most local leaders opt for good facts in advance.

THE BASIC SOCIAL IMPACT ASSESSMENT MODEL

The objective of the SIA process it to anticipate and predict social impacts in advance so that the findings and recommendations may become part of the planning and decision-making process. However, sociological research only recently has given attention to identifying measuring SIA variables in advance. Social indicators were developed by social scientists in the 1960s and 1970s to monitor social change and the general social health of the country. However, those measures were never widely utilized because the sample size was too small for use on the community or regional level. Furthermore, social indicators research assumed that the impact event had already occurred. Therefore, the results were only useful in understanding past change, not in advanced planning and policy making.

The model illustrated in Figure 4.1 depicts the approach utilized in uncovering the major social impacts of development projects. The assessment team first identifies similar projects that are presently operational and attempts to locate the impacts resulting from the planned change (the comparative study). Ideally, information about the community or area of study would be available both before and after the event to help in measurement. Social impacts then become the changes taking place between T_{1a} and T_{2a} (comparative study (a)). If available, a control study (c) where no event took place would help demonstrate the normal effects of social change (the difference between T_{1c}, T_{2c}, T_{3c}). The impact study (b) attempts to predict the change between T_{2b} and T_{3b} based on the research and information accumulated from comparative studies of similar impact settings.

Figure 4.1
The Basic Social Impact Assessment Model

Comparative T_{1a}-------$\overset{X_a}{\text{------}}$->$T_{2a}$ X = Development
study (a)

Impact study(b) T_{2b}-------$\overset{X_b}{\text{------}}$->$T_{3b}$

Control study(c) T_{1c}------------>T_{2c}-------------->T_{3c}---------------->T_{4c}
                 (Past)   (Present)   (Future)   (Far Future)

The basic strategy becomes one of identifying likely future impacts based on reconstructing the social impacts of past events. The SIA model (Fig. 4.1) may be thought of as a series of snapshots taken at different intervals. Missing information is then filled in based on data obtained from an extensive literature review. The SIA model provides a guide for understanding likely future impacts based on the reconstruction of past events.

Figure 4.2
Stages of Project Development

Planning/Policy   Construction/   Operation/   Decommission
Development $\rightarrow$ Implementation $\rightarrow$ Maintenance $\rightarrow$ Abandonment

---

The Stages of Project Development

All projects go through a series of steps or stages, starting with initial planning, then implementation and construction carrying through to operation and maintenance (Fig. 4.2). At some point the project might be abandoned or decommissioned, or official policy could change.

The social effects will be different for each stage. Local planners and community leaders may wish to focus only on one stage. For example, one community might be concerned about public reaction resulting from the initial siting of a hazardous waste disposal facility, another with the construction aspects of reservoirs, and a third might be faced with the loss of a high school that has been the focus of community pride for many years. The stage in project development is an important factor in determining impacts — and not all social impacts will occur at each stage.

Planning/policy development - refers to all activity that takes place from the time a project or policy is conceived to the point of construction activity on policy implementation. Examples include project design, revision, public comment, licensing, the evaluating of alternatives and the decision to go ahead.

Construction/implementation - begins when a decision is made to proceed. A permit is issued, or a law or regulation takes effect. The construction and implementation phase continues through complete implementation or the end of construction.

Operation/maintenance - is the stage after the construction is complete and/or the policy is fully operational. Some modifications in regulations and procedures might occur during the operation and maintenance stage. In addition, the project may be expanded or scaled down. During the operation and maintenance stage, the project should be monitored to determine if the social, economic, and environmental impacts that were predicted actually occurred.

Decommission/abandonment - begins when the proposal is made that the project or policy and associated activity will cease at some time in the future. As in the planning stage, the social effects of decommissioning begin when the intent to close down is announced.

The Project Setting

The projects and policy decisions that local communities must deal with range from school and plant closing to highway, reservoir, and power plant construction. They include such diverse activities as the introduction of new recreation facilities to the opening of a coal mine. Social impacts (as well as economic and physical changes) will vary depending upon the type of development. However, the general SIA model and the findings apply to most projects in of the United States and Canada.

- mineral extractions, both surface and underground mining as well as new oil and gas drilling;
- hazardous and sanitary waste sites, including the construction and operation of disposal sites for a variety of hazardous and sanitary wastes (Also included are facilities that burn or otherwise destroy chemical and toxic wastes);
- power plants mean both nuclear and fossil fuel electrical generating facilities and associated development;
- reservoirs include all water impoundments for flood control, hydro power, conservation, recreation, and cooling lakes; and
- industrial plants include the variety of manufacturing facilities built and operated by the private sector.

Applying Social Impact Assessment Variables

SIA variables point to measurable change in human populations, communities, and social relationships resulting from a development project or policy change. Drawing upon research on local community change, rural industrialization, reservoir and highway development, natural resource development, and social change in general, I have delineated a list of 26 social variables under the general headings of *population impacts, community/institutional arrangements, conflicts between local residents and newcomers, individual and family level impacts,* and *community infrastructure needs* (Fig. 4.3).

The 26 SIA variables shown in Figure 4.3 represent the types of effects arising from planned change in local communities. Research continues on the refinement of the list as well as on techniques by which each can be measured in advance of the impact event and, thus, be made more useful to local community leaders as well as to professional change agents. The following criteria were used in the selection of the 26 SIA variables.

• **An SIA variable is operative when a community may be altered by project development and policy change.** SIA variables do not refer to the total social environment, they explain only the consequences of the proposed impact event. Other portions of an environmental impact statement or planning document cover economic, physical, and land use change.

• **An SIA variable will tell the decision-maker or planner a specific consequence of the proposed action.** Such descriptors as increase, decrease, expand, and contract depend upon the type of project and the geo-political setting. The directionality of change is not assumed in the labeling of SIA variables.

• **An SIA variable always has a discrete, nominal, or continuous empirical indicator that can be measured, collected, and interpreted within the context of a specific social impact setting.**

• **All SIA variables are based upon data that can be collected or made available during the planning and decision stage as well as other stages in the development of the project or policy** (Fig. 4.2). Because SIA information is required before the event, we rely upon data that can be obtained in advance.

• **An SIA variable does not require, but may utilize, information from questionnaires of the general population.** Survey data vary in quality depending upon the amount of care taken in questionnaire design, sampling, and interviewing. However, results from survey research might contribute to the understanding of several SIA variables. Data from well designed questionnaires — addressed to limited objectives always enhance the understanding of community response to planned social change.

• **An SIA variable is not to be confused with such sociological labels as middle class, ethnicity, or small groups**. These labels define sociological concepts and situations but do not describe changes that take place in communities due to project development.

Figure 4.4 provides an abbreviated illustration of how the SIA variables (as listed in Fig. 4.3) might be interpreted within the context of both the type and the stage of a project. The first example is the siting of a hazardous waste facility. Perceptions about problems of public health and safety could emerge during the early planning stage. If the decision is made to go ahead, construction would be accompanied by an influx of temporary workers. In the case of the industrial plant, community infrastructure support might be added during construction, while changes in the industrial focus of the community might occur during the operation stage. These analytic procedures would be repeated for each of the SIA variables for each stage of the project. In short, the SIA process allows the user to identify and understand the SIA variables that apply to each stage of the project under consideration. Figure 4.4 further illustrates how the SIA variables become part of the SIA statement and serve as major sources of information for planners and decision makers.

Figure 4.3
Social Impact Assessment Variables: The Proposal List of Twenty Six

Population Impacts
Population change
Influx or outflux of temporary workers
Presence of seasonal (leisure) residents
Relocation of individuals and families
Dissimilarity in age, gender, racial or ethnic composition

Community/Institutional Arrangements
Formation of attitudes toward the project
Interest group activity
Alteration in size and structure of local government
Presence of planning and zoning activity
Industrial diversification
Enhanced economic inequities
Change in employment equity of minority groups
Change in occupational opportunities

Conflicts Between Local Residents and Newcomers
Presence of an outside agency
Introduction of new social classes
Change in the commercial/industrial focus of the community
Presence of weekend residents (recreational)

Individual and Family Level Impacts
Disruption in daily living and movement patterns
Dissimilarity in religious practices
Alteration in family structure
Disruption in social networks
Perceptions of public health and safety
Change in leisure opportunities

Community Infrastructure Needs
Change in community infrastructure
Land acquisition and disposal
Effects on known cultural, historical, and archaeological resources

Figure 4.4
Social Impact Assessment Variables by Project Setting and Project Stage

	Project Stage			
Project Settings	**Planning/Policy → Development**	**Construction/ → Implementation**	**Operation/ → Maintenance**	**Decommission/ Abandonment**
Hazardous Waste Site	Perceptions of public health and safety	Influx of temporary workers	Relocation of families	Alteration in size of local government
Industrial Plant	Formation of attitudes toward the project	Change in community Infrastructure	Change in the industrial focus of the community	Change in employ-ment equity of minority groups

Measuring Social Impact Assessment Variables

SIA variables require data that can be obtained at the community or county level. Most census data as well as routine information required by state and federal agencies are available for county and municipal units. The U.S. census has demographic information for each census tract and for each city block within urban areas. In addition, public meetings, newspaper articles, and other ethnographic information provide a source of data for the SIA variables related to public involvement. The measurement of the SIA variables also requires information about project design. For example, the size of the project relative to the size of the community will be important in determining the significance of employment-related and community infrastructure variables. Source of information with which to measure the SIA variables include but are not limited to:

• **Project parameters**, refers to information provided by the project proponents or gathered from on-site visits, for example, numbers and workers, length of construction, size and boundaries of project, etc.

• **Census and secondary demographic data**, refers to information available from such sources as the Census and the Bureau of Economic Affairs. Vital Statistics, and other public and quasi-public organizations that collect routine data on a periodic basis.

• **Community/county data**, which include, for example, needs assessment information, details on government activity available from city and county planning, offices, school records, and data obtained from key informants, public hearings, and newspaper accounts.

• **Public involvement data**, copies from the process whereby the local community and/or the larger society provides systematic input into the proposed policy or project. In the context of the SIA model we see public involvement as a way of collecting data on SIA variables, not as something that is done and then gotten out of the way—like a public hearing. The intent of public involvement is to give citizens a source of input to the planning and decision making process. Because public involvement is required for most projects, we maintain that the process should be seen as an opportunity for collecting data.

SUMMARY

Social impact assessment developed along with environmental impact assessment during the early 1970s as a methodological tool with which to better understand the consequences of environmental alteration and as an input to environmental impact statements. The idea was that if adverse social, economic, and physical effects of development were known in advance, they could either be mediated or eliminated. For the most part, the assessment of biological and economic impacts has become a required input into every stage in the planning process. However, social changes are not always arrayed alongside economic, biological, and land use changes in the matrix that leads to the final decision.

The major difficulty in the application of SIA process has been an identifying and measuring the social impacts that occur with each project. Even if important social impacts were identified, few procedures have been developed for measuring their significance. When either social costs or benefits to local communities are arrayed against regional and national economic goals, social concerns generally finish a distant second. Social science research must establish that the effects on human populations alone are significant enough to alter the outcome of the decision process.

REFERENCES

Bowles, R. T. 1981. *Social Impact Assessment in Small Communities: An Integrative Review of Selected Literature*. Toronto: Butterworths.

Branch, K., Hooper, D.A., Thompson, J., and Creighton, J.C. 1985. *Guide to Social Impact Assessment*. Boulder, CO: Westview Press.

Burdge, R.J. 1985. Social Impact Assessment and the Planning Process. *Planning and Public Policy*. 11 (2):1-4.

Carley, M.J. and Bustelo, E.S. 1984. *Social Impact Assessment and Monitoring: Guide to the Literature*. Boulder, CO: Westview Press.

Finsterbusch, K. 1980. *Understanding Social Impacts: Assessing the Effects of Public Projects*. Beverly Hills, CA: Sage Publications.

Finsterbusch, K. 1985. State of the Art in Social Impact Assessment. *Environment and Behavior*, 17(2):193-221.

Chapter 5

UTILIZING SOCIAL IMPACT ASSESSMENT VARIABLES IN THE PLANNING MODEL[1]

Rabel J. Burdge

BACKGROUND

This chapter represents an extension of chapter four on the use of Social Impact Assessment (SIA) model in the planning process (Burdge 1987). In that chapter I suggested a comparative social impact assessment model to illustrate the application of social impact assessment variables to the project and policy setting.

Figure 5.1 lists the 26 variables presented in the previous chapter as indicators of social impacts that may be applied in the various stages of the impact assessment and planning process. For each of the social impact variables listed in Figure 5.1, an empirical measure has been developed (Burdge 1994). Data on social impacts gathered during the process of public involvement (Burdge and Robertson 1990) have been incorporated into several of the SIA variables. For each social impact variable, I provide a definition of the variable and a rationale for considering each of the variables in the environmental impact assessment and planning process.

The empirical development of the social impact assessment variables is based on the premise that the planning process relies upon documents and data collected during the initial environmental assessment (social assessment) and/or from a draft environmental impact statement. The social impact assessment statement is a component of the planning process that assists decision-makers in understanding changes that will likely take place at the community level.

Sources of information with which to measure the SIA variables include but are not limited to:

- **Project parameters** -- which designate information provided by the project proponents or gathered from on-site visits, for example, numbers of workers, length of construction, size and boundaries of project, etc.

- **Census and secondary demographic data** -- refers to information available from such sources as the Census Bureau, Bureau of Economic Affairs, Vital Statistics, and other public and quasi-public organizations that routinely collect summary financial, demographic and health data.

[1]Abridged from the original. Rabel J. Burdge. 1990. Utilizing Social Impact Assessment Variables in the Planning Model. *Impact Assessment Bulletin*, 8(1/2):85-100. Reproduced here with permission of the author and the publisher.

• **Community/county data** -- includes for example, needs assessment information, details on government activity available from city and county planning offices, school records, and data obtained from key informants, public hearings, and newspaper accounts.

• **Public involvement** -- refers to the process whereby the local community and/or the larger society provides systematic input into a proposed policy or project. In the context of the SIA model we see public involvement as a way of collecting data on SIA variables, not as something that is done and gotten out of the way — like a public hearing (Burdge and Robertson 1990). The intent of public involvement is to give citizens a vehicle for input to the planning and decisionmaking processes. Because public involvement is required for most projects, we maintain that the process should be used as a way of collecting data on social impacts.

As shown in Figure 5.1, the twenty-six (26) social impact assessment variables are arranged under the headings of *population impacts, community/institutional arrangements, conflicts between local residents and newcomers, individual and family level impacts, and community infrastructure needs*.

These 26 social impact assessment variables come from the social science research literature accumulated by scholars who have studied the impacts of development on an ex-post facto basis (Bowles 1981; Branch *et al*. 1984; Carley and Bustelo 1985; Finsterbusch 1980; and Leistritz and Ekstrom 1986). The social impact assessment variables listed here occur repeatedly in most project and policy settings. The SIA variables listed in Figure 5.1 are not intended to be comprehensive, but rather ones that we think can be measured in advance of the development event.

CATEGORY I: POPULATION IMPACTS

Variable 1: Population Change
Definition: The movement of people either into or out of a specified geo-political area, over a specified period of time as a result of the project.

Rationale: The magnitude and rate of population change has important implications for community infrastructure requirements and may be a major determinant of other financial and social impacts in the project area. Three key indicators are important: the size of population change, the density of population in the impact area, and the rate of influx or outflux.

Variable 2: Influx or Outflux of Temporary Workers
Definition: The temporary movement into or out of a specified geo-political area, over a specified period of time, as a result of the project.

Rationale: Some of the social impacts in a project setting can be traced to the number and composition of the construction and associated workers who are introduced into the impact area.

Some of the impacts of the workers are temporary (i.e., housing and health needs), while others may be permanent - such as unused infrastructure capacity.

Figure 5.1
The Social Impact Assessment Variables:
The Proposed List of Twenty Six (26)

Population Impacts

1. Population Change
2. Influx or outflux of temporary workers
3. Presence of seasonal (leisure) residents
4. Relocation of individuals and families
5. Dissimilarity in age, gender, racial or ethnic composition

Community/Institutional Arrangements

6. Formation of attitudes toward the project
7. Interest group activity
8. Alteration in size and structure of local government
9. Presence of planning and zoning activity
10. Industrial diversification
11. Enhanced economic inequities
12. Change in employment equity of minority groups
13. Changing occupational opportunities

Conflicts Between Local Residents and Newcomers

14. Presence of an outside agency
15. Introduction of new social classes
16. Change in the commercial/industrial focus of the community
17. Presence of weekend residents (recreational)

Individual and Family Level Impacts

18. Disruption in daily living and movement patterns
19. Dissimilarity in religious practices
20. Alteration in family structure
21. Disruption in social networks
22. Perceptions of public health and safety
23. Change in leisure opportunities

Community Infrastructure Needs

24. Change in community infrastructure
25. Land acquisition and disposal
26. Effects on known cultural, historical and archaeological resources

Variable 3: Presence of Seasonal (Leisure) Residents

Definition: A permanent but seasonal increase or decrease in the population of the impact area resulting from project development.

Rationale: Recreational and leisure facility development often leads to recreational or seasonal housing. In turn, this may lead to rapid development of mobile homes, motels, gas stations, etc., on nearby private land. Such development may be a source of negative impacts if local zoning laws are inadequate. If the numbers of seasonal residents are high, the community may come to depend entirely upon the support income derived from seasonal residents.

The continual fluctuation in the population of a community is likely to have a substantial effect on the community's infrastructure, employment patterns, business practices and other aspects of daily living to include high cyclical unemployment, service shortages, negative aesthetic impacts and severe traffic congestion. Students at educational institutions might also be considered permanent, but seasonal residents.

Variable 4: Relocation of Individuals and Families

Definition: The number of people who are relocated, voluntarily or involuntarily, as a result of the project or development.

Rationale: Whether voluntary or involuntary, any type of relocation is stressful for the individuals concerned. For planning purposes, the severity of the impact will generally depend both on the numbers to be relocated as well as the distance. However, the research has demonstrated that certain categories of relocatees, e.g., the elderly, poor, long-time residents and minorities suffer more from displacement, because re-establishing former life and friendship support systems for these individuals is difficult.

Variable 5: Dissimilarity in Age, Gender, Racial and Ethnic Composition

Definition: The introduction into the impact area of a sizeable group of persons dissimilar to the resident population in one or more of the characteristics of age, gender, race or ethnicity.

Rationale: Changes in population composition resulting from the project may necessitate change in community infrastructure and the provision of support services to meet the changes in demand. Other social impacts may include disruption of traditional social and power structures and problems of newcomer integration into the community.

CATEGORY II: COMMUNITY/INSTITUTIONAL ARRANGEMENTS

Variable 6: Formation of Attitudes Toward the Project

Definition: The positive or negative feelings, beliefs or positions expressed by residents of the impacted area regarding the proposed project or policy change. (A Public Involvement Variable.)

Rationale: If possible, the SIA should include information on attitudes toward the project obtained from persons in the impact area. Furthermore, an assessment of attitudes towards the project will provide information as to the "community climate" that will prevail during both the construction and operation phases. Public attitudes may be crucial in deciding whether to proceed and whether alterations in plans are necessary (where mitigation is needed). Knowledge of residents' views of their community will also allow a better understanding of how changes induced by the project will influence the impact area.

Variable 7: Interest Group Activity

Definition: The formation, or renewed activity, of formal and informal interest organizations stating positions for or against the project or policy change. (A Public Involvement Variable.)

Rationale: Interest groups and organizations are identifiable forces active in the community that represent sub-categories of the population which stand to gain or lose by the proposed project or change in policy. Their membership characteristics and attitude toward the project should be determined in the full-scale SIA since they play an important role in shaping community response to the project and its effects. A consistent finding in social impact assessment research is that community interest groups always emerge, both for, as well as against the project.

Variable 8: Alteration in the Size and Structure of Local Government

Definition: A change in the number and type of positions necessary to operate local government activities within the impacted area.

Rationale: Changes in the size and complexity of local government generally occur if the project results in an increase or decrease in government related activity. For example, present funding and staffing levels may prove inadequate to meet demands for planning, rapid infrastructure and service expansion, tax collection, and other types of government support due to population change.

Local government may begin to operate more formally and bureaucratically as the volume and complexity of its responsibility increase. For example, as the size of the population increases, local government may take on more community services. This may place a strain on that government and lead to structural alteration. As government becomes more professional and formal it could lead to feelings of alienation on the part of long time residents. There may also be disruption of traditional power structures as newcomers gain political control, thus exacerbating resentment among long-term residents.

Variable 9: Presence of Planning and Zoning Activity

Definition: The presence of a government agency or organization that has jurisdiction within the impact area for development, planning, zoning and/or land use regulation.

Rationale: If such agencies/regulations are not operational in the impact area they may have to be introduced if consequences of project development are to be managed successfully. Coping with growth or decline will be easier if planning, zoning, or special tax and service districts are in place in the impact area prior to the proposed development or policy change.

Variable 10: Industrial Diversification

Definition: The number and variety of private sector industries (manufacturers, retailers, services, etc.) within the project impact area.

Rationale: Project development could lead to industrial diversification in the local economy, both directly through its presence as an employer and consumer of equipment, supplies and services produced by other industries or indirectly through goods and services produced by its employees. If project purchases are made within the area, other sectors of the community economy will experience growth.

Research has shown that business and industrial diversity must be present within the community if the benefits of development are to accrue within the impact area. Also, if the project is temporary in nature, induced diversification may not necessarily lend stability to the local economy since it is dependent solely on the presence of the project as the major consumer. The point here is that if the local economy has diversity it will be better able to absorb the impact event and benefit. Development could lead to diversification, but research has shown that the capacity has to be present for the benefits to take place.

Variable 11: Enhanced Economic Inequities

Definition: The degree to which employment opportunities of the proposed project or development match the job skills of the unemployed in the impact area.

Rationale: Project justification often hinges on the expectation that the proposed project will contribute to the employment needs of the impacted area. One such contribution would be jobs for locals that are presently unemployed. This social impact variable analyzes the match between jobs available from the project and the occupational skills of the locally unemployed.

Variable 12: Change in Employment Equity of Minority Groups

Definition: The degree to which employment opportunities of the proposed project match the job skills of minorities to include low-income, younger persons, ethnic and racial categories and women.

Rationale: Jobs resulting from project development tend not to be distributed equitably either geographically or socially. When assessing the combined negative impacts (costs) and positive impacts (benefits), patterns must be identified where matches are present, e.g., whether one group is significantly benefiting, while another is negatively impacted in many different ways. Assessors should be aware that the project may indirectly increase or decrease social inequity in the impact area. This measure expands the variable on enhanced economic inequities and attempts to determine if benefits will be extended to specific categories of the unemployed or indigenous populations that otherwise might not have employment opportunities.

Variable 13: Changing Occupational Opportunities

Definition: The degree to which the proposed project or development alters the occupational profile of the impacted area.

Rationale: The creation of new occupational opportunities means that local labor may be drawn from the unemployed, those not previously considered part of the labor force (e.g., housewives may enter service industries experiencing project-induced growth), or they may be drawn away from those presently employed. The resulting change in occupational opportunities may lead to changes in family income, class-level and even life-styles. Those not participating in the new occupational opportunities may also find their job situation changing. The different types of jobs available in the community may mean a requirement for a different sets of skills, which could attract new members to a community and may bring about social conflict.

Other, indirect effects of increased employment opportunities may include the retention of young adults in the community who otherwise might have left. Project development may also discourage local youths from acquiring higher education levels and remain in non-skilled positions.

CATEGORY III: CONFLICTS BETWEEN LOCAL RESIDENTS AND NEWCOMERS

Variable 14: Presence of an Outside Agency

Definition: Permanent residence in the project area of a government agency or private sector organization (the project proponent), that has not previously been in the community and whose management and control is external to the area.

Rationale: The presence of an agency or organization which is responsible for making decisions affecting the community and yet is externally controlled and not responsive to local needs and priorities may prove to be a major source of dissatisfaction among area residents. This variable refers to the degree of acceptance of a new, more bureaucratic neighbor in community decision making which might lead to the loss of local autonomy. The presence of a new employer may also significantly alter existing social and power structures within the community.

Variable 15: Introduction of New Social Classes

Definition: The appearance (or disappearance) of a group of people that either expand an existing social class or establish a new social class (based on educational level, income or occupation) in the impact area.

Rationale: The appearance in the community of a group of people who, because of their education, income and/or occupation, have a different lifestyle than those of the majority of long-term residents may change the political and power relationships within the community. Socio-economic characteristics may affect how the newcomers perceive the community and how the community perceives the newcomers. Differences may hinder acceptance and integration. The social class of newcomers may also affect their degree of involvement in community organizations and activities.

Variable 16: Change in the Commercial/Industrial Focus of the Community

Definition: A change in the traditional commercial/industrial or private sector focus of the community.

Rationale: If the project under consideration is large in terms of number of employees and income, and/or the impacted area is of low economic diversification, a change in the *focus* of the community may take place. If the area is known as a retirement, college, farming, ranching or other type of community, the concern is whether the introduction of the project will change this traditional character. If it does, this may alter existing social relationships and affect residents' lifestyles and their perceptions of their community. It may also affect the image outsiders have of the area and in turn influence future settlement patterns.

Variable 17: Presence of Weekend Residents (recreational)

Definition: Refers to the influx of temporary weekend or vacation type visitors who have no permanent home in the community.

Rationale: One of the most important social impacts is the *weekend resident syndrome*. By that we mean the people that come to an area to partake of a particular recreational, historical or cultural opportunities, that was created by the development. The weekend residents may exploit or use the new project, yet contribute very little in return to the impact area.

CATEGORY IV: INDIVIDUAL AND FAMILY LEVEL IMPACTS

Variable 18: Disruption in Daily Living and Movement Patterns

Definition: changes in the routine living and work activities of residents in the impact area caused by alteration to the visual environment, noise and odor levels, transportation routes or the amount of vehicular traffic resulting from the project or development.

Rationale: Project construction and operation may cause adverse environmental change leading residents in the vicinity to alter their movement patterns and social habitats in order to minimize exposure to project related activity. Such adverse impacts include increased traffic congestion, noise, odor, air or water pollution and impacts on the visual quality of an area. The latter is important because it can affect residents' perceptions of their community (which in turn may affect how willing they are to invest time and money in the area and how likely they are to move elsewhere). A change in the community image may also influence whether outsiders will visit, live or establish businesses in the area.

Variable 19: Dissimilarity in Religious Practices

Definition: Introduction into the impact area of a new group with religious values, beliefs and practices different than those of the resident population.

Rationale: This may be a source of social impacts if, for example, the host community is dominated by a single religious group and that religion has a strong influence on local lifestyles and political decisions. If the influx population does not share the religion or lifestyle of the area then conflict is likely. For example, rural Mormon towns in the mountain west of the US have strong norms against public smoking and drinking. Alternatively, the project could bring in a new religious group with practices different from those of the community.

Variable 20: Alteration in Family Structure

Definition: An increase or decrease in one or more of the family status categories (e.g., married, never married, female head of household, with/without children) as a result of the project.

Rationale: Typically, the construction phase of a project will bring large numbers of young males into the community. Many will be single and those who are married may not be accompanied by their families — if the length of employment is brief or local housing is in short supply. If newcomers are predominantly young and male, their integration into the community may be difficult if the community is traditional and family-oriented. Some Environmental Impact Statements suggest that certain social pathologies will come to an area as a result of population influx. Notable among such problems are drunkenness, increased crime and general rowdiness and harassment, basically, a violation of traditional rural community norms.

In addition, change in the family structure of the area may lead to significant change in service demands. A project development may also keep persons in the impact area that might otherwise leave, thereby altering the composition of existing family structures. For example, dependency ratios tend to be higher in rural areas due to the large number of children and older people. If opportunities change, more younger persons in the work force may stay in the impact community.

Variable 21: Disruption in Social Networks

Definition: The termination or disruption of normal community social interaction (including friendship and kin relations) by project activity and development.

Rationale: The normal flow of informal communication in an area may be disrupted by the project. An example would be the construction of physical barriers to existing vehicular or pedestrian routes. Such disruption will affect some social groups more than others. For example, persons with low incomes may be unable to afford the increased time and expense to continue former relationships. The elderly and physically disabled may be cutoff from support networks. The disruption of social networks will always occur in the case of significant population relocation, particularly if accompanied by water impoundment, highway development, and pipeline construction, among others.

Variable 22: Perceptions of Public Health and Safety

Definition: Perceptions, attitudes or beliefs on the part of residents in the impact area that their physical health and safety as well as their mental well-being will be jeopardized by the proposed project or activity (A Public Involvement Variable).

Rationale: Projects to include nuclear power plant construction and operation and hazardous (nuclear and chemical) waste site construction and operation may lead to perceived risk and stress among local residents. While the public's assessment of risk is subjective in nature, their fears should not be dismissed as irrational or unimportant. If there is a widespread belief that the project will endanger their (and future generations') health, community satisfaction will be diminished, acceptance of the project and workers will be hindered and perceptions and interpretation of subsequent positive benefits will be altered.

Variable 23: Change in Leisure Opportunities

Definition: An increase or decrease in leisure/recreational opportunities due to changes in the management of natural resources within the impacted area.

Rationale: The number and type of leisure opportunities available in a community has an important influence on residents satisfaction with their community. Recreational developments may add to, or change the nature of, available leisure opportunities. Not only may residents be affected but outsiders' perceptions of the community may change and thereby influence the number of people and businesses that relocate in the future. Furthermore, the development of a major recreation area will produce a large influx of temporary *weekend* or *vacation* residents to a community. Social impacts ascribed to temporary residents will alter a community in much the same way as seasonal residents.

CATEGORY V: COMMUNITY INFRASTRUCTURE NEEDS

Variable 24: Change in Community Infrastructure

Definition: The increase or decrease in the demands for, and supply of basic infrastructure services and facilities within the impacted area.

Rationale: Project development can alter the demands placed on private and community facilities and services. For example, the population influx that accompanies construction may result in the expansion or building of new facilities or, alternatively may lead to a reduction in community service levels. If capital investments are made in new facilities, communities may be faced with excess capacity during the operation phase of the project. Impacts on housing should be dealt with since projects often lead to increased demand for existing housing and thus increase prices and rents above those customary for the local economy.

In the long-term, the revenues local government derive from the project may lead to expansion of infrastructure. In the short-term however, local government may face financial problems since expenditures on services are likely to be needed before revenues from the project become available.

This variable must be included in a SIA since the cost and quality of public services have an important influence on residents' well-being and satisfaction with their community. The change in community infrastructure is the most frequently included variable in the *socio-economic* component of an Environmental Impact Statement.

Variable 25: Land Acquisition and Disposal

Definition: The number of acres of land that will shift from present use classification or ownership as a result of the project or policy change.

Rationale: Land acquisition or disposal resulting from the project represents more than just a financial loss or gain to the community. If the project is a controversial one, land acquisition may be resented by local residents. If private land is to become publicly owned due to the project, this may mean a loss to the local tax base since federal owned property is not subject to local, state or provincial taxes. Such a tax loss may mean public services and facilities in the area are reduced and residents negatively impacted. Governmental assistance may be necessary if increased demands on community infrastructure results from project induced population growth. If the project is to be sited on land which is already publicly owned, a change in land management policy may considerably affect local residents. For example, wilderness designation will reduce access to the land and restrict former uses such as logging and grazing, which may have been important to the local economy. Where the project means changes in land use patterns, for example, the issuing of permits allowing private development on public land may lead to rapid commercial development in areas lacking adequate zoning controls.

Variable 26: Effects on Known Cultural, Historical and Archaeological Resources

Definition: The proposed destruction, diminution or alteration of one or more of the known cultural/historical/or archeological resources within the impact area.

Rationale: There is often great community sentiment and pride invested in the cultural, historical and resources of an area. Thus, their destruction or diminution could mean not only the loss of valuable historic data but may also lead to an increase in public opposition to the project and may delay project approval. The loss of such resources may be perceived by residents as detracting from the community and may reduce local support for the project.

NEXT STEPS IN THE DEVELOPMENT OF THE SOCIAL IMPACT ASSESSMENT VARIABLES

1. Establish the predictability of utilizing advanced indicators of social impact assessment variables. Included under this step will be the need to establish data sources and analytical procedures which may be applied in advance of the impact event.

2. Develop an understanding of which social impact assessment variables apply to specific project and development settings. Based on a review of known social impact assessment literature as well as available planning documents and environmental impact statements, we will develop a list of the social impact variables that must be considered by the decision-maker for different types of development projects.

3. Develop a list of information and data that the social impact assessment variables require of each project setting from the project proponent.

4. Continue to develop new data sources for the social impact variables through a careful review of models utilized in other types of economic, demographic and sociological projections.

5. Develop criteria for recognizing the point at which the finding of significant social impacts will lead to a decision to stop the project or provide the basis for alternatives and for mitigation.

We should remember the following quote when doing planning in both First and Third World settings:

Social consequences of development always occur, can be measured and are borne at the community and local level — projects are justified and sold on the basis of regional and national economic goals —

Rabel J. Burdge, 1969

REFERENCES

Bowles, R.T. 1981. *Social Impact Assessment in Small Communities: An Integrative Review of Selected Literature.* Toronto: Butterworths.

Branch, K., D.A. Hooper, J. Thompson and J.C. Creighton. 1984. *Guide to Social Impact Assessment.* Boulder, CO: Westview Press.

Burdge, R.J. 1987. The Social Impact Assessment Model and the Planning Process. *Environment Impact Assessment Review,* 7(2):141-150.

Burdge, R.J. 1994. *A Community Guide to Social Impact Assessment*. Middleton, WI (P.O. Box 620863: The Social Ecology Press.

Burdge, R.J. and R.A. Robertson. 1990. Social Impact Assessment and the Public Involvement Process. *Environmental Impact Assessment Review,* 10(1/2):81-90.

Carley, M.J. and E.S. Bustelo. 1984. *Social Impact Assessment and Monitoring: Guide to the Literature*. Boulder, CO: Westview Press.

Finsterbusch, K. 1980. *Understanding Social Impacts: Assessing the Effects of Public Projects*. Beverly Hills, CA: Sage Publications.

Leistritz, F.L. and B.L. Ekstrom. 1986. *Social Impact Assessment and Management: An Annotated Bibliography*. New York: Garland Publishing.

THE METHODOLOGY OF SOCIAL IMPACT ASSESSMENT

Chapter 6

ENVIRONMENTAL IMPACT STATEMENTS AND THE SOCIAL SCIENTIST[1]

Rabel J. Burdge and Sue Johnson

THE NATIONAL ENVIRONMENTAL POLICY ACT: CREATION OF EISs

An optimistic reader of the National Environmental Policy Act (NEPA) of 1969 would pick out Section 2, calling for...*a national policy which will encourage productive and enjoyable harmony between man and his environment...and stimulate the health and welfare of man* as an implicit welcome to the social scientist in policymaking. Further, in Section 102 (A), the NEPA legislation calls for the utilization of... *a systematic, interdisciplinary approach which will insure the integrated use of the natural an social sciences and the environmental design arts in planning and in decision-making which may have an impact on man's environment*, in preparing an Environmental Impact Statement.

Others would note that of the four and one-half pages of the Act, less than one-half of a page is devoted to discussing the impact of projects on people. Rather, the concern and central thrust of the legislation is clearly on the physical environment and what projects may do to harm it. Nonetheless, social scientists who participate in the preparation of an EIS must follow the same guidelines as other disciplines in discussing probable impacts of projects. Figure 6.1 shows the relevant components of Section 102 of NEPA which prescribe the contents of an Environmental Impact Statement. NEPA also calls for the study, development and description of *appropriate alternatives to recommended courses of action in any proposal which involves unresolved conflicts concerning alternative uses of available resources*, and Figure 6.2 gives an example of an outline for an EIS that allows for a full description of alternatives while preserving the letter and intent of the legislation.

The draft EIS is circulated among appropriate Federal, State and local agencies, to the President, the public and to the Council on Environmental Quality (CEQ), whose major responsibility it is to *appraise programs and activities of the Federal Government in the light of the policy set forth in Title I of this act; to be conscious of the responsive to the scientific, economic, social, esthetics, and cultural needs and interests of the Nation; and to formulate and recommend national policies to promote the improvement of the quality of the environment*. Importantly, CEQ is only empowered to make recommendations to the President, it cannot stop projects except through political influence. CEQ can and does question the quality and comprehensiveness of

---

[1]Abridged from the original. Rabel J. Burdge and Sue Johnson. 1975. Social Impact Assessment: What are we doing here? Presented at the Meeting of the Rural Sociological Society. San Francisco, CA. August. Not previously copyrighted.

Figure 6.1
Typical Outline for Current EIS

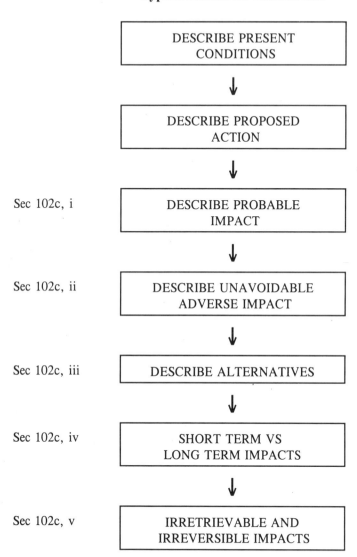

Source: *Environmental Impact Statements: A Handbook for Writers and Reviewers*, Illinois Institute for Environmental Quality, PB-226276, University of Illinois at Urbana-Champaign, August 1973.

Figure 6.2
Proposed Outline for EIS

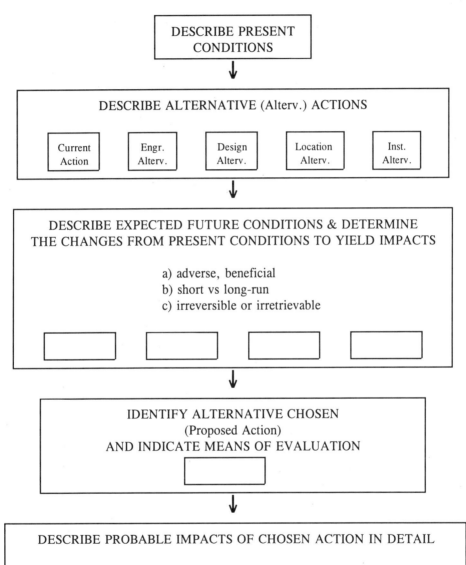

DESCRIBE PRESENT
CONDITIONS

↓

DESCRIBE ALTERNATIVE (Alterv.) ACTIONS

| Current Action | Engr. Alterv. | Design Alterv. | Location Alterv. | Inst. Alterv. |

↓

DESCRIBE EXPECTED FUTURE CONDITIONS & DETERMINE
THE CHANGES FROM PRESENT CONDITIONS TO YIELD IMPACTS

a) adverse, beneficial
b) short vs long-run
c) irreversible or irretrievable

↓

IDENTIFY ALTERNATIVE CHOSEN
(Proposed Action)
AND INDICATE MEANS OF EVALUATION

↓

DESCRIBE PROBABLE IMPACTS OF CHOSEN ACTION IN DETAIL

a) unavoidable impacts which remain

DESCRIBE TECHNIQUES TO BE EMPLOYED
TO MINIMIZE HARM

EIS's according to guidelines published in the *Federal Register*, Vol. 38, No. 147, Wednesday, August 1, 1973.

Given the complexity of the requirements of an EIS, agencies either organize multi-disciplinary teams on the assumption that groups like this will miss fewer significant effects than groups from like-disciplines, or they issue checklists of what are considered important parameters to be included.

THE SOCIAL COMPONENT OF AN EIS: SOCIAL IMPACT ASSESSMENT

If a social scientist participates in the EIS process, what will they contribute in fulfillment of Section 102 guidelines? Social impacts vary, of course, depending upon the nature of the proposal project. Eigermann (cited by Wolf, 1974:2) offers the following guidelines to what an SIA should minimally include:

- Categories of impact stimuli (what in the proposed development will lead to change).
- A baseline from which changes may be measured (description of present conditions)
- Quantitative and qualitative impact measures, or what is likely to change, how much and in what direction, for example; direct, indirect, intended - unintended, reversible-irreversible, random-systematic, among others.
- Temporal dimension, or frequency and duration of change, immediate or delayed.
- Spatial dimensions, or where the change is likely to occur, concentrated-dispersed.

Given the time and money constraints for doing an SIA the above goals would be difficult. Conducting a general survey of the affected population is out of the question, even if it is desirable. Therefore, we must rely upon secondary data sources as outlined in Chapters 2, 3, 4 and 5. Checklists of impact categories, as shown in Table 7.1, can be of two basic kinds: one outlines the components of the proposed project and its impacts, such as what is likely to happen in the design phase, the construction phase, and the operation phase. The other approach is to outline indicators of effects on environmental factors. Which means identifying criteria for environmental change against which projects can be measured.

The next step in impact assessment is to determine what the effects are and how we will measure and evaluate them. First we must figure out how to measure the impact itself, and then its relative value must be weighed in terms of how it will affect a human population. In the first case, measurement of impact, we are looking for data about changes in the environment due to natural resource alteration. In the second case, the effect of the impact on a human population, we make informed judgements, or survey the general population. In terms of levels of measurement, we need at least an ordinal scale to talk about direction of impact (e.g. more or less recreational facilities). An interval scale of magnitude of impact is preferable so we could say, for instance, the lose of farm land in acres will lead to a decline in the standard of living of the local community. (A ratio scale is usually not meaningful in an EIS context). Categories of impact, their measurement of magnitude, direction and degree, can then be placed in a matrix form as a guide to decision-making for which is the best project or alternative. (Illinois Institute for Environmental Quality 1973).

Once the matrices of alternatives are complete, values must be attached to them. If the affected public is not consulted, as is usually the case, the social scientist hired to do an SIA must do it. In essence, relative values are attached to various amounts of change in environmental quality for various indicators. This evaluation is based, necessarily, on value judgements by the EIA team.

In assessing impact, attention needs to be paid to how the history of the community will help in understanding response to planned change. Perception data needs to be gathered by survey research or through the reputational method. The community members and the leadership should be made aware of what has been said about how their community will be altered due to development for it may affect adjustment.

The most common social impact discussed in an EIS is an unelaborated statement of the increased economic activity expected from a project. Given the extensive utilization of cost-benefit analysis as the rationale for development, this emphasis is not surprising. Many times, however, the way agencies use these data to justify projects is biased in favor of project benefits. For example, recreation benefits are based on projected attendance, which are systematically overstated because the calculations do not consider competing recreation opportunity.

Most SIA components include only a simple listing of potential impacts. There is usually some demographic data on current population and expected growth, and possibly, statements about likely disruptions of the community. Even if social impacts are mentioned, it is rare to see any plan or program to ameliorate or mitigate significant impacts such as large-scale relocation of families; especially when compared to intervention strategies for plants, animals, air, water and landscape.

As a social scientist we would expect some consultation of pertinent literature, some theoretical guidance based on research and a delineation of the population to be impacted. Rarely is this the case, however. Agencies say that it is too expensive and time-consuming to conduct primary social research; these statements to the contrary, it is the best source of propositions about the likely impact of projects. (See Friesema and Culhane 1974, for an evaluation of current EIAs).

CONSTRAINTS ON THE SOCIAL SCIENTIST AS SIA PRACTITIONER

There are several reasons for this sad state of affairs in SIA, beyond the emphasis of NEPA and time and money constraints on the practitioner. As Friesema and Culhane (1974:5) have pointed out:

> *All the social science which appears in an EIS is marshalled as project justification, as if the EIS were an advocacy statement, and operates within the basic assumption that the project (or a similar, acceptable alternative) is surely desirable. If the negative social impacts are so obvious that they simply have to be acknowledged, they will be fudged over sufficiently, so that neither the decision-makers nor other reader can use the EIS to estimate those impacts.* There are few exceptions to this pattern.

A impact statement approved by the Huntsville Army Corps of Engineers is a case in point. The proposal would require the relocation of over 500 families and businesses of a rural village (U.S. Army Corps of Engineers, 1974). This is a social impact of considerable magnitude. The EIS devoted about six paragraphs (out of 136 pages) to the negative effects of relocation; all expressed in qualitative terms so that no estimation of the magnitude of personal and financial loss was given.

As a sub-contractor the SIA practitioner must deliver his or her part of the EIS. However, the contract is written such that the agency has final say over the uses (or misuses) and interpretations of the data. This means that a social impact study could appear in the draft EIS in a highly-truncated form — with the negative impacts ignored or misinterpreted. Short of litigation, the assessor will have difficulty reinstating their findings to the impact statement.

Agency staffs are usually strong in the natural and engineering sciences which means that what input social scientists do have is often misunderstood or ignored (see Chapter 13). Other constraints include being denied access to important information on the grounds of *sensitivity*, or that the agency may set stringent restrictions on what data are collected and utilized. Proponents of projects often make decisions independent of the EIS and comments by interested agencies and the public are merely incorporated into the public record, with no intent to include them in the decision-making process. This minimal bureaucratic compliance to the letter and spirit of the NEPA legislation is not uncommon (Carter 1975:46).

SOCIOLOGICAL CONSIDERATIONS IN IMPACT ANALYSIS

The natural resource development project is a causative factor, the baseline is the initial or *before* condition, and the selection of social impact measures the hypothesis among dependent variables and the *cause* of change. The relationship between the variables, the direction and magnitude of predicted change are problems of cause and effect. Predictions about social impacts are usually based on implicit notions of causality, whether theory, observational or literature derived. The exploration of impacts is what Jacobs (1961) calls an exercise in *organized complexity*, or the many interactions of events. We are dealing with impacts on a social system, be it a neighborhood a community or an entire city.

New models are needed to clarify the basic philosophical and sociological issues underlying man-environment relations. The contributions of applied sociology have been *spotty and do not cumulate to provide a coherent and convincing basis for action in major institutional settings* (Street and Weinstein 1975: 65). Our inability to make precise and reliable predictions about the future, which will be necessary if we meet the real needs of SIA, has its roots in our inability to manipulate crucial variables that would test our theories and hypotheses. Moreover, since humans can influence their future, and our predictions influence that behavior, we are caught in a self-renewing, ever-changing situation. This, at present, condemns us to what Popper calls *short-run social forecasting* for *piece-meal planning* (quoted by Street and Weinstein 1975:67).

Jobes (1974) points to the need for a generalists (ecological) perspective in the study of man/environment relationships, and that specialization and desire for precision within sociology have worked to militate against the ecological approach. Community studies and human ecology are both sources of empirical findings and theory for the

SIA practitioner, yet *sociologists may find antecedents to man-environment studies in sociology but their findings will be neither broad enough nor specific enough to provide adequate guidelines* for the environmental sociologist (Jobes:1974:6).

We raise these issues because our efforts and those of others (Finsterbusch 1975; Mack 1974; Drucker, Clark and Smith 1973; Johnson and Burdge 1974; Burdge and Johnson 1977, operating within standard social science perspectives, are attempting to make accurate predictions of future social impacts of projects while in the planning stage. Friesema and Culhane (1974) argue that the epistemological and methodological complexities of making precise and useable predictions are so great as to make it almost impossible to discuss anticipated social impacts of projects. However, we have faith that given sufficient time and effort viable predictive methodologies will emerge and that social impact assessment is the best place to begin.

Within the EIS framework, we need research on the typology or taxonomy of developing communities (Jobes 1974:6) and their major characteristics, as well as a propositional inventory of the existing literature. The time and money limitations means that not every EIS can have a social research component, though a few might serve as case studies.

Several researchers (in addition to the authors) are working on methodologies for assessing the social impact of projects (See Wolf 1974: 21-31; Finsterbusch 1975; Drucker, Clark and Smith 1972; and Smith 1970). In terms of meeting the requirements of an EIS, a comparative diachronic model has the virtues of providing an empirical basis for predictions (from matched projects, already operating), some indication of magnitude of likely changes as well as providing a time frame for studying the impact and predicting likely impact (before project, during construction, initial or near-initial operations phase, and after some years of operation). It has the shortcomings of difficulties in matching projects, the imprecision of predictions and expensive and length of needed research. At the present stage of development it is best for large-scale, either/or developments, rather than projects that must choose among alternative.

THE POLITICS OF ENVIRONMENTAL IMPACT ASSESSMENT

The EIS is a *public* document, designed impact to bring in environmental, local community and public interest groups which in the past have been left out of the decision-making process. These interest groups often disagree on project goals and even if it should be undertaken at all. The tendency of the agency to take on an advocacy role toward their projects often has the effect of polarizing opposition groups, creating adversarial relationships.

The willingness of opposition groups to engage in litigation if their interests are not represented makes agencies more likely to allow them access. However, as Friesema and Culhane (1974) point out, access and effectiveness are quite differently; to be effective, comments to a draft EIS must be technically sound, detailed, and contain a well-developed and justified argument against what is being proposed. Participation in the EIS review process offers the social scientist a chance to have an effective say in what happens with a project. Since the agency is mandated to formally consider any data or argument, no matter how threatening, detailed critiques of agency positions and the EIS can stop, delay or modify a project. However, the common response, of agencies, is to *ignore or creatively misinterpret* the comments so that the draft and final EIS remain almost identical. In this case, intervention on the part of social scientist than can take a different cast: since most projects require the cooperation of other agencies besides the proposing agency, and EIS comments are a matter of public record, the social scientist as advocate can use this information as the basis for an effective appeal to other agencies to stop or modify projects. If this fails, legal intervention is still possible because of the procedural complexities of NEPA and agency resistant and failure to show *good faith* in complying (Friesema and Culhane 1974; 7-11). The advocate approach requires the social scientist to take one side in the EIS process and often to face the prospect of being involved in court proceedings.

There are some important considerations underlying both the social scientist as advocate *and* the organizational constraints that operate to make agencies generally unresponsive to criticism and difficult to budge from their own advocate role. A practical question intervenes as well, does playing advocate stop or modify projects or do most projects proceed as planned in spite of vigorous opposition?

Moreover, being an *expert witness* in court, or in giving a deposition and being examined by agency attorneys can be a stress-inducing experience and can damage the social scientists' personal/professional credibility. The tendency of social scientists to qualify our statements can make us appear less than authoritative, compared to agency economist and engineers, and further weaken our credibility in the cycs of the court.

Agency behavior in the EIS process also holds out little hope of their abandoning the advocate role. Unfortunately, EISs have little relationship to such decisions as to location design, construction, or operation of public projects. Most EISs are predicated on the project as planned, with only lip service given to alternatives. The EIS needs to be integrated with the planning for a project rather than treated as a separate, formal requirement; agencies like the Forest Service have shown that this integration can be achieved and lead to wise decision-making. Unfortunately, most other agencies have been unwilling to abandon the advocate role and integrate project planning with the preparation of EISs. There seems to be an unwillingness to make plans public until they are practically finalized. At that point the investment in planning and the laying of their prestige on the line make it unlikely that the agency will take an EIS seriously, or to respond to public pressure to alter or cancel a project.

RECOMMENDATIONS FOR SOCIAL SCIENCE INVOLVEMENT IN THE NEPA PROCESS

This section outlines personal and professional alternatives open to social scientists who want to get involved in the EIS process and suggestions for improving the social components of an EIS. The two concerns are supportive — not mutually exclusive.

Social Scientists in Land Management Agencies

There are several fruitful activities we as a profession or as individual social scientists can undertake to see that the social impacts of public projects are given more serious consideration. The most obvious route is to work as a research social scientists for an agency which must file EISs. The major function of a social scientist in an agency would be education; that is providing *basic perspectives for thinking about the world* and communicating the real limitations of the discipline to one's co-worker (Street and Weinstein 1975:67). These authors go on to argue that sociologists cannot do good applied work *until they recognize and communicate the limits as well as the potentials of what they are doing.* We feel this is an important role for the sociologists employed by an agency, as well as providing *technical assistance* in the drafting guidelines for EISs and trying to provide the best research input possible in the situation.

Guidelines for SIA

It would be helpful if the professional social science organizations would draft guidelines for what an adequate social impact assessment might include. A 1974 conference sponsored by the Rockefeller Foundation and Cornell University provides several generalizations as to the conditions favoring the utilization of social science research. These are:

- The earlier in the research process that there is interaction between the researcher and the research user, the greater is the probability of utilization
- The more coordinated the research process is with the decision-making process of the research user, the greater is the probability of utilization
- The more congruent findings are with the preferences of the users and their clientele the greater is the probability of utilization (Cornell/Rockefeller Conference, Draft, 1975: 26-28).

Generalizations about Social Impacts

We need to gain support within the discipline of sociology for expanding our knowledge base about social impacts. In other words, a few dedicated researchers need to take social impact assessment seriously, and begin doing systematic research on social impact, perhaps to test the propositions that could be derived from a literature search. Sources include community studies, human ecology, the sociology of natural resources as well as the rural industrialization studies of the late 1950s and early 1960s. Monies for this kind of research would have to be sought through normal funding agencies and not the land management agencies which do EIAs and SIAs.

We need to build a series of generalizations about impacts derived from basic research in order to have an empirical basis for our predictions. Moreover, if we are going to help agencies who plan public projects, we need to work on quantifying the range and extent of social impacts. One way to do this is develop standardized impact measures. For example, what is the real cost of health care for each additional person in a community; what is the true cost of an increase in the crime rate; or the costs of expanding community facilities to meet construction phase demands? If we could begin to estimate these costs within a tolerable range of error, then we can begin to evaluate the real costs of public projects.

Role of the Social Scientist

As mentioned above, we hope that professionally sanctioned guidelines for participation in the EIS process and setting minimum standards for SIA will emerge. We also need a realistic assessment of what a social scientist can contribute to the EIS process so that the field is not misrepresented or claims are made which cannot be kept.

Similarly, instead of having agencies issue checklists for assessing social impact we would like to see a call for truly multidisciplinary teams in the preparation of EISs. This would ensure inclusion of the social sciences in EISs, and probably work to improve the overall environmental assessment process. We also suggest that input from the impacted population be included in an EIS.

Public Involvement Research

We need more research on ways in which the public may be involved in the EIS decision-making process. What we know about public involvement is not at the moment a part of the NEPA process. Presently, most public input is from highly motivated special interest groups. We need to find ways to ensure that the public is involved early and represented throughout the decision-making process.

SIA Research Under Contract

The sociologist should retain control over the collection, interpretation, and presentation of data rather than signing it over as property of the agency. Secondly, the sociologist should keep and retain the right to future analysis of the data. This task is difficult because most agencies insist on the right to have a final say over data interpretation and whether it will be included in an EIS. Outright misrepresentation or misinterpretation of data by the agency can be stopped by litigation, however, the expense is beyond most of us. Professional societies can provide guidelines for standard contracts for sociological work in SIA. However, as free-lance consultants, or as members of the University and college communities, we are in a better position to negotiate with agencies.

Conclusion

In conclusion, the current status of SIA for EISs is one of confusion and a source of professional role uncertainty. What is being done is often mundane, tedious and of questionable quality and impact. NEPA holds the promise for social scientists having an effective say in public policy-making; however, to date, our performance has not lived up to its potential, largely due to the temptations of easy money and a disregard the long-term impact on the discipline of doing shoddy SIA work.

REFERENCES

Burdge, Rabel J. and Sue Johnson. 1977. Socio-cultural Aspects of the Effects of Resource Development, in *The Social Consequences of Environmental Change: A Handbook for Environmental Planning*. James McEvoy III ed. New York: John Wiley, pp 241-279.

Carter, Luther J. 1975. The Environment, A *Mature* Cause in Need of a Lift. *Science* (January) 187 (4171): 45-48.

Cornell/Rockefeller Conference. 1974. State of the Art on Methodology for Studying Environmental Perception, Beliefs, Values and Attitudes and State of the Art on Utilizing Perception, Attitude and Opinion Research. Ithaca, N.Y.: Cornell University (October 21-24).

Dornbusch, David M. *et.al.* 1974. *A Generic Methodology to Forecast Benefits From Urban Water Resource Improvement Projects*. San Francisco: David M. Dornbusch and Co.

Drucker, Philip, J.E. Clark, and L.D. Smith 1973. *Sociocultural Impact of Reservoirs on Local Government Institutions*. Lexington: Kentucky Water Resources Research Institute. Research Report No. 65.

Friesema, H. Paul and Paul J. Culhane. 1974. The Environmental Impact Statement Process: Technical Assessment or Political Advocacy. Presented at the meeting of the Society for the Study of Social Problems, Montreal, Canada, August.

Finsterbusch, Kurt. 1975. *A Methodology for Analyzing Social Impacts of Public Policies*. Vienna, Va.: The BDM Corporation. May.

Gold, Raymond L. 1974. Social Impacts of Strip Mining and Other Industrializations of Coal Resources. in *Social Impact Assessment*. C.P. Wolf, ed. Milwaukee: Environmental Design Research Association 5, pp 123-146.

Illinois Institute for Environmental Quality. 1973. *A Handbook for Writers and Reviewers*. PB 226276, Urbana, IL. University of Illinois: August.

Jacobs, Jane. 1961. *The Death and Life of Great American Cities*. New York: Random House.

Jobes, Patrick. 1974. Random Thoughts on Environmental Sociology. in *Environmental Sociology 4*. C.P. Wolf ed. November, pp. 5-8.

Johnson, Sue and Rabel J. Burdge. 1974. A Methodology for Using Diachronic Studies to Predict the Social Impact of Resource Development. Presented at the meeting of the Rural Sociological Society, Montreal, Canada, August.

Mack, Ruth P. 1974. *Criteria for Evaluation of Social Impacts of Flood Control*. Phase I Report Submitted to the Connecticut River Basin Supplemental Flood Management Study. New York: Institute of Public Administration, March.

Smith, Charles R. 1970. *Anticipation of Change, A Socioeconomic Description of A Kentucky County Before Reservoir Construction*. Lexington: University of Kentucky Water Resources Institute, Research Report No. 28.

Street, David P. and Eugene A. Weinstein. 1975. Problems and Prospects of Applied Sociology, *The American Sociologist*, 10 (May): 65-72.

U.S. Army Corps of Engineers. 1974. *Final Environmental Statement, R.D. Bailey Lake*, Huntington, West Virginia.

Wolf, Charles. 1974. Social Impact Assessment: The State of the Art. in *Social Impact Assessment*. C.P. Wolf, ed. Milwaukee: Environmental Design Research Association 5, 1-44.

Chapter 7

SOCIAL COMPONENTS OF ENVIRONMENTAL IMPACT STATEMENTS[1]

Rabel J. Burdge, William R. Burch, Jr., Raymond Gold, Girard Krebs, Sue Johnson, Ted. L. Napier

BACKGROUND

Nothing has created quite the flow of bureaucratic paperwork and bureaucratic structures as the preparation of Environmental Impact Statements. While representing an initial political attempt to safeguard the natural environment and its living creatures, these documents have become legal instruments to examine changes ranging from the issuance or mining permits in Kentucky to the basis for a lawsuit closing down an air force base in Kansas City. In short, the impact of the legislation has been far greater than it's makers had intended. While some may argue that the law has hindered progress, cut down on jobs, and at times slowed the flow of critical resources, all agree that the NEPA legislation has allowed the country to think in a very systematic way about the impacts of policy and development decisions.

In the initial writing and interpretation of NEPA, it was thought that only physical, biological, and economic concerns should be considered. The impacts on the human population were not thought to be a part of the environment. However, it soon became obvious that construction of reservoirs, the mining of coal, and the building of highways had as much impact on the human population as on the physical environment. Based on similar events and legal interpretations, the social component of Environmental Impact Statements was born.

The President's Council on Environmental Quality (CEQ) was the agency responsible for interpreting the link between NEPA (National Environmental Policy Act) and human populations. In the 1974 regulations, CEQ pointed out that qualifying actions must be major, must clearly be a federal action, must have significant effect, and must involve the *quality of the human environment...either by directly affecting human beings or by indirectly affecting human beings or by indirectly affecting human beings through adverse effects on the environment.* Furthermore, each environmental statement should *utilize a systematic, interdisciplinary approach which will insure the integrated use of the natural and social sciences and the environmental design arts in planning and decision making which may have an impact on man's environment.* (CEQ 1974) The quality of the human environment provision and the interdisciplinary

[1]Abridged from the original. Rabel J. Burdge, *et.al.* 1978. Social Components of Environmental Impact Statements. in *Environmental Impact Analysis: Emerging Issues in Planning.* Ravinder K. Jain and Bruce L. Hutchings eds. Urbana, Illinois: University of Illinois Press, pp. 117-132. Reproduced here with permission of the authors and the publisher.

approach of the law clearly makes sociology an integral component of all required environmental impact statements.

Some agencies erroneously lump the sociological and economic components of an impact assessment statement together and simply refer to it as *socioeconomic*. A *sociological impact* is the change that will likely occur in the human populations that are directly a part of the system and the social institutions, such as the schools, communities, and families that occupy the impacted space.

This paper is divided into two parts: (1) a categorization of environmental impacts as a starting point or a way of thinking about similarities in impacts (**levels of protocols**); and (2) types of variables that sociologists and other social scientists may call upon in studying impact assessment which we ranked according to ease in obtaining data.

These two areas constitute more of an outline of a research program for sociologists, and not a table of contents for an impact statement. This chapter includes parts of the individual works of each author. The debate of always having to quantify was dismissed as necessitating the loss of important data and of forcing a requirement to accept the data of another discipline (namely economics). This portion of our deliberation includes a systematic way of looking at a social impact assessment regardless of the type of project, and a suggestion of the source of variables that might be used in such a study.

After considerable haggling over wording the authors suggest the following definition. A *social impact assessment* is an analysis of past and present impingements upon social conditions and processes and a projection of likely future consequences of proposed interventions in social interactions and relationships between and among people. These interventions are ordinarily combinations of natural resource and artifactual development. Our definition of SIA clearly indicates that the social pertains solely to interactions and relationships between and among people. Although hyphenated, social matters, for example, socio-economic, socio-biological, and so on, are obviously related to interactions between and among people, they are ancillary and subordinate to the SIA researchers' central and overriding concern with the social milieu *per se*.

THE CATEGORIZATION OF PROJECTS

The authors created a systematic way to think about the different types of projects that might be subject to environmental impact assessment (Figure 7.1). Protocols here refer to a plan or outline which represents a programmatic approach to social impact assessment.

Because they deal with highest level abstraction by applying to all projects, the general protocols are the most abstract and therefore least amenable to site-specific operationalization. The site-specific protocols are those which the research sociologist delineates in doing SIA, and therefore the hierarchy of levels of protocols from I through IV are the levels which are made operational in the actual "measurement" of site-specific social impact. Thus, in these levels, we observe a sharpening of focus; crystallization in the rules of correspondence between members of analytical categories and empirical referent; and transition in the criteria for mapping parameters of variables into empirical referents.

Establishing correspondence between this scheme and schemes in which other environmental sociologists have wrestled with establishing guidelines for SIA, it seems that it is level IV which is the focus of uncertainty. Note that there are no entries in Figure 7.1 for site-specific protocols. The next section suggests data sources that might be included at the site level.

We feel that the taxons in level II (Figure 7.1) are justified in terms of the types of activities involved. Resource extraction is an activity in environments which has obvious differences when compared to constructing a building or complex of buildings. We anticipate differential social impacts from construction of for transportation corridors when compared to non-renewable natural resource intervention. In brief, some level II activities result in alterations of environments which extend over broad areas, for example, surface mining of coal by area stripping which affects thousands of contiguous areas of land, extending over many square miles. Other level II activities in environments result in a narrow band of surface alterations which may be temporary dislocations, for example, the installation of water lines for provision of domestic water to households and other occupied units. While this chapter has reasonably exhausted level II taxons in terms of the nature of activities in environments, the committee's experience is limited to certain agencies, particularly the Army Corps of Engineers and the Bureau of Land Management. A further problem, that is difficult to handle under this taxon or any other systematic scheme is change in administrative designations. For example, the land in Alaska is presently being divided among federal agencies, the state, and native Alaskans. While no physical changes may take place after land transfer, the potential must be considered since every Federal Agency manages with different goals. It is our rationale that the similarity within a particular field protocol will be greater than that across level II. For example, it seems reasonable that area strip mining for coal is differentiated from urban renewal, which in turn is differentiated from reservoir construction in terms of parameters of social and cultural impacts. The further delineation and specification of level II and level III protocols, represents an important future task.

Figure 7.1, level III, is a taxonomic extension from level II, and the principles which apply in the explication of level II apply on level III by extension. Note that as we move from level II to level III, we move toward crystallization in actual design and implementation of an approach to analysis.

SUGGESTED SOCIAL IMPACT VARIABLES AND DATA SOURCES

It is at level IV where specific research settings are available. Only in concrete research on the SIA of site-specific projects will an instrument by found (be it a survey questionnaire, an open or closed interview schedule, or an operational research design) which produces data from some source.

Table 7.1 lists sources of data that can be used for research into social impacts. Data sources range from periodic censuses to personal interviews. As one moves down the list from category I to category VII, one moves from highly aggregated data about political units to measurements of behavior and attitudes of individuals. These data become more reflective of what is happening to community residents and their institutions. Also, as one goes down the list to category VI, the data are available in shorter time periods, making possible the monitoring of short-term impacts and the

Figure 7.1
Prospectus for Research Design in Social Impact Assessment

	All Projects				
I. General Protocols					
II. Field Protocols	**Resource Extraction** Renewable Nonrenewable	Land Use Manipulation	Building Construction	Transportation	Utility Delivery Systems
III. Local Protocols	Forestry Deep mining Agriculture Strip mining 　　　　　　　a. coal 　　　　　　　b. sand 　　　　　　　c. limestone 　　　　　　　d. copper 　　　　　　　e. etc.	Reservoirs Small Watersheds Stream Channelization Stream Flow Alteration Recreational Development Wildlife Habitat Estuary Modification	Power Plants Schools Urban Development & Redevelopment Shopping Centers Industrial Parks	Highways Airports Bike Paths Canals Harbors Dredging Locks Railways Subways Trolleys Trams	Sewers Water Lines Power Lines Pipe Lines Telephone Lines
IV. Site-Specific Protocols[a]					

[a]See Table 7.1 on lists of social impact variables and data sources

Table 7.1

Suggested Variables and Data Sources for Social Impact Assessment

I. **U.S. BUREAU OF CENSUS PUBLICATIONS**
   A. Census of Population
      1. Area and Population Size
      2. Urban population proportion
      3. Labor force composition
      4. Productivity of the population
      5. Extreme incomes
      6. Educational attainment
      7. In- and out-migration

   B. Census of housing
      1. Dwelling
      2. Household modernity
      3. Owner-occupied homes

   C. Census of agriculture
      1. Value of farm products sold
      2. Average farm size
      3. Agriculture tenure classes

   D. Census of business and industry
      1. Per capita retail sales
      2. Economic complexity
      3. Unemployment rate
      4. Government complexity

II. **STATE RECORDS**
   A. Marriage rate
   B. Birth rate
   C. Death rate
   D. School attendance records
   E. Public assistance payments
   F. Local educational expenditures
   G. Permits for resource or mineral removal
   H. Reported criminal activity

III. **PRIVATE RECORDS AND REPORTS**
   A. Per capita disposable income
   B. Median family income
   C. Bank receipts

IV. **COUNTY AND OTHER LOCAL RECORDS**
   A. Improved local highways
   B. Record of deed transfers
   C. Value of real property
   D. Per capita local expenditure for education
   E. Land-use patterns
   F. County relief expenditures
   G. Other Measures

V. **STATE AND FEDERAL AGENCY REPORTS**
   A. Cooperative extension service
   B. Soil conservation service
   C. Farmer's home administration
   D. Department of Health, Education, and Welfare

VI. **ARCHIVE INFORMATION**
   A. Newspaper reports
   B. Official transcripts of public hearings
   C. Cost benefits analysis of present and proposed projects

VII. **DATA FROM PERSONAL INTERVIEWS**
   A. Personal and family background variables
   B. Socioeconomic status
   C. Attachment to place and ancestral ties
   D. Identification with community
   E. Previous occupational and geographic mobility
   F. Attitudes toward and knowledge of resource development in general
   G. Quality of individual and family life
   H. Participation in public decision making
   I. Institutional variables

updating of predictions. The attempt in this section is to move from somewhat vague concepts to concrete empirical indicators that can be used and understood by informed and educated lay and professional people interested in this process. This is not a laundry list of social science variables, but rather variables that have been found through investigation to be related to the impacts of natural resource development.

Many of the variables listed under census data have surrogate measures which are available more frequently and which serve the dual purposes of being aids in interpolating trends between censuses and of being useful for monitoring short-term impacts.

U.S. Bureau Of Census Publications

Census data are reported and available down to the census tract level. Certain other forms of information are summarized by municipal place or county. Much of the information is available and relatively comparable for decennial periods since 1930. More recent censuses are available electronically. Data on agriculture, business, industry, and manufacturing are collected and reported in five-year intervals. Occasionally, special census reports are available for selected areas. In addition, the monthly survey of the labor market provides important data on nationwide occupational and employment trends. Generally speaking, the more recent the information, the more reliable.

Census Of Population - Information in this section is based on the decennial population census. Interpolation of data from other sources provides estimates during inter-census years.

Area and Population Size - Total population is the most frequently cited and readily available statistic for any political unit. Increases and decreases in population size are some of the most significant indicators of social change, although the reasons why are often complex and intertwined. We would expect most rural counties to lose population as they have in the past. However, if population loss was less than the average or if it actually increased, it may be due in part to resource development. However, the total area of a county is an indicator of capacity to absorb impact. Changes in population density (persons per square mile) may also be due to development.

Extreme Incomes - Traditionally, rural areas have been two-class societies: the rich and the poor. A measure of this is the percentage of the population having very low incomes (usually below the poverty line) plus the percentage of families having a very high income. Generally, economic development is associated with the emergence of a sizable middle class. The measure is calculated by adding the top and bottom quartiles of family income for the county. This measure is then compared to a similar figure for the comparison region.

Census of Housing - The decennial census of housing is collected in conjunction with the regular census of the population. Information is given on the same political units. Because indicators of housing quality have changed over the last fifty years, comparison of recent data with that of the past is sometimes difficult.

Dwelling Condition - This refers to the percent of the dwelling units in the county that are sound and have all plumbing facilities. Although a particular resource development may take many years to produce an improvement in the quality of housing, generally, if overall economic conditions improve, this will show up as improvement in dwelling conditions.

Census of Agriculture - The census of agriculture is collected every five years and includes food and fiber, in addition to horticultural and floricultural crops.

Value of Farm Products Sold - The total value of all agricultural products sold is available for each county from the agriculture census, and the interim reports are available from the crop reporting service of the State Departments of Agriculture. In an impacted community, the total value of farm products sold is likely to decrease relative to non-impacted areas if farmland is taken out of production, unless land conversion result is higher dollar yield uses.

Census of Business and Industry - As in the case of agriculture, censuses of business and industry and manufacturers are available on a five-year basis, with many special censuses conducted in interim periods. The *County and City Data Book* also includes much of the information. Some of the information in this section is not available for all census periods in recent decades. An increase in most of the indicators in this section would show a movement away from a traditionally agriculture-based economy.

Per Capita Retail Sales - The average per-person dollar sales in the county are available through the census bureau and are often available by county from a State Bureau of Business Affairs or the equivalent agency. As development in a particular region increases, the amount of dollar trade is expected to increase.

State Records

As professional statisticians find more employment in state agencies, the level of record keeping in these agencies improves. However, certain states did not keep birth, death, and marriage records until the late 1930s. Many of the variables in this section are indicative of the vitality and cohesiveness of the community. Many are available on a monthly as well as on an annual basis.

School Attendance Records - The average daily school attendance for eligible children is summarized on a school district basis. Rural education levels continue to lag behind urban areas and, in particular, suburban areas where many middle class persons live. A percentage increase in school attendance would indicate future higher levels of education and a greater influx of the middle class. School attendance records are, of course, different from increases and decreases in the number of students, which is reflective of population changes.

Public Assistance Payments - Total federal and state welfare payments include everything from social security to the rent supplement program. These numbers are available by county on a monthly and weekly basis. The only problem is that they must be combined into a single index. The total of public assistance payments provides an indication of federal and state participation in the economy. It also provides an index, *albeit* indirect, of the poverty level of the county. Any improvement in the economy coming from development should lessen the amount of public assistance payments.

Private Records and Reports

Private records refer to non-local, state, or federal statistics, including statistics from business, manufacturing, and sales organizations. A problem with the use of these data is that most are summarized as aggregates of political units. As such, many may not be reported for rural counties.

Median Family Income - This statistic is reported by the Department of Commerce as well as by many private business agencies and organizations. It is particularly crucial for measuring inflation rates and monitoring the buying power of persons in the county. The only problem with this statistic is that it may not be available for all counties every year. Despite these difficulties, the measure has the virtue of being the most easily understood economic statistic available for the family unit.

County And Other Local Records

This phase of the analysis brings us closer to the actual development as we begin the process of monitoring secondary data that may show changes as a result of project impacts. Depending on the particular variable being assessed, monthly, weekly, or even daily, information may be obtained. In the case of deed transfers, the County Clerk records deed transfers on a daily basis, and these are reported in the county newspaper. If no newspaper is available, the information may be obtained by visiting the courthouse. Deed transfers may be an early warning that development is about to occur or may be an indicator of speculative activity associated with some forms of resource development. Deed transfers may occur prior to the local acquisition phase and then again during the period of second-home and commercial development. In the case of reservoir development, such activity has been found to be particularly intense if the proposed facility is near an urban area.

State and Federal Agency Reports

Each of the agencies issues periodic reports of its environmental activity. The information contained in agency reports may deal with efforts to expand sewage treatment or, as in the case of the National Park Service, to provide more open space and parkland. Researchers will find much value in the records of the interrelationships of these agencies with the institutions and the people in local communities. A proposed resource development could also bring about jurisdictional disputes among various federal and state agencies.

Archive Information

Archive information refers mainly to newspaper accounts; however, important information is available from public hearings and the agency reports based on proposed project activity. These data must be collected and summarized by persons trained in content analysis and library research. The idea is to assembly opinions, attitudes, and descriptions of situations in the community that have developed or may develop as a result of the project. Because each source of information is biased in that it represents agency, official, or editorial opinion, it must be treated as information representing a special viewpoint. Other sources, such a as the transcripts of hearings about a project, are located with the agency responsible for the hearings. Archive information is very important in developing social impact statements because it deals with the actual event being studied. It also represents an important transition between the aggregate data discussed previously and data on social units impacted by a development project.

Data From Personal Interviews

To assess the full force of actual and perceived impact of resource development, interviews with both community leaders and a sample of the population should be conducted. This section lists categories of variables that sociologists and other social scientists are studying in relation to resource development. Although the research effort is just beginning, many significant findings have been uncovered.

Attitudes and knowledge toward resource development and development in general refer to response to attitude scales and specific inquires about the form of development under consideration. These scales provide an indication both of the general attitude and of the past knowledge of the population regarding proposed development. Attitude scales are helpful not only to describe the characteristics of those holding positive and negative attitudes toward the development, but also help to describe those people who have no attitudes toward the project. Knowledge of project development reflects a general awareness of the population regarding areas affected, dates, potential benefits or costs, and sponsoring agencies.

USES OF SOCIOLOGICAL PROTOCOLS AND VARIABLES

This chapter concludes with a rationale and recommendations for the inclusion of the protocols and variables outlined in the previous pages in any environmental impact statement. For modelling procedures endorsed by the authors we refer to chapters 2, 3, and 4 of this book in the development of the comparative diachronic model which provides a method of monitoring social impacts over time as well as a data collection framework. The authors suggest some of the following reasons for using the variables and protocols listed herein for SIA:

- To find out what is specific to field and local protocols (Figure 7.1) and to given developmental situations and settings, and what is present in social impacts associated with all categories of resource and artifactual development;
- To check out findings, recommendations, predictions, and so on;
- To monitor (and feed back resultant data to those concerned) the continuing impact of development on the lives of target area residents;
- To build data banks for use in subsequent SIAs;
- To help those concerned become better prepared to avoid and alleviate social impacts;
- To facilitate development-related planning, decision making, and decision implementing processes;
- To better understand the relationship between social and other environmental impacts and to foster common frames of reference, universes of discourse, and classification schemes for assessing all manner of impact;

• And to contribute to the emerging fields of environmental sociology and sociological practice and to the established field of social change.

Sociologists have a long history of research in social change and community analysis. Environmental and social impact assessment represents an opportunity to use some of these experiences to address a practical problem. Other disciplines mentioned in the NEPA legislation will have integrative material which will help expand the approaches to the problem and better understand the consequences of induced physical change on both the human and biological environment. Our general position within the discipline of sociology is that alterations in human behavior will almost always occur whether the disruptions be physical or social. The amount of time and variables necessary to specify all that changes is, as a practical matter, impossible. Our goal is to provide a usable framework within which the most obvious and disruptive consequences of physical change may be understood.

BIBLIOGRAPHY

Burchell, Robert W., and David Listokin. 1972. *The Environmental Impact Handbook*. New Brunswick, N.J.: Center for Urban Policy Research.

Burdge, Rabel J. and Sue Johnson. 1977. Socio-cultural Aspects of the Effects of Resource Development. in *The Social Consequences of Environmental Change: A Handbook for Environmental Planning*. James McEvoy, III and Thomas Dietz eds. New York: Wiley, pp. 241-279.

Cottrell, W.F. 1951. Death by Dieselization: A Case Study in the Reaction to Technological Change. *American Sociological Review*, 16(3): 358-365.

Dornbusch, David M., *et.al.* 1974. *A Generic Methodology to Forecast Benefits from Urban Water Resource Improvement Projects*. San Francisco: David M. Dornbusch and Co.

Drucker, Phillip, J. E. Clark, and L.D. Smith. 1973. *Sociocultural Impact of Reservoirs on Local Government Institutions*. Lexington: University of Kentucky Water Resources Research Institute, Research Report No. 65.

Finsterbusch, Kurt. 1975. *A Methodology for Analyzing Social Impacts of Public Policies*. Vienna, Virginia: BDM Corporation (BDM/W-75-079-TR), 1975.

Johnson, Sue, and Rabel J. Burdge. 1974. A Methodology for Using Diachronic Studies to Predict the Social Impact of Resource Development. Presented at the Meeting of the Rural Sociological Society. Montreal: Quebec, Canada, August.

Johnson, Sue, and Rabel J. Burdge. 1975. Sociologists and Environmental Impact Statements: What Are We Doing Here? Presented at the Meeting of the Rural Sociological Society, San Francisco, California. August.

Mach, Ruth P. 1974. *Criteria for Evaluation of Social Impacts of Flood Control.* New York: Institute of Public Administration, *Phase I Report Submitted to the Connecticut River Basin Supplemental Flood Management Study*, March.

Randall, Alan, B. Ives, and C. Eastman. 1974. *Benefits of Abatement of Aesthetic Environmental Damage from Four Corners Power Plant.* Fruitland, N.M.: New Mexico State University, Agricultural Experiment Station, Bulletin 618.

Smith, Charles R. 1970. *Anticipation of Change, a Socioeconomic Description of a Kentucky County before Reservoir Construction.* Lexington: University of Kentucky Water Resources Institute, Research Report No. 28.

Wolf, C.P. ed. 1974. *Social Impact Assessment: Man-Environment Interactions.* Stroudsburg, PA: Dowden, Hutchinson and Ross.

Chapter 8

SOCIAL IMPACT ASSESSMENT, KNOWLEDGE AND DEVELOPMENT[1]

Roy E. Rickson, John S. Western and Rabel J. Burdge

INTRODUCTION

A classical problem in social science is how knowledge shapes policy and political action. The problem is central to social impact assessment as the process is designed to influence development policy and politics. Knowledge and politics, separately and together, shape development and the impact assessment process. Aside from its formal role, impact assessments are often done in tense political situations where groups attempt to influence research designs or discredit the professional competence of assessors. Important questions are how much knowledge from impact assessment is independent of politics or, alternatively, whether political interests and power dominate the process from initial design to how data are collected, processed, interpreted and communicated.

In order to answer these questions we need to know how social impact assessment fits with development, a broader definition of development than conventional economic growth. Accordingly, this chapter gives particular attention to (1) applying social theory to impact assessment, (2) seeing assessment as part of a general learning process that is fundamental to development rather than an appendage to it and (3) reviewing two bodies of sociological theory that have potential for understanding the impact assessment process.

Theory and Politics

It is only through the use of relevant social theory that professionals assessing development know what to ask (what data to collect) and what data mean when they have it. Otherwise, we are neither certain of what to ask, in the first place, nor how to interpret responses to our questions. As Kaplan notes...*A theory is not just the discovery of a hidden fact; the theory is a way of looking at the facts, of organizing and representing them* (1964:309).

Impact predictions are ultimately conclusions from theory supported more or less by the data we collect. The contrast is an ad hoc atheoretical process disallowing the accumulation of knowledge and experience in defining and dealing with development problems. In these circumstances, political goals and power rather than knowledge

---

[1]Abridged from the original. Roy E. Rickson, John S. Western and Rabel J. Burdge. 1990. Social Impact Assessment, Knowledge and Development. *Environmental Impact Assessment Review*, 10(1/2): 1-10. Reproduced here with permission of the authors and the publisher.

easily dominate development decisions. Of course, attempts by political groups to control the research process are not precluded by having valid knowledge. Groups and individuals involved in situations where impact assessments are conducted will always evaluate data in terms of what it means for their social, political or economic agenda.

Neither social science data nor biological data are immune from political interest or, at times, militant advocacy. Political misuse and corruption of the process occur when SIA through restrictive legislation or connivance serves narrow political interests rather than comprehensive public needs. There is then the scientific question of having valid, generalizable knowledge and the political question of making sure that knowledge is public rather than private. The two dimensions of impact assessment are inseparable and are strongly related to SIAs effectiveness as an aid to development policy and decision-making (Burdge 1987).

Impact Assessment and Development

The concept of development implies a more comprehensive process than simple economic growth. Rather than seeing it as only some end-product of material or economic growth, *development* can be defined as the ability of an organization, community or society to change (transform itself) as the result of research and planning (Dunn 1971). *Growth*, on the other hand, is a scalar concept meaning only an increase in the scale of things -- e.g., population, employment, money.

Development, as presented here, requires a learning process where there is a research framework such as SIA for accumulating knowledge about alternatives for development and their potential impacts. It requires sufficient public awareness and mobilization so that public groups know about development alternatives and how each would potentially affect them; knowledge, in other words, is public rather than private and can be used by various groups in their responses to development alternatives. As we discuss below, impact assessment often engenders conflict and that, up to a point, group conflict increases the overall quality and quantity of community knowledge. Critical analyses of SIA suggest that if its theory and practices are to contribute to either dimension of development we need to (1) more fully relate modern social theory and research to social impact assessment and (2) to understand better what happens to knowledge in the political process of applying it to development problems.

SOCIAL THEORY AND IMPACT ASSESSMENT

Sociologists study a diversity of phenomena and the discipline encompasses frameworks which focus on attitudes and values to macro-level theories that concentrate on population, social structure and social change. Analyses of community social structures, a particular focus of social impact assessment, should explicitly refer to the social actors involved and the critical processes associated with relationships between actors (Blau 1977). Actors' in social impact assessments include, among others, persons, families, communities and organizations. The latter may refer to a variety of organizations ranging from business, industrial firms, and government agencies to environmental associations and neighborhood groups.

Relationships between *actors* vary from cooperation based on common goals to sharply conflicting goals and attempts at domination. All social actors respond or perceive change through values based on cultural traditions and structural commitments which have emerged over time. The former refer to individual and group conceptions of what is desirable or important to them while the latter are patterns of social relationships which are accepted as legitimate, *right* and proper. Development often has severe impacts on group and individual values (conceptions of the desirable) and patterns of social relationships (how they relate to others in their families and communities).

Theory and research in sociology helps us to understand how persons, communities and organizations respond to change, how they perceive and use impact information; and, how relationships between actors affect how information is used. Two areas of sociological theory and research are especially pertinent to this purpose: community studies, especially research on the relationship between conflict, public participation and knowledge diffusion, and organizational and interorganizational analysis.

Local communities are a focus of social impact assessment because this is where the costs and benefits of change are most acutely experienced (Burdge 1987). Government agencies are formal organizations responsible for formation and implementation of environmental and social policies. Their relations with other organizations and the general public (other agencies, local citizen groups, private industry, business, or development firms) are instrumental to policy-formation and the applications of impact assessment information.

Community Analysis

Impacts of rapid economic growth have been principal subjects of social and environmental assessment. Growth is generated by elites seeking to expand job opportunities, home building, industrial and commercial investment. Socioeconomic costs and benefits of growth programs are seldom, if ever, distributed equally across groups or perceived to be so distributed by groups involved (Gibson *et al.* 1988). Costs, of course, are more than economic as some groups may see community economic growth as a direct assault on their social values, family honor and cultural heritage. As a theory of human conduct, conventional economics cannot explain human responses based on these types of values (Gross 1986; Milbrath 1984). Costs therefore encompass a host of social and economic data.

Conflict and Decision-Making

Inequities, real and perceived, are inevitable dimensions of impact assessment and engender controversy and local conflict. First of all, assessment data are often collected where there is tension or overt conflict (Gibson *et al.* 1988). Secondly, conflict theory orients the scholar, assessor and planner to a number of significant factors. These include the existence and identification of different interest groups, the distributional effects of projects and programs on community social structure, and possible strategies to alleviate different concerns and tensions either among community groups or across communities (Halstead *et al.* 1984).

How conflict affects decision-making is a subject of community theory. One perspective is that conflict, by increasing public interest and awareness reduces the relationship between social class and political participation (Nowak *et al.* 1982). Because of increased involvement by diverse community groups, knowledge by groups of development alternatives increases. Knowledge includes knowing about criteria for the selection and implementation of technology and knowledge by decision-makers of what different groups are willing to accept. As general public knowledge increases, elites are forced to consider a broad rather than narrow array of alternatives increasing decision-making rationality.

Elites commonly attempt to avoid conflict for many different and understandable reasons. Common assumptions about conflict is that it is an impediment to rational decision-making. In conventional economic and political theory, conflict is an impediment to rational decision-making where rationality is contingent on a relatively exclusive relationship between scientist and decision-maker; the role of the scientist is to reduce a problem to a set of alternatives derived from extensive research using rigorous and objective criteria. Typically, the professional relates only to elite *decision-makers* who take the information and apply it directly to conditions defined as problems. This type of decision-making narrows rather than expands the range of alternatives and consequences considered; agendas for decision-making are controlled by a few, knowledge of development alternatives is restricted to an elite and rationality, defined as maximizing knowledge of alternatives, is minimized.

Because of the importance of professionals as arbitrators in disputes about development, groups of various kinds may recruit scientists and other professionals to support their own points of view. Scientific work, in such cases, takes on an ideological role (Stryker 1989). It can, depending upon the level and duration of conflicts and how many different groups are able to employ scientific talent, function as a means for increasing public knowledge or as a substitute for political control. An extensive literature finds that the scientist or technical professional, in certain conditions, becomes a legitimizer rather than an independent collector and contributor of information (Schnaiberg 1980; Rickson 1976).

A number of circumstances affect the type of information scientists present to decision-makers. Even if they are not classical legitimizers actively seeking to ingratiate themselves with community or organizational elites, scientists learn that transmitting information to decision-makers that challenges their goals and possible *hidden agendas* is a complex, sensitive, and occasionally dangerous, business (Taylor 1984; Rickson 1976).

Power

Power is associated with conflict; defined simply, it is the ability of a person or group to know about, mobilize and then influence decision-making; that is, to *make a difference* in something important to them. It is a means by which groups may influence whether projects or programs are assessed and what type of data will be collected, whether theoretical assumptions and data will be concealed or enter the public debate. The distribution of power at the community level, for example, determines at least initially how much public knowledge, attention and public reaction there will be to proposed community projects and programs. In highly dominated communities, public participation in decision-making and public knowledge about programs are generally low, and both highly related to socioeconomic status and social class. That is, the higher the socioeconomic status of a person, the more likely are they to participate or belong to active political groups and know about plans for economic growth, alternatives to implement those plans, and the distribution across groups of social and environmental costs (Nowak *et al*. 1982).

A principal test of power is the ability of an elite to control political agendas in a community or society keeping issues such as pollution or poverty *out of mind* if not *out of sight* (Lukes 1977). Coincidentally, overt conflict in these types of communities tends also to be low because individuals and groups are neither mobilized to express interests nor grievances, nor do they have access to information from, say, social impact assessments that would stimulate interest and mobilization.

Conflict and Impact Assessment

Impact assessment is often seen as a technocratic means to reduce conflict, as a scientific procedure to replace or obviate need for direct political action by groups. Assessors often work in situations where conflict is intense — sometimes operating on the premise that their data will explicitly resolve conflicts. Its role in dispute resolution depends upon the degree to which impact assessment practices are integrated with the dynamics of community change and development. Simplistic views about communities and the people in them are unfortunately persistent in the impact assessment literature and are held by some ecologists, engineers and others with little or no social science training (Gibson *et al.* 1988).

Impact assessment should be seen as a long-term process allowing for community affects to accumulate or thresholds to be reached. Assessment procedures are most effective as an aid in resolving disputes if they are applied over time and adjusted to needs as they emerge. Community change is a gradual process and the cumulative effects of projects or policies need to be examined over time. In summary, community research literature on power, conflict and decision-making finds that (1) as conflict increases, up to a point, people and groups learn more about issues and decision-making or policy alternatives and (2) public participation diversifies as awareness and participation by low and middle income people increases (Nowak *et al.* 1982). Overall community knowledge increases as participants introduce information perhaps lacking in original impact assessments or investigations commissioned by leaders.

The kind of conflict we refer to is integrative rather than divisive and generally stimulates rather than impedes learning and public involvement by persons and groups. Because there is more information at the collective and individual level, in these circumstances, the chances of making decisions which are politically and scientifically acceptable over time are increased (Nowak *et al.* 1982; Sabatier 1979). Decisions are more likely to be scientifically rational because there will be more and different kinds of information about both socioeconomic and environmental impacts of different development plans.

Rationality, in this definition, depends upon a certain level of community pluralism and the potential for groups to challenge impact assessments or decisions which they perceive to be unfavorable to them. Conflict, at a certain level, improves both the quantity and quality of information. As we have argued, using contemporary research, there will be more information of different types and, because of groups challenging information they see as costly to them, researchers must specify the accuracy or validity of their research findings. We emphasize the term *conflict at a certain level* because as in most natural phenomena there are important threshold effects. The outcome of a series of rational actions undertaken separately by highly committed groups can prove to be irrational for all. Inertia can result, as we suggest above, both from domination as well as from groups hopelessly divided by age old hatreds or specific economic interests.

The effectiveness of social impact assessment as a means to evaluate development alternatives depends upon both theoretical and political factors, and more basically on an understanding of communities as social institutions. Communities have a basis for rational change through impact assessment when there is a proper distribution of power so that community or political action can be altered in line with research findings and accumulated knowledge. Public mobilization and participation contributes information which must be considered by government agencies and other organizations involved in programs for economic growth. How organizations collect, interpret and apply information is critical to the impact assessment process.

Organizational Analysis

Organizational research is a complex field including studies of many different types of organizations. Research topics are equally varied from studies of managerial effectiveness to the dynamics of regulatory relationships between government agencies, public groups and industrial firms. In this chapter, we are primarily concerned with government agencies, as organizations, and how their needs and behavior affect impact assessment practice and decisions about development.

Government bureaucracies have the power to, in practice, define or redefine how impact law and policy are applied. The purpose of impact assessment law is to require private or public developers to routinely use impact assessment procedures and there the weigh findings equally with predicted economic benefits (Taylor 1984). However, ambiguities of impact assessment law, as with environmental law in general, allow agencies great discretion and they may decide to follow the letter of law in one circumstance while redefining and perhaps ignoring it in another. Agencies are pressured by external groups to define law and policy in their favor. When agencies relate to a diversity of external groups the relative power of any single group is decreased reducing the chances of undue influence.

Some organizational theorists see the ability of an organization to learn and positively respond to public protest and new information as basic to rationality (Wilensky 1967). Rationality is defined by them as a pattern of improvement in intelligence over time by using more and varied types of information; an increase in an organization's average capability to consider new information, collect information on its own, interpret and apply it is fundamental to rationality (Wilensky 1967; Taylor 1984). The reverse is bureaucratic rigidity or inertia in which organizations resist change and discredit any information challenging conventional conceptions of development. Resistance to change or promotion of special political interest can also be the result of agency *capture*.

The Capture Model

Agency capture is a situation in which agency-industry relationships result in (1) concealment or selective interpretation of quantitative or qualitative information about impacts or (2) collusion between agency regulators and their industry clientele to actively subvert the original intention of legislation and legislators (Sabatier and Mazmanian 1979). A basic hypothesis is that in the long run, government agencies are controlled by the industries they relate to. The model is applicable to any private or public interest groups and is of course not exclusive to the industry-agency relationship. If *captured* by powerful interests, agencies enforce law, apply policy and report data in a manner desirable to them. Agency behavior becomes a way for developers to substantially evade the law while securing agency legitimization of its operations. This *...creates or sustains an impression that induces acquiescence of the public in the face of private tactics that might otherwise be expected to produce resentment, protest and resistance* (Edelman 1964: 56). Professionals are then pressured to act as legitimizers (Rickson 1976); research by professionals, rather than neutral or objective, is used by agencies to control public opinion and facilitate private interest goals (Stryker 1989).

Impact assessment laws, according to Hill and Ortolano (1978), have had limited success in forcing government agencies to weigh environmental and social factors equally with economic and technical factors in either regulation or plans for growth. Research by government agencies can function as a substitute for action, allowing agencies to evade active regulatory pressure on developers. Schnaiberg (1980) argues that impact assessment reports function mainly to control public opinion about the social and environmental consequences of development rather than promoting fundamental change.

Other researchers suggest that agency capture by private interests is far from inevitable (Sabatier and Mazmanian 1979). Significant variables sustaining agency power in their contacts with powerful interests are access to professional and technical expertise, and legal and political resources. Inertia is common to bureaucracy, but organizations vary greatly in their capacity for innovation and ability to respond creatively rather than submissively to external pressures (Rickson and Ramsey 1984). Broad based agencies employing highly trained professionals are capable of resisting capture more than narrow based or single purpose agencies. Active and highly mobilized public groups supportive of agency goals and initiatives reduce the possibility of general capture by private interests (Sabatier and Mazmanian 1979).

Survival and effectiveness of a government agency depends upon legitimacy and money (Benson 1978). Legitimacy is related to an agency's ability to consolidate financial and political support. When agencies are diverse, having related but different tasks, there are a number of different constituency groups which can offer political support (legitimacy). Single purpose agencies having less room to maneuver, have fewer legal, political and technical resources to respond to conflict over impact assessments and must therefore respond cautiously to public and private initiatives.

SUMMARY AND CONCLUSIONS

If impact assessment is to achieve its fundamental goals of balancing science and politics in policy-formation and implementation, it is necessary that we understand more fully the social structure in which assessment information is gathered, analyzed and applied. Two general theoretical areas in sociology help us to do this-community and organization theory. Rationality is an aim of social impact procedures. Achieving rationality requires that decision-makers have a variety of options available to them and knowledge of the distributive effects of each on individuals, groups and organizations in communities. The research literature on community politics and decision-making suggests that this is most likely to occur when there is a sufficiently pluralistic structure so that there is enough public mobilization for conflict to occur and to force, if necessary, assessment information to become public.

Because impact assessments often engender conflict themselves and are undertaken when there is conflict, theory focusing on community conflict is directly applicable to understanding this process. Research on environmental and general political participation in communities shows clearly that knowledge and political or environmental participation are jointly associated with social class. However, as conflict increases, up to a certain point, participation and knowledge are decreasingly class based and more and better information (both technical and political) is reported.

Active groups are more likely to know different sides of an issue and how decisions or policies are apt to affect them. Additionally, groups who are unlikely to participate on a routine basis are drawn into conflicts and contribute information; for example, the nature of their values and their interpretations of projects and potential impacts. An ideal model of the role of impact assessment would therefore be that community rationality is a joint product of integrative political conflict and research such as environmental or social impact assessment.

The politics of survival influence how government agencies use information including that derived from social impact assessments. A possible consequence of SIA is that it improves the intelligence capacity of government agencies; it influences what kind information they routinely collect and the weight they give it in their decisions. Impact information can function to fundamentally refashion decision-making by public agencies promoting to include, as part of their routine information gathering procedures, the concerns, values and knowledge of those at the local level who must accept the positive and negative consequences of intervention.

REFERENCES

Benson, J.K. 1978. The interorganizational network as a political economy. In *Organization and Environment*. L. Karpik ed. London: Sage Publications.

Blau, P.M. 1977. *Inequality and Heterogeneity: A Primitive Theory of Social Structure*. New York: The Free Press.

Burdge, R.J. 1987. The Social impact assessment model and the planning process. *Environmental Impact Assessment Review*, 7 (2):141-150.

Derman, W. and S. Whiteford eds. 1985. *Social Impact Analysis and Development Planning in the Third World*. Boulder, CO: Westview Press.

Dunn, E.S. 1971. *Economic and Social Development*. Baltimore: Johns Hopkins University Press.

Edelman, M. 1964. *The Symbolic Uses of Politics*. Boston: Little and Brown.

Gibson, D.M., R.E. Rickson and J.S. Western. 1988. *World Heritage Listing of Queensland's Wet Tropical Rainforest: Assessment of Social Impact.* Commonwealth of Australia Department of the Arts, Sport, Environment, Territories and Tourism, Canberra.

Gross, E. 1986. The rationality of symbolic actors. *British Journal of Sociology,* 38(2):139-157.

Kaplan, A. 1964. *The Conduct of Inquiry: Methodology for Behavioral Science.* San Francisco: Chandler.

Halstead, J.N., R.A. Chase, S.H. Murdock and S.L. Leistritz. 1984. *Socioeconomic Impact Management.* London: Westview Press.

Hill, W.H. and Ortolano, L. 1978. NEPA's effect on the consideration of alternatives. *Natural Resources Journal,* 18(2):285-311.

Milbrath, L. 1984. *Environmentalists: Vanguard for a New Society.* Albany: State University of New York Press.

Lukes, S. 1977. *Power: A Radical View.* London: Macmillan.

Nowak, P.J., R.E. Rickson, C.E. Ramsey and W.J. Goudy. 1982. Community conflict and models of political participation. *Rural Sociology,* 47(4):333-349.

Rickson, R.E. and C.E. Ramsey. 1984. Comparative bases of industry change. *Water Resources Bulletin,* 21(1):89-97.

Rickson, R.E. 1976. Knowledge management in industrial society and environmental quality. *Human Organization,* 35(3):239-251.

Sabatier, P. and S. Mazmanian. 1979. The conditions of effective implementation: a guide to accomplishing policy objectives. *Policy Analysis,* 5(3):481-504.

Schnaiberg, A. 1980. *The Environmental: From Surplus to Scarcity.* New York: Oxford University Press.

Stryker, R. 1989. Limits of technocratization of the law. *American Sociological Review,* 54(3): 341-359.

Taylor, S. 1984. *Making Bureaucracies Think: The Environmental Impact Strategy of Administrative Reform.* Stanford, CA: Stanford University Press.

Wilensky, H.L. 1967. *Organizational Intelligence: Knowledge and Policy in Government and Industry.* New York: Basic Books.

Chapter 9

GUIDELINES AND PRINCIPLES FOR SOCIAL IMPACT ASSESSMENT[1]

The Interorganizational Committee on Guidelines and Principles for Social Impact Assessment

SECTION I - INTRODUCTION

Since passage of the National Environmental Policy Act (NEPA) of 1969, environmental impact assessment has become the key component of environmental planning and decision making in the United States. More recently, agency planners and decision makers have recognized a need for better understanding the social consequences of projects, programs and policies. In response to this need a group of social scientists formed the Interorganizational Committee on Guidelines and Principles for Social Impact Assessment (SIA), with the purpose of outlining a set of guidelines and principles that will assist agencies and private interests in fulfilling their obligations under NEPA, related authorities and agency mandates.

By *social impacts* we mean the consequences to human populations of any public or private actions—that alter the ways in which people live, work, play, relate to one another, organize to meet their needs and generally cope as members of society. The term also includes cultural impacts involving changes to the norms, values, and beliefs that guide and rationalize their cognition of themselves and their society.

In this monograph, however, we define *social impact assessment* in terms of efforts to assess or estimate, in **advance**, the social consequences that are likely to follow from specific policy actions (including programs, and the adoption of new policies), and specific government actions (including buildings, large projects and leasing large tracts of land for resource extraction), particularly in the context of the U.S. *National Environmental Policy Act of 1969* or "NEPA" (P.L. 91-190, 42 U.S.C. 4371 *et seq.*).

A central requirement of NEPA is that before any agency of the federal government may take "actions significantly affecting the quality of the human environment" that agency must first prepare an Environmental Impact Statement (or EIS). Preparing an EIS requires the integrated use of the social sciences.

The social science components of EISs are called social or socioeconomic impact assessments, or simply SIAs. Several federal agencies have moved to develop SIA guidelines, but most have not. Even within agencies that have SIA guidelines there is variation on how the social component of NEPA is to be implemented. Since the passage of NEPA there has never been a systematic, inter-disciplinary statement from

---

[1]Abridged from the original. Listed alphabetically, the initial version of this chapter was prepared by Rabel J. Burdge, Peter Fricke, Kurt Finsterbusch, William R. Freudenburg, Robert Gramling, Arnold Holden, Lynn Llewellyn, John S. Petterson, James Thompson, and Gary Williams. Comments were received from Hobson Bryan, Tom Greider, Larry Leistritz, Lambert Wenner and C. P. Wolf.

the social science community as to what should be the content of an SIA, even though the term *social impact assessment* was first used when the Department of the Interior was preparing the EIS for the Trans-Alaska pipeline in the early 1970s.

The purpose of this chapter is to present the central principles and some operational guidelines for use by federal agencies in conducting social impact assessments.

The individuals listed as authors represent both relevant social science disciplines and persons who have done SIAs both in federal agencies and the private sector, and those who have taught courses and conducted social impact assessment research through universities. The document on which this chapter is based is the first systematic and interdisciplinary statement to offer guidelines and principles to assist government agencies and private sector interests in using SIA to make better decisions under NEPA and related authorities (see Section II). These guidelines and standards are equally important for those communities and individuals likely to be affected by proposed actions in order that they might conduct independent assessments or evaluate the adequacy of SIAs. Within these few pages we cannot cover over two decades of research on "social effects" much less every contingency that may occur in the course of implementing a proposed project or policy change. However, we do provide a broad overview, focusing less on methodological details and more on the guidelines and principles for the preparation of technically and substantively adequate SIA's within reasonable time and resource constraints.

SECTION II
LEGAL MANDATES AND ADMINISTRATIVE PROCEDURES FOR SOCIAL IMPACT ASSESSMENT

Section II of this chapter provides a brief overview of the legal mandates and the administrative procedures that shape SIAs done in the context of environmental impact statements; Section III provides a basic model for social impact assessment; Section IV outlines the steps in doing an SIA; and Section V provides principles and guidelines for doing social impact assessment. We conclude with a list of easy-to-obtain references.

Prior to the enactment of the National Environmental Policy Act, analysis of the social consequences of major projects often was fragmented and lacking in focus. For example, when construction-related impacts of public works projects were at issue, attention was generally centered on economic considerations. The prevailing view was that money could compensate for any adverse impacts. There was minimal concern for social impacts even if entire neighborhoods had to be displaced so long as comparable housing could be located elsewhere. There was even less concern for the distribution or "equity" of these impacts on different populations. Also lost in this process was the importance people attach to their communities and neighborhoods; and particularly to long-standing social networks that form the basis of support both for daily living and during periods of extreme stress and hardship.

The passing of NEPA created a different, but somewhat vague, set of requirements for federal agencies; among these is the integrated use of the social sciences in assessing impacts on the human environment. Over the years, the legal definition of "human environment" has undergone substantial modification as a result of court decisions stemming from NEPA-related litigation. The Council on Environmental Quality's (CEQ) *Regulations for Implementing the Procedural Provisions* of the

National Environmental Policy Act (40 CFR 1500-1508) point-out that the "human environment" is to be "interpreted comprehensively" to include "the natural and physical environment and the relationship of people with that environment" (40 CFR 1508.14). Agencies need to assess not only so-called "direct" effects, but also "aesthetic, historic, cultural, economic, social, or health" effects, "whether direct, indirect, or cumulative" (40 CFR 1508.8).

The CEQ Regulations also contain another key provision that should be noted "...economic or social effects are not intended by themselves to require preparation of an environmental impact statement" (40 CFR 1508.14). However, when an EIS is prepared "and economic or social and natural or physical environmental effects are interrelated, then the environmental impact statement will discuss all of these effects on the human environment" (40 CRF 1508.14). The EISs are thus intended to provide a kind of full-disclosure procedure for federal decision-makers, who are then expected to consider the negative as well as the positive implications of potential courses of action, and the unintended as well as the intended consequences, before they proceed.

NEPA also provides citizens with the opportunity to challenge agency decisions; again in this case, however, NEPA's provisions are often misunderstood. The greatest level of legal vulnerability for the agency is not created by taking actions that will create negative impacts. It comes from failing to consider or fully analyze those impacts in advance.

Most federal agencies are required to establish government-to-government relationships with American Indian tribes. The requirement is passed on to states, cities, and counties when federal funds are involved. The special status of American Indian tribes is recognized in the CEQ Regulations with early knowledge of projects, participation in the formulation of issues and data collection, and comments on drafts whenever a project can impact Indian people living on a reservation.

American Indian concerns are to be included in an EIS whenever a project affects any of their culture's resources on or off current reservation lands. American Indian rights in the SIA process have been expanded by the American Indian Religious Freedom Act (PL 95-341) and the Native American Graves Protection and Repatriation Act of 1990. Although neither act was specifically designed to affect the NEPA and SIA processes, both acts have resulted in special sections in EISs involving traditional Indian lands.

Figure 9.1 presents a brief chronology listing statutes and regulations that directly or indirectly mandate the conduct of social impact assessment. However, the NEPA requirements were first. They continue to have the broadest applicability in the U.S., and thus we focused on social impact assessment within that context.

SECTION III - A BASIC MODEL FOR SOCIAL IMPACT ASSESSMENT

The Link Between Environmental Impact Assessment
and Social Impact Assessment

Impacts on the social environment resemble biophysical impacts in several ways.

- Social and biophysical impacts can vary in desirability, ranging from the desirable to the adverse.

Figure 9.1
Statutes and Regulations that Mandate or Contain Provisions
for the Conduct of Social Impact Assessment

<u>Date</u>	<u>Law</u>	<u>Provisions</u>
1970	National Environmental Policy Act of 1969.	Calls for the integrated use of the social sciences in assessing impacts "on the human environment". Also requires the identification of methods and procedures...which insure that presently unquantified environmental amenities and values be given appropriate consideration.
1976	Magnuson Fishery Conservation and Management Act, as amended (16 U.S.C.A. 1801, et seg.).	Where a "system for limiting access to the fishery in order to achieve optimum yield" is deemed necessary, the Act requires the Secretary of Commerce and the Regional Fishery Management Councils to consider in depth the economic and social impacts of the system.
1978	U.S. Council on Environmental Quality 1978. (40 CFR 1500-1508). Regulations for implementing the procedural provision of the National Environmental Policy Act.	"'Human environment' shall be interpreted comprehensively to include the natural and physical environment and the relationship of people with that environment."
1978	Outer Continental Shelf Lands Act, as amended (43 U.S.C.A. 1331 et seg.).	"The term 'human environment' means the physical, social, and economic components, conditions and factors which interactively determine the state, condition, and quality of living conditions, employment, and health of those affected directly or indirectly" by the resource development activities in question.
1980	Comprehensive Environmental Response, Compensation and Liability Act (26 and 43 U.S.C.A. et. seg.).	Calls for working with affected publics through community relations programs and assessing community and state acceptance of Superfund plans affecting local populations.
1982	Nuclear Waste Policy Act.	Calls for the preparation of an EIS, specifies demographic limitations on siting the nuclear repository; inclusion of affected Indian Tribes in the siting process and impact assistance.
1986	Superfund Amendments and Reauthorization Act.	Work with an affected public through community relations programs and assessing the acceptance of plans by local communities.
1986	Council on Environmental Quality (40 CFR 1500-1508) re-issue of regulations implementing the procedural provision of the National Environmental Policy Act.	The treatment of incomplete or unavailable information is clarified.

- They also vary in scale—the question of whether a facility will create 50 or 1000 jobs, for example, or will have the potential to spill 50 or 1000 gallons of toxic waste.
- Another consideration involves the extent or duration of impacts in time and space. Like biophysical impacts, some social impacts can be of short duration, while others can last a lifetime; and some communities "return to normal" quite quickly once a source of disruption is removed, while others do not.
- Social impacts can also vary in intensity or severity, a dimension that is defined differently in different project settings, just as an objective biophysical impact (e.g., a predicted loss of 75 sea otters) might have a minor effect on populations in one location (e.g., off the coast of Alaska), while amounting to a significant fraction of the remaining population in another location (e.g., off the coast of California).
- Similarly, there are differences in the degree to which both types of impacts are likely to be cumulative, at one extreme, or mutually counterbalancing, at the other.

It is important to consider the social equity or distribution of impacts across different populations. Just as the biological sections of EISs devote particular attention to threatened or endangered plant and wildlife species, the socioeconomic sections of EISs must devote particular attention to the impacts on vulnerable segments of the human population. Examples include the poor, the elderly, adolescents, the unemployed, and women; members of minority and/or other groups that are racially, ethnically, or culturally distinctive; or occupational, cultural, political, or value-based groups for whom a given community, region, or use of the biophysical environment is particularly important.

In addition to the types of disturbances that can affect other species, humans are affected by changes in the distinctly human environment, including those associated with the phenomenon known as the *social construction of reality*. Persons not familiar with the social sciences are often tempted to treat social constructions as mere perceptions or emotions, to be distinguished from reality. Such a separation is not so easy to accomplish. We are careful to point out that the social construction of reality is characteristic of all social groups, including the agencies that are attempting to implement changes as well as the communities that are affected.

In the case of proposed actions that involve controversy, attitudes and perceptions toward a proposed policy change are one of the variables that must be considered in determining the significance of impacts (40 CFR 1508.27b[4]). During controversies, participants are often tempted to dismiss the concerns of others as being merely imagined or perceived.

There are two important factual reasons not to omit such concerns from SIAs and EISs, regardless of whether the views are widely accepted internally or come from an agency's critics. First, positions taken by all sides in a given controversy are likely to be shaped by (differing) perceptions of the policy or project, and the decision to accept one set of perceptions while excluding another, may not be scientifically defensible. Second, if the agency asserts that its critics are "emotional" or "misinformed," for example, it is guaranteed to raise the level of hostility between itself and community members and will stand in the way of a successful resolution of the problem.

In summary, some of the most important aspects of social impacts, involve not the physical relocation of human populations, but the meanings, perceptions, or social significance of these changes.

A Social Impact Assessment Framework

To predict what the probable impact of development will be, we seek to understand the past behavior of individuals and communities affected by agency actions, development, or policy changes.

We use a comparative SIA method to study the course of events in a community where an environmental change has occurred, and extrapolate from that analysis what is likely to happen in another community where a similar development or policy change is planned. Put another way, if we wish to know the probable effects of a proposed project in location B, one of the best places to start is to assess the effects of a similar project that has already been completed in location A. Specific variables to access project impacts are shown later in this section.

Based on the direction outlined in NEPA and the CEQ Regulations, we need to identify probable undesirable social effects of development before they occur in order to make recommendations for mitigation. As we point out in a later section, the appropriate federal agency (in cooperation with the local community) bears responsibility for coordinating mitigation efforts. The SIA model also allows us to address the issues of alternative plans and alternative impacts of a proposed project. Moreover, because social impacts can be measured and understood, recommendations for mitigating actions on the part of the agencies can be made. In Section IV we outline a procedure for mitigating potentially adverse impacts.

It is almost impossible to catalogue all dimensions of social impacts because change has a way of creating other changes. A freeway extension facilitates residential growth which leads to increased traffic and air pollution, creation of new schools, retail centers, and other services, and the decline of a downtown neighborhood.

In Figure 9.3 we have identified the basic social dimensions that can be measured which reflect fundamental and important characteristics of a community. Studied over time, these characteristics give us insight as to how social structure will be altered when change occurs. Faced with a proposal to implement a new ski area, for example, the community and the agency proposing the change can profit from the experience of other comparable communities that have already undergone a ski area development and thereby gain a reasonably accurate expectation of how the project will affect their community.

Forecasted impacts are the difference in the human environment between a future with the project and a future without the project. Since we cannot see the future, we look at similar communities that have experienced similar policies or projects in the past. The social impact assessment model is comparative. Our experience has shown that forecasts can be made about probable social impacts. The model also permits a restudy of the impacted community in the future to assess what the actual impact has been, so that the fit between forecasts and outcome can be matched.

One way to capture the dynamic complex quality of social impacts is to metaphorically take a series of snapshots over time as the development event or policy change unfolds and fill in what happened in between. Ideally, information about the community or geographic area of study is available both before and after the event to help in measurement. Social impacts then become the changes taking place between the two measurement points. The social assessor attempts to forecast the change associated with proposed activity, based on research and information accumulated from comparative studies of similar situations.

A strength of the comparative SIA model is that with appropriate data sources (those which can be collected frequently, such as land transfer records) it allows for an interpretation of dynamic events and can provide monitoring of short-term impacts. This kind of frequent monitoring provides a continual source of evaluation or check on the direction of forecasts made about social impacts.

Stages in Project/Policy Development

All projects and policies go through a series of steps or stages, starting with initial planning, then implementation and construction, carrying through to operation and maintenance (see Figure 9.2). At some point the project might be abandoned or decommissioned, or official policy could change. Social impacts will be different for each stage. Scoping of issues prior to analysis may lead the assessor to focus only on one stage. For example, one community might be concerned about public reaction resulting from the initial siting of a hazardous waste disposal facility; another with the construction aspects of reservoirs; and a third might be faced with a change in the designation of adjacent public land from timber production to wilderness use. The specific stage in life of the project or policy is an important factor in determining effects. Not all social impacts will occur at each stage. Figure 9.2 illustrates the stages in project development.

Planning/Policy Development - Planning/policy development refers to all activity that takes place from the time a project or policy is conceived to the point of construction activity or policy implementation. Examples include project design, revision, public comment, licensing, the evaluating of alternatives, and the decision to go ahead. Social impacts actually begin the day the action is proposed and can be measured from that point.

Social assessors must recognize the importance of local or national social constructions of reality, which begin during the earliest of the four stages—the

Figure 9.2
Stages in Project/Policy Development

Stage 1. Planning/policy development

Stage 2. Construction/implementation

Stage 3. Operation/maintenance

Stage 4. Decommissioning/abandonment

planning/policy development stage. We often assume that no impacts will take place until Stage 2 (construction/implementation) begins on a project—through dirt-moving operations, for example, or the start-up of construction activities. However, real, measurable, and often significant effects on the *human environment* can begin to take place as soon as there are changes in *social or economic* conditions. From the time of the earliest announcement of a pending policy change or rumor about a project, both hopes and hostilities can begin to mount; speculators can lock up potentially important properties, politicians can maneuver for position, and interest groups can form or redirect their energies. These changes occur by merely introducing new information into a community or region.

Construction/Implementation - The construction/implementation stage begins when a decision is made to proceed, a permit is issued or a law or regulation takes place. For typical construction projects, this involves clearing land, building access roads, developing utilities, etc. Displacement and relocation of people, if necessary, occurs during this phase. Depending on the scale of the project, the buildup of a migrant construction work force also may occur. If significant in-migration occurs, the new residents may create a strain on community infrastructure, as well as creating social stresses due to changing patterns of social interaction. Communities may have difficulties in responding to the increased demands on school, health facilities, housing and other social services. Further stresses may be created by resentments between newcomers and long-time residents, by sudden increases in the prices for housing and local services, and even by increased uncertainty about the future. When new policies are implemented, local economies and organizations may change, and old behaviors are replaced with new ways of relating to the environment and its resources.

Operation/Maintenance - The operation/maintenance stage occurs after the construction is complete or the policy is fully operational. In many cases, this stage will require fewer workers than the construction/implementation phase. If operations continue at a relatively stable level for an extended period of time, effects during this stage can often be the most beneficial of those at any stage. Communities seeking industrial development will often focus on this stage because of the long-term economic benefits that may follow from a development. It is also during this stage that the communities can adapt to new social and economic conditions, accommodation can take place, and the expectations of positive effects—such as stable population, a quality infrastructure, and employment opportunities—can be realized.

Abandonment/Decommissioning - Abandonment/decommissioning begins when the proposal is made that the project or policy and associated activity will cease at some time in the future. As in the planning stage, the social impacts of decommissioning begin when the intent to close down is announced and the community or region must again adapt, but this time to the loss of the project or an adjustment to a policy change. Sometimes this means the loss of the economic base as a business closes its doors. At other times, the disruption to the local community may be lessened or at least altered if one type of worker is replaced by another, as in a case such as the Hanford Facility in Washington State, where nuclear production facilities have been closed down, but employment has actually increased as environmental cleanup specialists have been hired to help deal with the contamination at the facility. In other cases, disruption may be exacerbated if the community is not only losing its present economic base, but has lost the capacity to return to a former economic base. Morgan City, Louisiana which had been the self-proclaimed "shrimp capital of the world" in the 1950s is a good example of a community that lost its capacity to return to a former economic base. During the 1960s and 1970s the employment in this community shifted to offshore oil development. When oil prices collapsed in the 1980s, the community found it could not return to the shrimp industry because shrimp-processing facilities had closed down and most of the shrimp boats had been allowed to decay or left the area.

The Project Type and Setting

Projects and policy decisions which require and benefit from social impact assessment range from prison and plant sitings, to highway, reservoir, and power plant construction, to managing old growth forests to maintain a biologically diverse region. Accordingly project types may range from isolated wilderness areas to urban neighborhoods, each with special characteristics that can affect social impacts. Social impacts (as well as economic and physical changes) will vary depending upon the type of development. The following examples of project types, settings, and policy changes are taken from the *Digest of Environmental Impact Statements*, published by The Information Resource Press:

- Mineral extractions, including surface and underground mining as well as new oil and gas drilling.
- Hazardous and sanitary waste sites, including the construction and operation of disposal sites for a variety of hazardous and sanitary wastes (also included are facilities that burn or otherwise destroy chemical and toxic wastes).
- Power plants, including both nuclear and fossil fuel electrical generating facilities and associated developments.
- Reservoirs, including all water impoundments for flood control, hydropower, conservation, and recreation; and cooling lakes and diversion structures.
- Industrial plants (manufacturing facilities built and operated by the private sector, e.g., refineries, steel mills, assembly lines).
- Land use designations, e.g., from timber production to wilderness designation.
- Military and governmental installations, including base closures and openings.
- Schools, public and private, including primary, secondary, and university.
- Transportation facilities, including airports, streets, terminals.
- Linear developments, including subways, railroads, power lines, aqueducts, bike paths, bridges, pipelines, sewers, fences, walls and barrier channels, green belts, and waterways.
- Trade facilities, including businesses and shopping centers.
- Designation of sacred sites.
- Parks and preserves, refuges, cemeteries, and recreation areas.
- Housing facilities, including apartments, office buildings, and hospitals.

Identifying Social Impact Assessment Variables

Social impact assessment variables point to measurable change in human population, communities, and social relationships resulting from a development project or policy change. After research on local community change, rural industrialization, reservoir and highway development, natural resource development, and social change in general, we suggest a list of social variables under the general headings of: 1) *Population Characteristics*; 2) *Community and Institutional Structures*; 3) *Political and Social Resources*; 4) *Individual and Family Changes*; 5) *Community Resources*.

Population Characteristics - mean present population and expected change, ethnic and racial diversity, and influxes and outflows of temporary residents as well as the arrival of seasonal or leisure residents.

Community and Institutional Structures - mean the size, structure, and level of organization of local government including linkages to the larger political systems. They also include historical and present patterns of employment and industrial diversification, the size and level of activity of voluntary associations, religious organizations and interest groups, and finally, how these institutions relate to each other.

Political and Social Resources - refer to the distribution of power authority, the interested and affected publics, and the leadership capability and capacity within the community or region.

Individual and Family Changes - refer to factors which influence the daily life of the individuals and families, including attitudes, perceptions, family characteristics and friendship networks. These changes range from attitudes toward the policy to an alteration in family and friendship networks to perceptions of risk, health, and safety.

Community Resources - include patterns of natural resource and land use; the availability of housing and community services to include health, police and fire protection and sanitation facilities. A key to the continuity and survival of human communities are their historical and cultural resources. Under this collection of variables we also consider possible changes for indigenous people and religious sub-cultures.

At this point in discussing a SIA model we have demonstrated a conceptual procedure for both examining and accumulating information about social impacts. We have also outlined a matrix which demonstrates that social impacts will be different depending upon the project type and the stage of development. The next step in the development of the social impact assessment model is to suggest the social impact variables for stages in project development given different project types and settings.

Combining Social Impact Assessment Variables, Project/Policy Stage, and Setting

The four stages of project/policy development affect the social processes which produce changes in characteristics of the community or region. Social impact assessment specialists must construct a matrix to direct their investigation of potentially significant social impacts. Sample matrices are shown in Figures 9.3 and 9.4.

For each project/policy stage, the assessor should identify potential impacts on each social variable identified in the matrix. This approach ensures that no critical areas are overlooked. We emphasize that Figure 9.3 does not represent all social impact assessment variables that may be of interest for any project. It is presented to illustrate

A No change
B w/change

Figure 9.3
Matrix Relating Project Stage to Social Impact Assessment Variables[2]

Social Impact Assessment Variable	Planning/Policy Development	Implementation/ Construction	Operation/ Maintenance	Decommissioning/ Abandonment
Population Characteristics				
Population change				
Ethnic and racial distribution				
Relocated populations				
Influx or outflow of temporary workers				
Seasonal residents				
Community and Institutional Structures				
Voluntary Associations				
Interest Group Activity				
Size and structure of local government				
Historical experience with change				
Employment/income characteristics				
Employment equity of minority groups				
Local/regional/ national linkages				
Industrial/commercial diversity				
Presence of planning and zoning activity				
Political and Social Resources				
Distribution of power and authority				
Identification of stakeholders				

[2]These variables are suggestive and illustrative and are only intended to provide a beginning point for the social assessor. Taylor *et al.* 1990 (as well as the U.S. Forest Service manual) use the four major categories of: population change; life style; attitudes, beliefs and values; and social organization. Burdge 1994, uses the five categories of: population impacts; community and institutional arrangements; conflicts between local residents and newcomers; individual and family level impacts and community infrastructure needs. Branch *et al.* 1984, uses four categories of social impact assessment variables in their social organization model: direct project inputs, community resources, community social organization; and indicators of individual and community well being.

Social Impact Assessment Variable	Planning/Policy Development	Implementation/ Construction	Operation/ Maintenance	Decommissioning/ Abandonment
Interested and affected parties				
Leadership capability and characteristics				
Individual and Family Changes				
Perceptions of risk, health, and safety				
Displacement/ relocation concerns				
Trust in political and social institutions				
Residential stability				
Density of Acquaintanceship				
Attitudes toward policy/project				
Family and friendship networks				
Concerns about social well-being				
Community Resources				
Change in community infrastructure				
Native American tribes				
Land use patterns				
Effects on cultural, historical, and archaeo- logical resources				

Figure 9.4
Social Impact Assessment Variables, by Project/Policy Setting (type) and Stage

		Project/Policy Stage		
Project/Policy Settings (type)	**Planning/Policy Development**	**Construction/ Implementation**	**Operation/ Maintenance**	**Decommission/ Abandonment**
Hazardous Waste Site	Perceptions of risk, health and safety	Influx of temporary workers	Trust in political social institutions	Alteration in size of local government
Industrial Plant	Formation of attitudes toward the project	Change in community Infrastructure	Change in employment/ income characteristics	Change in employment equity of minority groups
Forest Service to Park Service Management	Interested and affected parties	Trust in political and social institutions	Influx of recreation users	Distribution of power authority

the issues which represent the beginning of such a task. The task for the assessor is to spell out the magnitude and significance of impacts for each cell like those identified in the illustrations.

Figure 9.4 provides an abbreviated illustration of how SIA variables (as suggested in Figure 9.3) might be applied within the context of both the setting type and the stage of a project. The first example is the siting of a hazardous waste facility. Perceptions about problems of public health and safety could emerge during the early planning stage. If a decision is made to go ahead, construction would be accompanied by an influx of temporary workers. In the case of the industrial plant, community infrastructure support might be needed during construction, while changes in the industrial focus of the community might occur during the operational stage. These analytic procedures would be repeated for each of the SIA variables for each stage of the project. Procedures for accomplishing this task are outlined in Section V *principles for doing social impact assessment.*

SECTION IV - STEPS IN THE SOCIAL IMPACT ASSESSMENT PROCESS

The social impact assessment itself should contain the ten steps outlined in Figure 9.5. These steps are logically sequential, but often overlap in practice. This sequence is patterned after the environmental impact assessment steps as listed in the *CEQ guidelines.*

1. Public Involvement — Develop an Effective Public Involvement Plan to Involve all Potentially Affected Publics.

This requires identifying and working with all potentially affected groups starting at the very beginning of planning for the proposed action. Groups affected by proposed actions include those who live nearby; those who will hear, smell or see a development; those who are forced to relocate because of a project; and those who have interest in

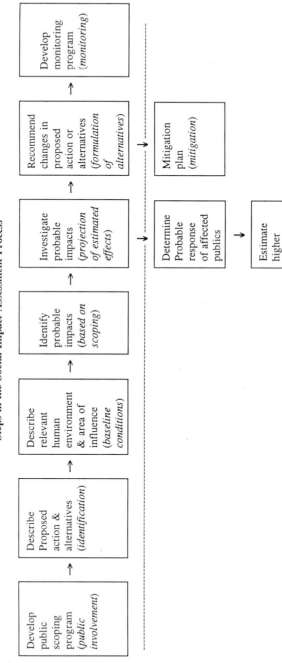

Figure 9-5
Steps in the Social Impact Assessment Process

Include Interested and Affected Publics in all Steps of the Social Impact Assessment Process

a new project or policy change but may not live in proximity. Others affected include those who might normally use the land on which the project is located (such as farmers who have to plow around a transmission line). Still others include those affected by the influx of seasonal residents who may have to pay higher prices for food or rent, or pay higher taxes to cover the cost of expanded community services. Once identified, representatives from each group should be systematically interviewed to determine potential areas of concern/impact, and ways each representative might be involved in the planning decision process. Public meetings by themselves are inadequate for collecting information about public perceptions. Survey data can be used to define the potentially affected population. In this first step, the pieces are put in place for a public involvement program which will last throughout the environmental and social impact assessment process.

2. Identification of Alternatives — Describe the Proposed Action or Policy Change and Reasonable Alternatives.

In the next step, the proposed action is described in enough detail to begin to identify the data requirements needed from the project proponent to frame the SIA. At a minimum, this includes:

- Locations
- Land requirements
- Needs for ancillary facilities (roads, transmission lines, sewer and water lines)
- Construction schedule
- Size of the work force (construction and operation, by year or month)
- Facility size and shape
- Need for a local work force
- Institutional resources

The list of social impact assessment variables shown in Figure 9.3 is a guide for obtaining data from policy or project proponents. Sometimes the description of the proposed alternatives may not include all the information needed for an SIA. Another problem is the provision of summary numbers when desegregated numbers are needed. For example, the social assessor may be given numbers for the total peak work force of a construction project, when information is needed on local, in-migrating, and nonlocal commuting workers for each phase of construction.

3. Baseline Conditions — Describe the Relevant Human Environment/Area of Influence and Baseline Conditions.

The baseline conditions are the existing conditions and past trends associated with the human environment in which the proposed activity is to take place. This is called the baseline study. For construction projects, a geographical area is identified along with the distribution of special populations at risk; but for programs, policies, or technology assessments, the relevant human environment may be a more dispersed collection of interested and affected publics, interest groups, organizations, and institutions. The generic set of dimensions for investigation listed below would include the following aspects of the human environment for construction projects and geographically-located programs and policies (the social impact assessment variables listed in Figure 9.3 require similar information):

- **Relationships with the biophysical environment**, including ecological setting; aspects of the environment seen as resources or problems; areas having economic, recreational, aesthetic or symbolic significance to specific people; residential arrangements and living patterns, including relationships among communities and social organizations; attitudes toward environmental features; and patterns of resource use.
- **Historical background**, including initial settlement and subsequent shifts in population; developmental events and eras, including experience with boom-bust effects, as well as a discussion of broader employment trends; past or ongoing community controversies, particularly those involving technology or the environment; and other experiences likely to affect the level or distribution of the impacts on local receptivity to the proposed action.
- **Political and social resources**, including the distribution of power and authority; the capacities of relevant systems or institutions (e.g., the school system); friendship networks and patterns of cleavage or cooperation among potentially affected groups; levels of residential stability; distributions of socio-demographic characteristics such as age and ethnicity; presence of distinctive or potentially vulnerable groups (e.g., low income); and linkages among geo-political units (federal, state, county, local and inter-local).
- **Culture, attitudes and social-psychological conditions**, including attitudes toward the proposed action; trust in political and social institutions, perceptions of risks; relevant psychological coping and adjustment capacity; cultural cognition of society and environment; assessed quality of life; and important values that may be relevant to or affected by the proposed action.
- **Population characteristics** including the demographics of relevant groups (including all significant stakeholders and sensitive populations and groups); major economic activities; future prospects; the labor markets and available work force; unemployment and underemployment; population and expected changes; availability of housing, infrastructure and services; size and age structure of households; and seasonal migration patterns.

The level of effort that is devoted to the description of the human environment should be commensurate with the size, cost, and degree of expected impacts of the proposed action. At a minimum, the existing literature on comparable or analogous events, knowledgeable experts, and readily available documents such as government reports should be consulted. On-site investigations and the use of previous field studies and surveys are recommended, as well as rapid appraisals and mini-surveys.

4. Scoping — After Obtaining a Technical Understanding of the Proposal, Identify the Full Range of Probable Social Impacts that will be Addressed Based on Discussion or Interviews with Numbers of all Potentially Affected.

After initial scoping, the social impact assessor selects the SIA variables for further assessment situations. Consideration needs to be devoted both to the impacts perceived by the acting agency and to those perceived by affected groups and communities. The principal methods to be used by experts and interdisciplinary teams are reviews of the existing social science literature, public scoping, public surveys, and public participation techniques. It is important for the views of affected people to be taken into consideration. Ideally, all affected people or groups contribute to the selection of the variables assessed through either a participatory process or by review and comment on the decisions made by responsible officials and the interdisciplinary team.

Relevant criteria for selecting significant impacts comparable to those spelled out in the CEQ Regulations (40 CFR 1508.27) include the:

- Probability of the event occurring;
- Number of people including indigenous populations that will be affected;
- Duration of impacts (long-term vs. short-term);
- Value of benefits and costs to impacted groups (intensity of impacts);
- Extent that the impact is reversible or can be mitigated;
- Likelihood of causing subsequent impacts;
- Relevance to present and future policy decisions;
- Uncertainty over possible effects; and
- Presence or absence of controversy over the issue.

5. Projection of Estimated Effects — Investigate the Probable Impacts.

The probable social impacts will be formulated in terms of predicted conditions without the actions (baseline projection); predicted conditions with the actions; and predicted impacts which can be interpreted as the differences between the future with and without the proposed action. The empirical procedure is based on the social impact assessment model outlined in Section III.

Investigation of the probable impacts involves five major sources of information: 1) Data from project proponents; 2) Records of previous experience with similar actions as represented in reference literature as well as other EISs; 3) Census and vital statistics; 4) Documents and secondary sources; and

5) Field research, including informant interviews, hearings, group meetings, and surveys of the general population. The investigation of the social impacts identified during scoping is the most important component.

Methods of projecting the future lie at the heart of social assessment, and much of the process of analysis is tied up in this endeavor. In spite of the long lists of methods available, most fall into the following categories:

- **Comparative method;**
- **Straight-line trend projects** (taking an existing trend and simply projecting the same rate of change into the future);
- **Population multiplier methods** (each specified increase in population implies designated multiples of some other variable, e.g. jobs, housing units);
- **Scenarios** 1) logical–imaginations based on construction of hypothetical futures through a process of mentally modeling the assumptions about the variables in question; and 2) fitted empirical—similar past cases used to analyze the present case with experts adjusting the scenario by taking into account the unique characteristics of the present case;
- **Expert testimony** (experts can be asked to present scenarios and assess their implications);

- **Computer modeling** (involving the mathematical formulation of premises and a process of quantitative weighing of variables); and
- **Calculation of "futures foregone"** (a number of methods have been formulated to determine what options would be given up irrevocably as a result of a plan or project, e.g., river recreation and agricultural land use after the building of a dam).

The record of previous experience is very important to the estimation of future impacts. It is largely contained in case reports and studies and the experience of experts. Variations in the patterns of impacts and responses in these cases also should be registered. Expert knowledge is used to enlarge this knowledge base and to judge how the study case is likely to deviate from the typical patterns. The documents and secondary sources provide information on existing conditions, plans, reported attitudes and opinions; and contribute to the case record. The field research involves interviews with persons who have different interests at stake, different perspectives, and different kinds of expertise. Wherever feasible, it should also involve a search through a wide range of documentation that is often available (in forms that range from official statistics and the minutes of meetings to the patterns of coverage and letters to the editors). The opinions of various individuals and groups toward the proposed change should also be part of the record. Surveys are valuable to assess public opinion properly, because spokespersons for groups do not always represent the views of the rank-and-file. Statements at public meetings and by spokespersons should not be used as projections, but as possible impacts to be evaluated through other means.

6. Predicting Responses to Impacts — Determine the Significance of the Identified Social Impacts.

This is a difficult assessment task often avoided, but the responses of affected parties frequently will have significant subsequent impacts. After direct impacts have been estimated the assessor must next estimate how the affected people will respond in terms of attitude and actions. Their attitudes before implementation predicts their attitudes afterwards, though there are increasing data that show fears are often overblown and that expected (often promised) benefits fail to meet expectations. This literature should be consulted.

The actions of affected groups are to be estimated using comparable cases and interviews with affected people about what they expect to do. So much depends on whether local leadership arises (and the objectives and strategies of these leaders), that this assessment step often is highly uncertain, but at least policy makers will be notified of potential problems and unexpected results. This step is also important because adaption and responses of affected parties can have consequences of their own—whether for the agency that proposes an action (as when political protest stalls a proposal) or for the affected communities, whether in the short-term or in the longer-term (as in the previously noted example of Morgan City, Louisiana).

Patterns in previous assessments guide this analysis, and expert judgment and field investigations are used to see whether the study case is following the typical patterns or how it is developing uniquely. Being able to show potentially affected people that significant impacts are being incorporated into the assessment is critical to the success of this step.

7. Indirect and Cumulative Impacts — Estimate Subsequent Impacts and Cumulative Impacts.

Indirect impacts are those caused by the direct impacts; they often occur later than the direct impact, or farther away. Cumulative impacts are those impacts which result from the incremental impacts of an action added to other past, present, and reasonably foreseeable future actions regardless of which agency or person undertakes them (see 40 CFR 1508.7). A community's residential and retail growth and pressures on government services following the siting of a major project are examples of indirect and cumulative impacts. While they are more difficult to estimate precisely than direct impacts, it is very important that indirect and cumulative impacts be clearly identified in the SIA.

8. Changes in Alternatives — Recommend New or Changed Alternatives and Estimate or Project Their Consequences.

Each new alternative or recommended change should be assessed separately. The methods used in step five (estimation), apply here but usually on a more modest scale. More innovative alternatives and changes probably should be presented in an experimental structure. Expert judgment and scenarios are helpful in developing project and policy alternations. The number of iterations here will depend upon time, funding, and the magnitude of the project or policy changes.

9. Mitigation — Develop a Mitigation Plan.

A social impact assessment not only forecasts impacts, it should identify means to mitigate adverse impacts. Mitigation includes avoiding the impact by not taking or modifying an action; minimizing, rectifying, or reducing the impacts through the design or operation of the project or policy; or compensating for the impact by providing substitute facilities, resources, or opportunities (see 40 CFR 1508.20).

Ideally, mitigation measures are built into the selected alternative, but it is appropriate to identify mitigation measures even if they are not immediately adopted or if they would be the responsibility of another person or government unit. (Federal legislation which mandates mitigation measures is shown in Figure 9.6).

We suggest a sequencing strategy to manage social impacts modeled after one used with wetland protection and other natural resource issues. During the first sequence, wetlands managers strive to *avoid* all adverse impacts. In the second sequence, managers strive to *minimize* any adverse impacts that cannot be avoided. During the third sequence, managers *compensate* for adverse impacts. Compensation for the loss of a wetland, for example, could be to acquire a different wetland, enhance a degraded site, or create a new wetland. The amount of compensation can be based on the type of wetland or resource lost, the severity of the impact, and the location of the wetland mitigation site.

The first two steps of sequencing—*avoiding and minimizing*—can apply to the project itself or to the host community or the impacted region. For example, the project may be revised to avoid or minimize adverse social impacts (e.g., extend the construction period to minimize in-migration), or the community may be able to take steps to attenuate, if not avoid, any adverse effects. Application of the sequencing concept for the mitigation of adverse social impacts requires that the assessor first rank

Figure 9.6
United States Federal Legislation and Executive Orders
Addressing Resource Development and Socioeconomic Mitigation

Date	Federal Law	Socioeconomic Mitigation
1920	Mineral Leasing Act (41 Stat 449)	Allowed 37.5% of receipts to be returned to local governments for schools and roads; required protection of subsistence habitats.
	Coastal Energy Impact Program	Places Federal government in a secondary role behind State and local governments.
1969	National Environmental Policy Act	Required human and community conditions to be considered in the assessment process.
1975	Federal Coal Leasing Amendments Act	Increased percent of revenues for socioeconomic mitigation.
1976	Federal Land Policy Management Act	Required revenues received by States to go to impacted areas.
1976	Mineral Leasing Act Amendments	Increased the amount of receipts to 50% and broadened categories of receipts that could be spent on courts, sewers, infrastructure, etc.
1978	Power Plant and Industrial Fuel Use Act	Federal government can pay for planning and land acquisition for housing and community facilities in coal/uranium development.
1978	Defense Economic adjustment programs Executive Order	Establishes economic adjustment committee and encourages uniform economic impact analysis and information sharing.
1981	Military Construction and Authorization Act	Allows up to $1 million of Federal funds per county for impacts.

the level of importance of each significant SIA variable determined during the estimated effects step.

The first step in evaluating potential mitigation for each variable is to determine whether the proponent could modify the project or proposed policy to avoid the adverse effects. For example, a road that displaces families could be rerouted. The next step in the sequencing process is to identify ways to minimize adverse social impacts. For example, most citizens are uncomfortable with the idea of locating a perceived as undesirable facility near their community. Attitudes (particularly negative ones) formed about the project cannot be eliminated, but might be moderated if the public has complete information about the proposed development, are included in the decision making process, or are provided with structural arrangements that assure safe operations.

There are at least three benefits of identifying unresolvable social impacts that may result from a proposed project. The first is identifying methods of compensating individuals and the community for unavoidable impacts. The second occurs when the community may identify ways of enhancing other quality of life variables as compensation for the adverse effects. The third happens when the identification of unresolvable social impacts makes community leaders and project proponents more sensitive to the feelings of community residents.

By articulating the impacts that will occur and making efforts to avoid or minimize the adverse consequences, or compensating the residents or the community for the losses, benefits may be enhanced and avoidable conflicts can be managed or minimized.

10. Monitoring — Develop a Monitoring Program.

A monitoring program should be developed that is capable of identifying deviations from the proposed action and any important unanticipated impacts. A monitoring plan should be developed to track project and program development and compare real impacts with projected ones. It should spell out (to the degree possible) the nature and extent of additional steps that should take place when unanticipated impacts or impacts larger than the projections occur.

Monitoring programs are particularly necessary for projects and programs that lack detailed information or that have high variability or uncertainty. It is important to recognize, in advance, the potential for "surprises" that may lie completely outside the range of options considered by the SIA. If monitoring procedures cannot be adequately implemented, then mitigation agreements should acknowledge the uncertainty faced in implementing the decision.

It is generally only at this stage that the community or affected group has the influence to "get it in writing." A recent example of a monitoring program with subsequent provision for mitigation was negotiated between the U.S. Department of Energy, the State of Texas and the Super Conducting Super Collider Laboratory. The process allowed for the payment of approximately $800,000 to local jurisdictions to monitor the impacts of the construction activity.

SECTION V
PRINCIPLES FOR SOCIAL IMPACT ASSESSMENT

In general, there is consensus on the types of impacts that need to be considered (social, cultural, demographic, economic, social-psychological, and often political impacts); on the need for the SIA to include a discussion of the proposed action (i.e., the proposed facility, project, development, policy change, etc.); on the components of the human environment where the impacts are likely to be felt (affected neighborhoods, communities, or regions); on the likely impacts (generally defined as the difference between the likely future of the affected human environment with versus without the proposed policy or project); and on the steps that could be taken to enhance positive impacts and to mitigate any negative ones (by avoiding them, if possible, by modification and minimization, and by providing compensation for any negative impacts that cannot be avoided or ameliorated).

As SIA textbooks point out (Burdge 1994; Branch et.al. 1984; Finsterbusch 1980; Freudenburg 1986; Taylor et.al. 1990) and as suggested by the Council on Environmental Quality (CEQ) *Regulations for Implementing the Procedural Provisions of NEPA* (U.S. Council on Environmental Quality 1986), the SIA practitioner should focus on the more significant impacts, should use appropriate measures and information, should provide quantification where feasible and appropriate, and should present the social impacts in a manner that can be understood by decision-makers and community leaders.

The following principles augment the guidance provided in earlier sections. These principles are benchmarks for conducting an SIA (Figure 9.7). They include the:

- Joint role of **SIA and public involvement** in identifying affected groups;
- Concept of **impact equity** (who "wins" and who "loses") as it concerns sensitive groups;
- **Focus of an SIA**—The possible impacts identified by the affected public and impacts identified through social science expertise;
- **Explicit identification of methods, assumptions, and determination of significance;**
- **Feedback** to project planners;
- **Use of SIA practitioners** to do SIA;
- **Establishment of mitigation and monitoring** as a joint agency-community responsibility;
- **Identifying appropriate data sources** for SIA; and
- **Planning** for gaps in data.

1. Involve the Diverse Public — Identify and Involve all Potentially Affected Groups and Individuals.

A public involvement and conflict management program can beneficially be closely integrated with the development of the social impact assessment process. A lack of understanding still exists among many decision-makers as to how public involvement fits within the planning process. Public involvement can complement and fit within the SIA process by identifying potentially affected groups, and by interpreting the meaning of impacts for each group. Public involvement plays an important role in recruiting participants for the planning process who are truly representative of affected groups. Public involvement should be truly interactive, with communication flowing both ways between the agency and affected groups.

2. Analyze Impact Equity — Clearly Identify Who will Win and Who Will Lose, and Emphasize Vulnerability of Under-Represented Groups.

Impacts should be specified for differentially affected groups and not just measured in the aggregate. Identification of all groups likely to be affected by an agency action is central to the concept of impact equity. There can always be winners and losers as the result of a decision to construct a dam, build a highway or close an area to timber harvesting. However, no category of persons, particularly those that might be considered more sensitive or vulnerable as a result of age, gender, ethnicity, race, occupation or other factors, should have to bear the brunt of adverse social impacts. While most proposed projects or policies are not zero-sum situations, and there may be varying benefits for almost all involved, SIA has a special duty to identify those whose adverse impacts might get lost in the aggregate of benefits.

The impact assessment practitioner must be attentive to those groups that lack political efficacy; such as groups low in political or economic power which often are not heard, or do not have their interests strongly represented.

Figure 9.7
Principles for Social Impact Assessment

- **Involve the diverse public**
  *Identify and involve all potentially affected groups and
  individuals*

- **Analyze impact equity**
  *Clearly identify who will win and who will lose and emphasize
  vulnerability of under-represented groups*

- **Focus the assessment**
  *Deal with issues and public concerns that "really count," not those
  that are "easy to count"*

- **Identify methods and assumptions and define significance in advance**
  *Define how the SIA was conducted, what assumptions were used and
  how significance were selected*

- **Provide feedback on social impacts to project planners**
  *Identify problems that could be solved with changes to the proposed
  action or alternatives*

- **Use SIA practitioners**
  *Trained social scientists employing social science methods will
  provide the best results*

- **Establish monitoring and mitigation programs**
  Manage uncertainty by monitoring and mitigating adverse impacts

- **Identify data sources**
  *Use published scientific literature, secondary data and primary data
  from the affected area*

- **Plan for gaps in data**

Examples abound in the literature of groups that could be considered sensitive, vulnerable, or low in power. The elderly have been identified as a category of persons sensitive to involuntary displacement and relocation. Children have suffered learning problems resulting from long-term exposure to various forms of transportation noise and local pollution (e.g., vehicular traffic, airports). Minorities and the poor are disproportionately represented in groups low in power; low-income, minority neighborhoods frequently were targeted in the 1960s as optimal sites for road construction and similar public works projects. Persons with some form of disability or impairment constitute another sensitive category with important needs. Farmers often are affected by transmission lines, water projects or developments that take large amounts of land. The special impacts to those persons should be highlighted in an SIA, not lost in summary statistics.

3. Focus the Assessment — Deal With Issues and Public Concerns that Really Count, Not those that are Just Easy to Count.

Impacts Identified by the Public - Social impact assessment practitioners must contend with stringent time and resource constraints that affect the scope of the assessment and how much can be done in the time available. Given such constraints, a central question emerges: "If you cannot cover the social universe, what should you focus on?" The answer is to focus on the most significant impacts in order of priority, and all significant impacts for all impacted groups must be identified early using a variety of rapid appraisal or investigative techniques. Clearly, impacts identified as important by the public must be given high priority. Many of these will surface during the NEPA scoping process or earlier if a survey is used to identify the potentially-affected populations. However, as noted earlier, some groups low in power that may be adversely affected do not necessarily participate in early project stages. It is essential that broadly-based public involvement occur throughout the life of the SIA; but additional means (e.g., key informants, participant observation, and where possible, surveys) often must be used to ensure that the most significant public concerns are addressed.

Impacts Identified by SIA Practitioners - SIA practitioners have the expertise to help prioritize issues using a review of literature and professional experience. Often they will suggest the study of issues unrecognized by either the public or the agencies.

4. Identify Methods and Assumptions and Define Significance — Describe How the SIA is Conducted, what Assumptions are Used and How Significance is Determined.

The methods and assumptions used in the SIA should be made available and published prior to a decision in order to allow decision makers as well the public to evaluate the assessment of impacts (as required by NEPA). Practitioners will need to consult the CEQ Regulations. Definitions and examples of effects (direct, indirect, and cumulative) are provided in 40 CFR 1508.7 and 1508.8; "effects" and "impacts" are used synonymously. The CEQ regulations are clear that an environmental impact statement has to focus on impacts found to be significant.

Significance in terms of context and intensity considerations is defined in 40 CFR 1508.27. Context includes such considerations as society as a whole, affected regions, affected interests and locality (e.g., when considering site-specific projects, local impacts assume greater importance than those of a regional nature). Intensity refers to the dimensions presented under Scoping in Section IV, as well as consideration of health and safety, endangered species or unique human resources, precedents and laws. While these criteria are helpful in judging significance, the SIA practitioner also needs to consult individual agency procedures for NEPA compliance. Some of these list additional social impacts that the agency must consider even if not always significant.

5. Provide Feedback On Social Impacts To Project Planners — Identify Problems That Could Be Solved With Changes To The Proposed Action Or Alternatives.

Findings from the SIA should feed back into project design to mitigate adverse impacts and enhance positive ones. The impact assessment, therefore, should be designed as a dynamic process involving cycles of project design, assessment, redesign, and reassessment. This process is often carried out informally with project designers prior to publication of the draft assessment for public comment; public comments on a draft EIS can contribute importantly to this process of feedback and modification.

6. Use SIA Practitioners — Trained Social Scientists Employing Social Science Methods will Provide the Best Results.

The need for professionally qualified, competent people with social science training and experience cannot be overemphasized. An experienced SIA practitioner will know the data, and be familiar and conversant with existing social science evidence pertaining to impacts that have occurred elsewhere, which may be relevant to the impact area in question. This breadth of knowledge and experience can prove invaluable in identifying important impacts that may not surface as public concerns or as mandatory considerations found in agency NEPA compliance procedures. A social scientist will be able to identify the full range of important impacts and then will be able to select the appropriate measurement procedures.

Having a social scientist as part of the interdisciplinary EIS team will also reduce the probability that an important social impact could go unrecognized. In assessing social impacts, if the evidence for a potential type of impact is not definitive in either direction, then the appropriate conservative conclusion is that it *cannot be ruled out with confidence*. In addition, it is important that the SIA practitioner be conversant with the technical and biological perspectives brought to bear on the project, as well as the cultural and procedural context of the agency they work with.

7. Establish Monitoring and Mitigation Program — Manage Uncertainty by Monitoring and Mitigating Adverse Impacts.

Crucial to the SIA process is monitoring significant social impact variables and any programs which have been put into place to mitigate them. As indicated earlier, the identification of impacts might depend on the specification of contingencies. For example, if the in-migration of workers during the construction phase work force is 1000, then the community's housing will be inadequate to meet the need, but if it is only 500, then the impact can be accommodated by currently vacant units.

Identifying and monitoring infrastructure needs is a key element of the local planning process. Two key points:

1. Monitoring and mitigation should be a joint agency and community responsibility; and

2. Both activities should occur on an iterative basis throughout the project life cycle. Depending on the nature of the project and time horizons for completion, the focus of long-term responsibility for monitoring and mitigation is not easily defined. Research shows that trust and expertise are key factors in choosing the balance between agency and community monitoring participation. Few agencies have the resources to continue these activities for an extended period, but local communities should be provided resources to assume a portion of the monitoring and mitigation responsibilities.

8. Identify Data Sources — Published Scientific Literature, Secondary Data, and Primary Data from the Affected Area.

These three sources should be consulted for all SIAs. Balance among the three may vary according to the type of the proposed action, as well as specific considerations noted below, but all three will be relevant.

Published Scientific Literature — The SIA should draw on existing, previously reviewed and screened social science literature which summarizes existing knowledge of impacts based on accepted scientific standards. Examples include journal articles, books, and reports available from similar projects. A list of easy-to-obtain, recommended sources is provided at the end of this monograph. Existing documentation is useful in identifying which social impacts are likely to accompany a proposed action. When it is possible to draw potentially competing interpretations from the existing literature, the SIA should provide a careful discussion of relative methodological merits of available studies.

As pointed out in Section III, the best guidance for future expectations is past experience; therefore, consideration of existing literature should err on the side of inclusiveness, not on exclusion of potentially relevant cases. Caution is needed when the SIA presents a conclusion that is contradicted by the published literature; in such cases, the reasons for the differences should be explicitly addressed. Anthropological data on rural and ethnically- and racially-diverse communities is best for understanding the cultural context of the impacted community.

Secondary Data Sources — The best known secondary sources of these are the Census, vital statistics, geographical data, relevant agency publications, and routine data collected by state and federal agencies. Examples of other secondary data sources include agency caseload statistics (e.g., from mental health centers, social service agencies and other human service providers, law enforcement agencies, and insurance and financial regulatory agencies); published and unpublished historical materials (often available in local libraries, historical societies, and school district files); compilations produced by booster and/or service organizations (such as chambers of commerce, welcome wagon organizations, and church groups); and the files of local newspapers. These secondary sources can be used in conjunction with key-informant interviews, to allow for verification of informant memories and to be alert for potential sources of bias in other data.

Primary data from the affected area — Survey research, oral histories and informant interviews are examples of primary data which may be collected to verify other data sources. If a social assessor concludes that community impacts will differ from those documented elsewhere, such conclusions must be based on the collection and analysis of primary data which specifically show why such alternative conclusions are more credible. Also, local residents often have important forms of expertise, both about local socioeconomic conditions and about the broader range of likely impacts. Because of its unique history and structure, each community may react to a development event or policy change differently than other communities.

9. Plan for Gaps in Data

SIA practitioners often have to produce an assessment in the absence of all the relevant or even the necessary data. The three elements of this principle are intended to supplement the guidance already provided by the CEQ Regulations at 40 CFR 1502.22.

When an agency is evaluating reasonably foreseeable significant adverse effects on the human environment in an environmental impact statement and there is incomplete or unavailable information, the agency shall always make clear that such information is lacking.

(a) If the incomplete information...is essential to a reasoned choice among alternatives and (b) the overall costs of obtaining it are not exorbitant, the agency shall include the information in the environmental impact statement.

Only if the relevant information "cannot be obtained because the overall costs of obtaining it are exorbitant or the means to obtain it are not known," is the EIS permitted a gap in relevant information. In such cases, however, the EIS needs to include: 1) a statement of relevance of the incomplete or unavailable information; 2) a summary of existing credible scientific evidence [that] is relevant; and 3) the agency's evaluation of the likely and possible impacts based upon theoretical approaches or research methods generally accepted in the scientific community (40 CFR 1502.22). The following three elements are acceptable procedures to the social science community when there are shortages of resources necessary to do the desired data collection.

It is more important to identify likely social impacts than to precisely quantify the more obvious social impacts - All assessors strive to identify and quantify significant impacts, thereby providing decision makers and the affected publics with information that is both as complete and as accurate as possible. In cases where this desirable goal cannot be met, *it is better to be roughly correct on important issues than to be precisely correct on unimportant issues.* Within the context of the social impact statement, there are two important differences between impact *identification* (what are the general categories or types of impacts that are likely to occur [see Figure 9.3]) and impact *evaluation* (precisely how significant are those impacts likely to be?).

Research has identified the social impacts of many types of actions, and the experienced SIA practitioner can identify plausible and potentially significant impacts relatively quickly and efficiently. On the other hand, an accurate evaluation is a resource-intensive process and deals with the question of significance. Research on the decision-making process has found that experts and policy makers were particularly prone toward premature closure. Given a partial listing of potential impacts experts tended to assume they have been given a complete list and in most cases, failed to recognize the potential impacts that had been omitted from consideration. While empirical estimates can appear to be quite precise, demographic and economic projections have been shown by empirical analysis to have an average absolute error in the range of 50-100 percent. We support the use of qualitative and quantitative measures of social impact assessment variables, but realize that the evaluation of significance has an important judgment component.

It is important to be on the "conservative" side in reporting likely social impacts - The purpose of the EIS is to provide an even-handed treatment of the potential impacts, offering *a scientifically reasonable assessment of the probable impacts in advance of the development event*. It is a very different matter from *providing solid proof* of impacts after the impacts occur and all the evidence is in! All EISs and SIAs are by their nature anticipatory.

Questions about the "proof" of impacts can be asked in an apparently scientific language, but cannot be answered with true confidence in advance of the actions in question. In assessing social and economic impacts, accordingly, if the evidence for a potential type of impact is not definitive in either direction, the conservative conclusion is that the impact *cannot be ruled out with confidence*, not that the impact is not proven. In cases of doubt, in terms of statistical terminology, the proper interpretation is the Type II test for power or sensitivity, and not the Type I test for the strength of consistency of an association.

The less reliable data there are on the effects of the projects or policy change, the more important it is to have the SIA work performed by competent, professional social scientists - Resource limitations will not always allow for SIA's to be done by experienced social scientists. The two following situations are ones in which it may be appropriate to proceed without professional social scientists' involvement in an SIA.
1. In cases where proposed actions are considered by persons within the agency with social science training, and by those in the potentially affected community, to likely cause only negligible or ephemeral social impacts.
2. In cases where a significant body of empirical findings is available from the social science literature, which can be applied fairly directly to the proposed action in question, and is *referenced, summarized*, and *cited* by the person(s) preparing the SIA section of the EIS.

If one of these two conditions is not present, the absence of professional social science expertise would be imprudent for both the agency and affected groups and communities; any SIA would be speculative and not well grounded.

SECTION VI - CONCLUSIONS

Social impact assessment is predicated on the notion that decision-makers should understand the consequences of their decisions before they act, and that the people affected will not only be appraised of the effects, but have the opportunity to participate in designing their future. The social environment is different than the natural environment because it reacts in anticipation of change, but can adapt in reasoned ways to changing circumstances if part of the planning process. In addition, persons in different social settings interpret change in different ways, and react in different ways. Perhaps because of this complexity, or the political consequences of making explicit the social consequences of projects and programs, social impact assessment has not been well-integrated into agency decision-making. The guidelines and principles presented herein are designed to assist agencies and other institutions in implementing SIA within the context of the NEPA process. If a well-prepared SIA is integrated into the decision-making process, better decisions will result.

SECTION VII - SOCIAL IMPACT ASSESSMENT LITERATURE

Textbooks and Guides

Branch, Kristi, Douglas A. Hooper, James Thompson and James C. Creighton. 1984. *Guide to Social Impact Assessment*. Boulder, CO: Westview Press, ISBN 0-86531-717-8.

Burdge, Rabel J. 1994. *A Community Guide to Social Impact Assessment* Middleton, WI (P.O. Box 620863). Social Ecology Press.

Freudenburg, William R. 1986. Social Impact Assessment. *Annual Review of Sociology*, 12:451-478.

Taylor, C. Nicholas, C. Hobson Bryan and Colin C. Goodrich. 1990. *Social Assessment: Theory, Process and Techniques*. Studies in Resource Management No. 7, Center for Resource Management, P.O. Box 56, Lincoln University, New Zealand.

Regulations and Administrative Procedures

Atherton, Carol Coop. 1977. Legal Requirements for Environmental Impact Reporting. in *Handbook for Environmental Planning: The Social Consequences of Environmental Change*. James McEvoy III and Thomas Dietz eds. New York: Wiley, pp 9-64.

Jordan, William S. III. 1984. Psychological Harm After PANE: NEPA's Requirements to Consider Psychological Damage. *Harvard Environmental Law Review*, 8:55-87.

Llewellyn, Lynn G. and William R. Freudenburg. 1990. Legal Requirements for Social Impact Assessments: Assessing the Social Science Fallout from Three Mile Island. *Society and Natural Resources*, 2(3): 193-208.

Meidinger, Errol E. and William R. Freudenburg. 1983. The Legal Status of Social Impact Assessments: Recent Developments. *Environmental Sociology*, 34:30-33.

U.S. Council on Environment Quality. 1986. *Regulations for Implementing the Procedural Provisions of the National Environmental Policy Act* (40 CFR 1500-1508). Washington: Government Printing Office, Washington, D.C. 20402.

Public Law 91-90, *The National Environmental Policy Act of 1969, as Amended* (P.L. 94-52 and P.L. 94-83) 42 U.S.C. 4321-4347.

SIA Methodology

Finsterbusch, Kurt and C. P. Wolf eds. 1981. *Methodology of Social Impact Assessment*. 2nd Edition. Stroudsburg, PA: Hutchinson Ross, ISBN 0-87933-401-0.

Finsterbusch, Kurt, Lynn G. Llewellyn, and C.P. Wolf eds. 1983. *Social Impact Assessment Methods*. Beverly Hills, CA: Sage, ISBN 0-8039-2142.

Finsterbusch, Kurt, J. Ingersol, and Lynn Llewellyn eds. 1990. *Methods for Social Analysis in Developing Countries*. Boulder, CO: Westview Press.

Leistritz, Larry and Steven H. Murdock. 1981. *The Socioeconomic Impact of Resource Development: Methods of Assessment*. Boulder, CO: Westview Press, ISBN 0-89158-978-3.

Rickson, Roy E., Tor Hundloe, Geoffrey T. McDonald and Rabel J. Burdge, eds. 1990. Social Impact of Development: Putting Theory and Methods into Practice. *Environmental Impact Assessment Review*, 10: (1/2): 357 pages.

Stoffle, Richard W., and others. 1990. Calculating the Cultural Significance of American Indian Plants: Paiute and Shoshone Ethnobotany at Yucca Mountain Nevada. *American Anthropologist*, 92(2): 416-432.

Research Findings

Elkind-Savatsky, Pamela. 1986. *Differential Social Impacts of Rural Resource Development*. Boulder, CO: Westview Press. 293 pp.

Finsterbusch, Kurt. 1980. *Understanding Social Impacts: Assessing the Effects of Public Projects*. Beverly Hills, CA: Sage.

Freudenburg, William R. and Robert Gramling. 1992. Community Impacts of Technological Change: Toward a Longitudinal Perspective. *Social Forces*, 70(4): 937-55.

Freudenburg, William R. and Robert E. Jones. 1992. Criminal Behavior and Rapid Community Growth: Examining the Evidence. *Rural Sociology*, 56 (4): 619-45.

Gramling, Robert and William R. Freudenburg. 1990. A Closer Look at 'Local Control': Communities, Commodities, and the Collapse of the Coast. *Rural Sociology,* 55(4): 541-58.

Greider, Thomas and Lorraine Garkovich. 1994. Symbolic Landscapes: The Social Construction of Nature and the Environment. *Rural Sociology,* 59 (2): forthcoming.

Gulliford, Andrew. 1989. *Boomtown Blues: Colorado Oil Shale, 1885-1985.* Niwot, CO: University Press of Colorado.

Llewellyn, L.G. 1981. The Social Cost of Urban Transportation. In *Transportation and Behavior.* I. Altman, J. Wohlwill and P. Everett eds. New York: Plenum Press, 169-202.

Stoffle, Richard W. and others. 1991. Risk Perception Mapping: Using Ethnography to Define the Locally Affected Population for a Low-Level Radioactive Waste Storage Facility in Michigan: *American Anthropologist,* 93 (3): 611-635.

Literature Reviews

Bowles, Roy T. 1981. *Social Impact Assessment in Small Communities: An Integrative Review of Selected Literature.* Toronto: Butterworths, ISBN 0-409-81611-6.

Carley, Michael J. 1984. *Social Impact Assessment: A Cross-Disciplinary Guide to the Literature.* Boulder, CO: Westview Press, ISBN 0-86531-529-9.

Leistritz, Larry and Brenda Ekstrom. 1986. *Social Impact Assessment and Management: An Annotated Bibliography.* New York: Garland.

Conceptual Guidelines

Burdge, Rabel J. 1994. *A Conceptual Approach to Social Impact Assessment: Collection of writings by Rabel J. Burdge and Colleagues.* Middleton, WI (P.O. Box 620863): Social Ecology Press.

Freudenburg, William R. and Kenneth M. Keating. 1985. Applying Sociology to Policy: Social Science and the Environmental Impact Statement. *Rural Sociology,* 50(4):578-605.

Gramling, Robert and William R. Freudenburg. 1992. Opportunity-Threat, Development, and Adaptation: Toward a Comprehensive Framework for Social Impact Assessment. *Rural Sociology,* 57 (2): 216-234.

Rickson, Roy E., Rabel J. Burdge and Audrey Armour eds. 1990. Integrating Impact Assessment into the Planning Process: International Perspectives and Experience. *Impact Assessment Bulletin,* 8: (1/2); 357 pages.

Peer-Reviewed Journals

American Anthropologist
Environmental Impact Assessment Review
Human Organization
Impact Assessment (formerly Impact Assessment Bulletin)
Project Appraisal
Rural Sociology
Society and Natural Resources

Chapter 10

TEACHING SOCIAL IMPACT ASSESSMENT AT THE COLLEGE LEVEL[1]

Rabel J. Burdge

Introduction

This chapter addresses the focus, need, rationale, content, location and audience for a college level course on social impact assessment (SIA). The author's perspective is sociological, but the wider contributions of the social sciences to social impact assessment are also included.

The substantive area labelled SIA grew out of a need to apply the knowledge of sociology and other social sciences in an attempt to predict *social effects* of environmental alteration for development projects subject to the NEPA (National Environmental Policy Act) legislation in the U.S. and EARP (Environmental Assessment and Review Process) in Canada. These legal and regulatory mandates required project proponents to assess the social effects of development in a variety of environmental impact projects in varying geo-political settings. Most of the early SIA procedures were developed by social scientists located within federal agencies or consultants hired by engineering and architectural firms that prepared the larger environmental impact assessment statements. These early impact assessors used social science labels in their environmental impact statements, but few of the concepts had a connection to prior literature on community and cultural change.

More recently, SIA in the U.S. has opted for models that require such data as the number and types of new workers as an input to predict quantitative social changes in the geo-political area of impact (Leistritz and Murdock 1981). The Canadian model focuses more on social action, with emphasis on helping the impacted population to adjust to impending change (Bowles 1981). What role university-based social scientists can and should play in the developing SIA field has remained a relatively open question.

The Focus of a Social Impact Assessment Course

This chapter identifies two approaches to the teaching of SIA, one labelled generic and the other the project level approach. The *generic approach* to SIA is taught from the perspective of sensitizing students to general social change. It assumes the presence of major impacts and a rather wide policy perspective. Furthermore, project impacts are seen as leading to radical shifts in the distribution of the population and in turn producing recognizable changes in how human groups relate to each other.

[1]Abridged from the original. Rabel J. Burdge. 1984. Teaching Social Impact Assessment at the College Level, *Impact Assessment Bulletin*, 3(2): 48-53. Reproduced here with permission of the author and the publisher.

Implicit in the generic approach to SIA courses is the notion of understanding social change through experience. Being sensitive to the existence of social impacts is seen as more important than actually being able to identify them. Often the objective of the generic type of social impact assessment course is to get the sociological (or social science) point of view across to the non-social scientists (generally engineers).

The *project level* approach to teaching SIA assumes that social change is ubiquitous, but that a new project or policy change alters the normal flow of social change. Furthermore, this approach stresses that impact events will vary in specificity, intensity, duration, and a variety of other characteristics. It then becomes important for students to understand what will be the social impacts of a particular development rather than only being aware that social change will take place. By utilizing past social science research the student is better able to understand what is likely to happen to human populations given different impact events. *The practical goal of social impact assessment is to anticipate likely areas of impact, to utilize the information in the planning process, and to plan appropriate mitigation.*

The project-oriented course assumes that social impacts are most observable at the local level — at least the direct effects. For most social impact variables the measuring and interpretation works best the more restricted the area of study. A problem in both teaching and research is identifying the sequencing and duration of social impacts. For example, the rapid influx of construction workers is easily observed, but the gradual shifting of power from old-timers to an outside agency is less obvious. An important goal of teaching SIA thus becomes one of identifying and understanding the consequences of change for human populations, given different types of impact events.

Although I favor teaching SIA within a project setting there are some problems in focusing on specific impacts. For one, not all social assessors use the procedures outlined under NEPA and EARP. However, teaching SIA from the generic standpoint might produce a course with little applicability or one similar to those on social change or community development. Whichever approach is taken, the major concepts and research findings should come from the community and social change literature.

What can the University Contribute to the Teaching of SIA?

SIA training materials and workshops are offered by a number of federal land management agencies and consulting firms (e.g. Branch *et al* 1984; U.S. Forest Service, 1982; and Social Impact Research 1983). What then, is left for a college level course? The following is a list of suggested contributions:

•Agency training is likely to be specific to a particular type of social impact setting (e.g., off-shore drilling or recreational development). Each agency must deal with the settings that their employees are likely to encounter even though a more general approach might be preferred. University teaching can show that similar types of social impacts occur in a variety of settings and through research establish empirical linkages.

•There appears to be minimal agreement among agencies as to the organization and procedures for doing EIA and SIA statements. The college level courses should emphasize a general approach that would be useful to a variety of organizations.

•Step-by-step procedures characterize the present approach by SIA and EIS practitioners. The substantive nature of the social impacts is seldom addressed during either training or implementation. College courses could help explain the likely social consequences of different developments and thereby connect the procedures of the environmental impact assessment to real life events as well as basic social science concepts.

•Many of the students who take an SIA course will not be social scientists, and the course will likely be their first exposure to the analysis and interpretation of sociological variables. I have found that students do not know what to look for in the way of a social impact variable. Therefore, they should first be taught what is a social impact assessment variable and then how to select and utilize them in impact analysis. Furthermore, the instructor should discourage the myth that social impacts which cannot be quantified are unimportant and should therefore be dismissed. However, proselytization can be unproductive if the questions of engineers and planners about quantification are simply dismissed as irrelevant.

•Teaching SIA helps move the focus of the social sciences much closer to the reality of public planning and decision-making.

•Social impact assessment is one of the few applied areas of the social sciences which has direct application to the project evaluation setting.

What Should be Taught in a University Social Impact Assessment Course?

I personally believe that SIA should be taught within a project or policy context as a substantive, knowledge/producing enterprise. In teaching SIA I have attempted to address the question... *What are the different social impacts in a variety of project settings and how can they be utilized in project decision making and/or in mitigating the impacts of development?* Below is a list of general topic areas that convey the essence of the material and should form the core of a college-level SIA course:

•What is social impact assessment?
•How does social impact assessment fit the planning process?
•The history of social impact assessment
•How does social science theory contribute to SIA?
•The initial social assessment (scoping)
•Steps in the social impact assessment process
•Integrating social impact assessment with the EIA process
•Social impact variables
•How are social impact variables measured and interpreted?
•Public involvement as a social impact assessment variable
•Developing mitigation measures for social impacts
•International applications of social impact assessment

It is important that the course not only deal with appropriate methods and procedures, but also include the most up-to-date research findings on a wide variety of social impacts. The major topics listed above form an agenda around which SIA research can be organized within or outside of a course. My course requires that each team of students complete a social impact assessment. The goal of the course is to be capable of doing social impact assessment and to understand social soundness analysis as practiced by the U.S. Agency for International Development (USAID 1978) and the World Bank.

Which Departments Should Teach Social Impact Assessment?

Except for a handful of universities (e.g., Washington State University, Texas A&M, Iowa State, and the Universities of Alabama, Illinois and Maryland) courses on SIA are seldom taught within either the anthropology or sociology curriculum. Many sociologists and anthropologists would probably say that SIA is what we have been doing all along, and that no more applied courses are needed. Rural sociology, for example, has a rich tradition of community/social change research that provides a large body of findings about how rural communities adjust to outside influences. Applied anthropology rightly claims that they have always studies social impacts, particularly where traditional and modern cultures meet. Such titles as *Old wine is new bottle*, reinforce the notion that SIA is really a relabelling of what we have been doing all along (Carter 1981). Of course, these critics forgot that SIA requires prediction in advance of the event.

SIA courses (or as portions of courses) can sometimes be found in Landscape Architecture, Architecture, Environmental Studies, Urbana and Regional Planning and Geography. In many cases, SIA is taught as an addendum to an existing planning course or as part of a course on environmental impact analysis. However, when taught within a non-social science department, the focus is likely to be on procedures (how to do it) rather than on understanding the nature of social impacts. This emphasis on procedures as opposed to analysis of impacts may be the crucial factor in distinguishing an agency workshop from the type of contribution that could be made by a social scientists teaching of SIA at the university level. For example, the matrix advocated by the Federal Environmental Assessment Review Office of Canada (FEARO 1978) is widely used within engineering to insure that all environmental impacts are considered. If included, social impacts are designed by either *+*, *-*, or *0*. Their importance is quickly lost in the overall analysis, particularly when summed against short run economic gain.

Who Should Take Social Impact Assessment Courses at the College Level?

We would hope that students interested in planning—and enrolled in departments such as those previously mentioned—would be first in line. These students need to understand how SIA and the planning process fit together. The monographs by Finsterbusch and Motz (1980) and Warheit *et al.* (1977) as well as other chapters in this book document the importance of SIA in the anticipatory planning process.

For students who receive only introductory social sciences training, an SIA course offers the opportunity to learn about human responses to and *societal* consequences of technological change. Advanced undergraduate and master's level students drawn mostly from engineering and the physical and biological sciences would particularly benefit from such exposure. For these students, SIA might be part of a general course on the human consequences of technological change.

Future resource managers in state and federal agencies will need to know how to do SIA within the context of the EIS process. Students headed for these positions come from university departments of forestry, parks and recreation, fish and wildlife, water resource management, and conservation.

It may be possible to get a job with the title of *social impact assessor* with either a federal or state agency in the U.S. More likely, SIA responsibilities would be combined with public involvement, community relations, and general planning activities. Another possibility is employment as an SIA consultant. At the 1982 International Conference on Social Impact Assessment, held in Vancouver, B.C., forty-one percent (92 of 224) of the participants from Canada listed a consulting firm affiliation.

If environmental impact analysis becomes a requirement for projects in developing countries, then persons who work with USAID (U.S. Agency for International Development) and the World Bank will need to know how to do social soundness analysis. The same social assessment requirements are emerging for international donor agencies from all developed countries. Any *national* from a developing country who gets involved with foreign assistance will also need to know about SIA.

The University Contribution to Social Impact Assessment

If SIA is to become something more than a response to government mandates, then relevant research questions must be conceptualized and a body of knowledge must begin to form around the topic. The objective of the SIA process is to anticipate and predict social impacts in advance of choices and events so that the assessor's recommendations may become part of the decision-making and planning process. However, sociological research has given scant attention to identifying and measuring social impact variables in advance. Social indicators were developed by social scientists in the 1960s and 1970s as a quantitative attempt to monitor social change and the general social health of the country. But those measures were never widely utilized, because results were seldom valid below the state level. Besides, these measures involved impact events that had already occurred, so that study results were useful only for after-the-fact policy adjustments.

I conclude by pointing out that the teaching of social impact assessment has some important benefits to offer the discipline of sociology. It does represent an important and continuing opportunity for sociologists to make a contribution in the policy arena. It does bring together sociologists both inside and outside the university. It does provide an opportunity for us to show how sociology can contribute in a meaningful manner to the solving of interdisciplinary problems. At present, the impacts that are identified by sociologists are best understood by policy-makers within the practical context of environmental decision-making. The larger social science community needs to legitimize SIA as a proper area for research and teaching even though its roots have been in applied problem areas. As the need for social science input to the anticipatory planning process is better understood, college level courses on SIA should become more popular.

REFERENCES

Bowles, Roy T. 1981. *Social Impact Assessment in Small Communities: An Integrative Review of Selected Literature.* Toronto, Butterworths.

Branch, Kristi, Douglas A. Hooper, James Thompson and James C. Creighton. 1984. *Guide to Social Impact Assessment.* Boulder, CO: Westview Press.

Carter, Novia. 1981. SIA: New Wine in Old Bottles, in Frank J. Tester and William Mykes eds., *Social Impact Assessment Theory, Method and Practices*. Calgary, Alb., Canada: Detseling Enterprises Ltd., 6147 Dalmarnock Circle, N.W.

FEARO. 1978. *Guide for Environmental Screening*. Federal Activities Branch, Environmental Protection Service and Federal Environmental Assessment Review Office, Ottawa.

Finsterbusch, Kurt and Annabelle Bender Motz. 1980. *Social Research for Policy Decision*. Belmont, California: Wadsworth Publishing Co.

Leistritz, Larry and Steven H. Murdock. 1981. *The Socioeconomic Impact of Resource Development: Methods of Assessment*. Boulder, CO: Westview Press.

Social Impact Research, Inc. 1983. *Socioeconomic Impact Management*, 4020 East Madison, Seattle, WA 98112 USA.

U.S. Agency for International Development. 1978. *AID Handbook*. U.S. Government Printing Office, Washington, D.C. pp. 4A-1 to 4A-11.

U.S. Forest Service. 1982. Guidelines for Economic and Social Analysis of Programs, Resource Plans, and Projects: Final Policy, *Federal Register*. 47(80) April 26, pp. 17940-17954.

Warheit, George J., Roger A. Bell, and John J. Schwab. 1977. *Needs Assessment Approaches: Concepts and Methods*. DHEW Publications, No.(ADM) 79-472, U.S. Government Printing Office, Washington, D.C.

CASE STUDIES IN SOCIAL IMPACT ASSESSMENT

UTILIZING SOCIAL HISTORY TO IDENTIFY IMPACTS OF RESOURCE DEVELOPMENT ON ISOLATED COMMUNITIES: THE CASE OF SKAGWAY, ALASKA[1]

Rabel J. Burdge, Donald R. Field, Stephen R. Wells

BACKGROUND

The dramatic social consequences of resource development are often played out and easily observed in isolated rural areas. Most important are the boom-bust cycles common to resource-dependent areas. Resource management agencies as well as private-sector developers are concerned about community response to growth and decline.

The boom-bust phenomenon is well known in the social assessment literature. The popular image is of a small North American community consumed by changes from external forces. The main thesis of this chapter is that by examining the social and cultural history of a community we can better understand how communities will adjust to future environmental and social impacts due to alternate periods of prosperity and recession.

Implicitly, the social impact assessor relies upon rural-urban continuum theory, which assumes that all changes will move a community from rural-to-urban. Little attention, however, is paid to looking at the community in terms of its historical context and experiences with the ups and downs of developing cycles. We present Skagway, Alaska, as a case example of how social history was useful in predicting how a resource-dependent community adjusts to development events. In a ninety-year span, Skagway has experienced not one, but six, major impact events. The first was the gold rush that led to a massive influx of people and subsequent mineral extraction and land exploitation. After the stampeders left, the community attempted to retain the spirit of that era by developing tourism. The decision to build the Alaska Highway in 1942 resulted in the U.S. Army occupation of Skagway during World War II (resource alteration in the form of transport enhancement). Designation of the area as a National Park in 1976 and events leading up to it meant dramatization, expansion, and protection of gold rush artifacts. The 1978 completion of the road to Carcross meant a land route from southeast Alaska to the interior of the Yukon Territory and the Alaska Highway.

[1]Abridged from the original. Rabel J. Burdge, Donald R. Field and Stephen R. Wells. 1989. Utilizing Social History to Identify Impacts of Resource Development on Isolated Communities: The Case of Skagway, Alaska. *Impact Assessment Bulletin*, 6(2):37-54. Reproduced here with permission of the authors and the publisher.

In 1983 the Yukon and White Pass railroad closed — a victim of declining revenue brought on by the new road and reduced shipments of minerals from the Yukon territory. In 1988 the 20.4-mile stretch of railroad from Skagway to White pass was reopened as a tourist attraction.

A Short History of the Development Events in Skagway

The Klondike Gold Rush of 1897-1898 brought thousands of people north to seek their fortunes in the Klondike.[2] The vast majority of these people and their goods got to the gold fields by following the protected waters along the coast of British Columbia an Southeastern Alaska to a terminus at the end of the Fjord-like Lynn Canal, about 100 miles north of Juneau (Berton, 1958; Bearss, 1970). At the end of the canal two boom towns, Skagway and Dyea, grew within six miles of each other. From each community a trail led the gold-seekers over the mountains of the Coast Range to the headwaters of the Yukon River. Dyea led to the Chilkoot Trail-shorter in distance but higher in elevation and not suited for pack animals. Skagway was the gateway to the White Pass - longer in distance but less of a climb and better suited to pack stock.

Skagway and Dyea competed for the business of the gold seekers by extolling the virtues of the routes they served. However, the trails were anything but virtuous. The Chilkoot and White Pass trails broke the hearts, bodies, and spirit of many of those bent on finding their fortune in Klondike gold. Yet the trails and the towns that lived and died with them caught the spirit of the two nations, and through the novels and poems of Jack London and Robert Service they became a collective part of the Canadian and U.S. folk history.

With the end of the Klondike gold rush, Dyea died. By 1900 the population had dwindled from thousands to 261 (U.S. Census, 1900), and five years later the only human activity in Dyea wa the homestead of one family. Skagway on the other hand persisted. Though population declined from a peak estimated at greater than 10,000 to 3,117 in 1900 and eventually to a plateau of about 500, the community continued to serve as the primary transportation link to and from the Yukon. In 1900 the White Pass and Yukon railroad was completed from Skagway to Whitehorse - 100 miles inland. Though gold seekers were no longer streaming into the Yukon, the railroad continued to haul goods and curious sightseers into the interior and to haul out gold and silver.

During the years after the gold rush, many of the original buildings in Skagway were moved from scattered locations to a more consolidated central business district. This created a gold-rush tone in the heart of the community, which was subsequently cultivated for tourism. These buildings together with the Chilkoot and White Pass trails and the many gold rush artifacts stashed away in public and private collections constitute a historic resource. Local and national interest in the preservation of this significant resource culminated in June 1976 with the creation by the U.S. Congress of the Klondike Gold Rush International Historic Park (P.L. 94-323). The park includes a historic zone within the central business district of Skagway and narrow strips of land

---

[2]The "Klondike" refers to the Klondike River which flows into the Yukon River at Dawson City, Yukon Territory. The gold was found in the beds of the small creeks that flowed into the Klondike (Bonanza Creek, Bear Creek, etc.). Dawson City is downstream from Whitehorse about 400 miles and upstream about 1,200 miles from where it flows into the Bering Sea.

along the two trails leading to the Canadian border at the summit of the Coast Range. Parks Canada then assumes jurisdiction for developing the park along the two trails and in Whitehorse and Dawson City.

Reasons for the Study

The National Park Service was interested in how the community of Skagway would adjust to the active presence of a government agency within the Skagway community. We wanted to know, what were the essential social impact variables that could be used to predict community response to social change? What has been the history of change in those variables and the relationship among them? What historical forces or factors, either external or internal, can be associated with those changes?

Answers to these questions were derived from archival research, content analysis of newspapers and public documents, open-ended interviews, and participant observation of the Skagway community done at intervals since 1974.

COMMUNITY THEORY AND SOCIAL IMPACT ASSESSMENT

Community studies represents the oldest and most important contribution by rural sociologists to the social science literature. During the 1920s and 1930s, much of the emphasis was on the definitions of the community, its structure and functions. Early theories on human ecology from the Chicago school as well as descriptive analysis, represented the major research approach (Wade, 1964). Data were obtained from field observations and comparisons among different rural communities.

In the post-World War II era, community research shifted to studies of social change in rural communities. Rural industrialization, declining community populations and the impact of new farming methods represent a few of the topics (Kaufman 1959). Many of the observed changes were adjustments to the out-migration of rural people, agricultural marketing practices, and new transportation systems.

In the 1970s and the 1980s, research knowledge obtained from the study of community change focused on the likely social consequences of change due to impacts brought about by some external event. Examples include the siting of a nuclear power plant, planning a national park, construction of a new pipeline system or the closing of a factory.

The conceptual and empirical task in social impact assessment is to understand the process of community adaptation to the external forces of change. In using our theory to locate key elements for study within the community, we must remember that social impact assessment (SIA) is anticipatory planning. Although rural sociologists are not accustomed to crystal-ball gazing, we feel that historical response to change will be a key factor in predicting the adaptation of the community to a future impact event.

As Wilkinson (1982) and others have pointed out, community analysis of impact events has relied upon the traditional rural-urban continuum to explain social change. Communities were placed along this scale depending upon the degree-to-which urban and rural characteristics were identified. The influx of outsiders due to development was presumed to move the community toward the urban end of that continuum. Although not explicitly stated in the SIA literature, rural values, social structure, and life styles were presumed to dominate in isolated areas. The impact event was seen as leading to a more urban type of social organization.

The implicit theory goes on to point out that, with the impact event, forces beyond the community were likely to exert increased control over local decision making. In effect, local community control was usurped. Another point, following from Wilkinson and others (1982), is that in communities (and in a region) in which change has been occurring with some regularity in the past, it would seem likely that social and personal mechanisms for coping with change would have developed. That observation supports our notion that previous community response is a powerful predictor of coping mechanisms.

Community Analysis and the SIA Process

The SIA process is intended to anticipate environmental impacts in advance of the event and then propose ways to mitigate those impacts. By reviewing the social history of Skagway, we should be able to predict what might happen in the community as new development events occur. The analysis reported here weds historical analysis with social impact assessment variables. *Social Impacts are defined as the impact of new technologies or resource alteration on the human populations and attendant social systems* (Freudenburg and Keating 1982:72). Superimposing a knowledge of the proposed project on a chronology of the communities' social history provides a clue as to whether the impacts will be significant.

Although impact events come in different levels of intensity and complexity and are instigated by all levels of government as well as private-sector organizations, they have a certain commonality and regularity, be it the boom-bust cycle of Skagway, coal development in eastern Kentucky, or siting nuclear wastes in New Mexico. Similar consequences can be expected for any type of resource development or alteration.

The following seven social impact variables were used to guide the historical social analysis of the Skagway community (Burdge 1987):

Population Influx-Outflux - Will the development involve significant influx of new people and has the community experienced significant population influx-outflux in the past?

Community Involvement - Will the project or policy be known in advance, and to what degree will the community be involved in the planning decision process?

Previous Impact Events - Does the community have a history of the same or similar social impacts?

Occupational Composition - What is the occupational composition of the persons who will be involved in the project and to what degree does it match with that of the host community?

Local Benefits - Will the benefits of the project accrue to private-sector or government agencies of the larger society or will they accrue to the local community?

Presence of Outside Agency - Will the proposed project bring to the community a new neighbor in the form of a temporary or permanent government agency or private-sector organization? Does the "new neighbor" have a history of attempting to mitigate the social impacts it creates? Has the community experienced occupation by an outside agency in the past?

Mitigation Measures - To what degree has the community acted as a unified decision making body in past dealings with outsiders? Does the community make decisions in response to a crisis or was some advanced planning involved (Dixon 1978:300)?

We now turn to the history of development events in Skagway, Alaska, to determine which, if any, of these social impact variables allow us to make statements about the impact of the Klondike Gold Rush Intern National Historic Park and subsequent changes in the region.

SOCIAL HISTORY OF SKAGWAY, ALASKA: 1896 to 1988

The social history of Skagway can be studies in three eras with specific development events taking place in each. The Gold Rush era lasted from 1896 to 1910. Then came the lean years from 1920 until the beginning of the Second World War. The third era coincides with the post-war boom in the U.S. and Canadian economy.

When we think of people living in frontier Alaska, we dwell on such notions as rugged individualism, self-sufficiency, subsistence hunting, egalitarianism, and rustic simplicity (many traits associated with rural living). Yet from the early days of the town, Skagway was a very urban place. The populace was urban in origin, highly educated, and cosmopolitan (Smith 1980), and the social relationships among those living there were characteristically urban. Skagway achieved its urban characteristics as a result of a massive and essentially immediate influx (of stampeders) from Seattle and the rest of the world. However, it was a flow through rather than a flow to Skagway. The influx was motivated not by an interest in Skagway *per se*, but rather by an interest in the gold fields that lay beyond. In that relationship to the Klondike and the Yukon lies the story of the birth, decline, and eventual recovery of, as one journalist put it, *The City of Fluctuating Fortune*, (Bond 1972). A city or town as a place to *flow through* is not unique to Skagway or to other parts of the sparsely populated northern and western parts of North America. In fact, the boom-bust cycle may be the rule rather than the exception. Dixon (1978) describes the history of Fairbanks in much the same way. The Trans-Alaska pipeline is only one event in a series of historical boom-bust cycles which represents a history of adjustment to externally imposed resource-related impacts.

A City in the Wilderness: 1896 to 1900

Sociologists label places urban when they are diverse, bureaucratic, hierarchical, technological, formal, commercially intense, specialized in function, and relatively removed from direct involvement with natural resources. During the gold rush years, social relationships within the city of Skagway could be characterized in those terms.

Skagway's urban nature was evidenced in many ways, of which we mention only a few here. The disregard for the lay of the land as seen in the grid pattern of the first plat of the townsite shows an attitude more sensitive to urban convention and tradition than to the more subtle characteristics of the land (Wade 1964). There was a high degree of specialization in the occupations and businesses of the community; wholesale and retail merchants were separated, and a buyer could choose among several suppliers of those goods and services. There were enough lawyers to justify a local Bar Association. At the peak of the rush at least ten doctors, seven churches, several movie houses, a multitude of saloons, an abundance of prostitutes, and an array of social and civic clubs were counted. Stores were of sufficient number to allow comparison shopping, competitive pricing, and abundant advertising. The impersonal and formal nature of social relationships and the large size and rapid rate of turnover of the population made the development of widespread personal friendship and informal communication networks unlikely and unreliable. The urban formality of naming streets, numbering avenues, and assigning each building on a street a consecutive number was necessary in a community composed of strangers. The ambitious bureaucratic structures of the quasi-government of Soapy Smith, the reigning con man of 1898, and later of the more formal government activities in the city were specialized in function, adhered to fixed rules, and were organized around a recognized hierarchy of authority.

Adapting to New Conditions: 1900 to 1910

From a city of between 10,000 and 20,000 people in 1898, Skagway showed a population of only 3,117 in 1900 and of about 1,000 in 1903 (Carson 1903). By 1910 it had a population of 872, and by 1920 the population had stabilized at about 500 residents. This abrupt population loss led to an emphasis on permanence rather than urban refinements in Skagway.

The bust cycle, as we label it today, was brought about by several factors, not the least of which was the gold had been discovered on the beaches of Nome, Alaska, in 1899. In addition, the demand for transportation into the interior fell off in proportion to the decline of the population of the Yukon Territory. From a high of 24,200 in 1901 the territory dropped to 8,500 in 1911 and to 4,200 in 1921 (Lotz 1970). The completion of railroad construction between Skagway and Whitehorse in July 1900 drastically reduced the number of jobs available in the region. The U.S. Army permanently closed Camp Skagway on September 30, 1904.

In spite of the dramatic decline in size, the town persisted. Emphasis was placed on solidifying its government and ordinances, providing for schools and sidewalks, and consolidating jobs, buildings and property ownership. Perhaps the most significant realization in these first years after the gold rush was the inklings of a potential tourist industry. The first excursion train ran part way up the line in July 1898 (Bearss 1970). The aura of the Klondike was much alive even six hundred miles from the actual diggings. Because of their appreciation for the role that Skagway had played in the Gold Rush, these early visitors were the first non-residents to place a value on Skagway that was intrinsic to the community rather than derived from its location relative to the Yukon.

In analyzing the Gold Rush era of Skagway, we find that rapid population influx was the major characteristic, represented by persons with an urban, middle-class background. The occupational structure of the community consisted of traders and railroad laborers, most of which were drawn from the ranks of the stampeders. No outside agency or business was present, although the U.S. Army did have a small encampment. The benefits of the Gold Rush accrued to the local power structure and business operations. The railroad, of course, get its start as the dominant feature of the community. When George Carmacks picked up the first gold nugget on Bonanza Creek in 1896, Skagway had little inkling about its future until the steamship Portland arrived in Seattle in the fall of 1897 with trunks of gold and tales of riches from gristly sourdoughs.

Lean Years: 1910 To 1941

After the gold rush, a much reduced but nevertheless steady volume of people and freight flowed through Skagway. Population levels stayed virtually constant between 1920 and 1940. The payroll of the railroad, when adjusted for the purchasing power of the dollar, changed very little. Between World War I and II tourism began to emerge as an important part of Skagway. Four steamship companies operating as many as sixteen ships provided service to Skagway in the summers, and cruise ships arrived several times a week each caring 200-300 passengers (Burnett 1972; U.S. Department of Interior 1945). The volume of visitors did increase to a high in 1927 and then dropped off again (Anonymous 1920:43). In fact, 1927 was the peak year for passengers riding the White Pass Railroad prior to 1962 (MacBride 1954).

The Second Boom: Army Occupation 1942-1945

Between 1942 and 1945 the White Pass and Yukon railroad was leased and operated by the U.S. Army in order to transport into the Yukon the men, material, and equipment needed to build the Alaska Highway. This meant that thousands of soldiers moved into and through Skagway. From operating two trains a week if the weather was good enough, the railroad under Army operation worked up to a peak of 38 trains one August day in 1942. The memories and methods of coping with a transient influx of temporary visitors (now in the form of soldiers) were kept alive by tourists and the activities developed by the community to cater to them.

The events of the war were physically, politically, and socially traumatic for Skagway. Relations with the Army were so strained that in July 1943 the City Council demanded the following as reparations: title to the federal Building and to the phone and sewer systems installed by the Army, the paving of the two main streets and of the cross street between them, construction of a small boat harbor, removal of the airport to the Dyea tidal flats, and the building of a connecting highway from Haines to the Alaska Highway. The highway from Haines was eventually built, the one main road was paved, and the Army did leave behind all the improvements necessary to build the airport.

The building of the Alaska Highway brought a second boom to Skagway and with it some now familiar social impacts. The population influx was large and somewhat permanent. An infrastructure was basically in place as a leftover from the Gold Rush. Again, the change was rapid and not known too far in advance. The decision to build the highway to Alaska was made quickly when it was thought that the Japanese would threaten the sea route to Anchorage. A new twist was the presence of an outside agency—named the U.S. Army. However, the town was now organized and able to demand and get certain mitigation measures. As before, the economy of Skagway was service oriented and directed to operating and maintaining the railroad.

Development in the Yukon: 1946 to 1975

In 1947, the post-war economic boom began in earnest; mining, prospecting, and oil exploration in the Yukon were stimulated by the Canadian government's $100 million Roads-to-Resources development program. The United Keno Hill Mines had been brought into production. The Alaska Highway was opened to general civilian use, and the military was actively building new defense and communication facilities in the north. By 1950 Whitehorse had its first southern-style subdivision, and the 1951 census showed that the Yukon Territory had surpassed the 1911 population level for the first time (World War II excepted). This growth in the Yukon implied economic health in Skagway as evidenced by the increased volume of shipments.

The decade from 1954 to 1964 was for the Yukon a decade of development based on resource exploitation and expanded government activity. Canadian government expenditures in the Yukon rose from $11 million in 1954-1955 to $23.4 million in 1962-1963. Claim-staking in the Yukon Territory from 1961 to 1963 far exceeded any similar activities in the previous 25 years. In 1965 at least 40 companies, as many individual prospectors, and three syndicated were actively seeking new ore bodies in the Yukon.

Tourism: 1945-1970

Tourism in Skagway underwent a parallel transformation. All visits had ceased during the war. Because the freight-hauling business of the railroad was in a post-war decline, there was an incentive to re-establish tourism and for the people of Skagway to work toward that goal.

In 1952, the National Park Service inventoried the recreation potential of Alaska. At that time Skagway was the fifth most heavily visited recreation site in the territory. Of the approximately 10,000 visitors who came to Skagway that year, 85 percent came by ship, 10 percent came by air, and the remaining 5 percent came over the mountains from the Alaska Highway by train (Stanton, 1953). A Park Service survey concluded that Skagway had great potential. That study also showed that for many of those respondents, the train trip on the White Pass and Yukon Railroad was the highlight of their Alaskan visit.

Just as the 1960s were years of development in the mining industry of the Yukon, they were years of growth in tourist visits to Skagway. Total rail passengers (visitor and resident) on the White Pass grew from 18,000 in 1960 to 42,000 in 1966. The Alaska Marine Highway ferry system began operating in 1962 and added greatly to the volume of people passing through Skagway. Although there were still only four cruise ships serving Skagway in the summer of 1963, between 10,000 and 20,000 visitors contributed about $94,000 in value added to the local economy. By 1968 visitation reached 35,000 visitors, up 27 percent from the previous year.

At this point in our historic analysis, Skagway has returned to a year-round population of about 700 people made up of long-time residents. A basic infrastructure is in place, and the railroad along with tourism provides a rather stable economy. However, the interest by the National Park Service looms on the horizon as well as increased involvement by the Alaskan Government brought on by statehood in 1959.

THE DEVELOPMENT OF THE GOLD RUSH PARK

The idea of preserving the artifacts and the spirit of the Gold Rush in a federal park had such a long history that many of the potential social impacts were mitigated by the passage of time and by the active involvement of the city's representatives in the development of the master plan for the park. Beginning in 1955, the continuing dialogue between the Park Service and the community allowed both to react and respond to the plans, proposals, and ambitions of the other. By the time the legislation creating the park was being considered by the U.S. Congress, there was no significant controversy presented in the hearings.

There was, however, an undercurrent of concern about the possible development of the Gold Rush Park to include the restriction of personal freedom (i.e., to fly airplanes over the passes, to ride horses in Dyea and on the Chilkoot trail, to drive and park in the historic district, etc.); the taking of property tax base as buildings and lots are acquired by the Park Service; an increase in the population of the community; and the fear of living in a "zoo or museum" after "the Park people get everything set up the way they want." However, a very positive development of the Klondike Park was the evolution of cooperation among the city, the state, and the Park Service in comprehensive planning for the Skagway Valley.

The Social Impacts of the Gold Rush Park

The presence of the park altered the flow of visitors through the community only by increasing the rate of that flow. The length of the visitor season was not significantly affected. A threshold had long since been passed where the level of visitation precluded personal (as opposed to personable) hospitality. From 1967 to 1983 the community was dominated by the flow of mine products coming from Yukon. The park posed no threat to that flow and consequently did not mitigate or supplement the social implications of it.

The most significant of the social changes associated by people in the community with the park were just as strongly associated with the opening of the Carcross Road (and connection to the Alaska Highway). These included fears of the loss of peace, security, and frontier autonomy. If such losses do in fact occur, it will not be possible to attribute them separately to one cause or another. In addition, given the implications of future events, such as the proposed construction of the MacKenzie Valley pipeline along the Alaska Highway, the economic benefits and costs of the Klondike park become very difficult to assess. However, the closing of the railroad in 1982 was easy to assess. The most important and consistent employment source (year around) in the community was gone.

Park Service personnel have expressed pleasure with the speed and warmth of their integration into the community. This can be explained by what at the time, in our opinion, were perceived local benefits to Skagway from the Klondike Park and because the park evolved as a cooperative effort of the Park Service and the community. The development of the Klondike Park was done with Skagway rather than to Skagway.

Since its inception, Skagway has been very much a community in transition. Without a full knowledge of the social history of the community one might attribute radical social impacts to the Gold Rush Park. However, the social history of the community uncovered the roots of how Skagway has been adapting to social change all along. Therein lies some protection for the National Park Service since there might be a temptation to blame negatively valued social change on the agency as newcomers and outsiders. In fact, they are but the second government agency to become a Skagway neighbor (fortunately for the Park Service the first one was not a good one).

Hindsight and Looking Ahead

This ethnographic study of Skagway has shown that knowing the past history of the community was the best predictor of how the community would adapt to the new park. The town, the railroad, the famous Chilkoot Trail, the Army, the Alaska Highway, the Gold Rush park, the Carcross Highway and now the loss of the railroad and its partial reopening for tourists illustrate that the town has always been a pass-through community. People have come up the Lynn Canal and over the mountains into the Yukon for almost a century. Depending upon the time in history, that activity has been a boom or a bust — a cycle with ups and downs. The establishment of the park represented a slight upturn on the boom cycle when it was developed and then opened, but the presence of the park could never cushion the loss of the complete operation of the railroad. For example, visitation to the park increased from 37,000 in 1979 to 48,000 in 1980, although there was some decline in subsequent years.

If we were looking at Skagway in 1955 through our historical assessment model, we might have been able to predict quite well what actually happened. Although Skagway would experience increased visitation as a result of the park, that would soon reach a plateau. The change did not come abruptly; the time from conception to operation for the park was 21 years. The park was but one impact event in a long chain, with more links being added all the time. The Carcross Highway was the next one, to be followed quickly by the closing and then the partial reopening of the White Pass and Yukon Railroad.

Although the occupational composition of the park employees was different from the skilled persons required to operate the railroad, they fit the service and administrative category that catered to the tourist industry. Benefits seem to exist more for the community at large rather than any segment of the local power structure. If anything, the stability in employment will benefit all. Although the Park Service does represent an outside agency, the community has a history of coping with them. It has demonstrated the collective ability to negotiate with the U.S. Army and the Alaska state government. Skagway residents have a good idea what mitigation measures are necessary and appear to have shown a collective notion as to how they might be achieved in the case of the National Park Service.

The future of the Skagway community will hinge on the future of the railroad. If the MacKenzie pipeline is built, the railroad will probably be fully reopened to haul construction materials to the interior of the Yukon. The tourist trade will stabilize and perhaps increase, for the railroad trip over White Pass is a highlight of the visit to Skagway (at least based on evidence from recent surveys of cruise-ship passengers [Field, et.al. 1985]). The number of hikers going over the trail has declined due to the difficulties in obtaining return transportation once the hike is completed.

REFERENCES

Anonymous. 1920. Skagway, the Gateway for the Tourists. *The Pathfinder of Alaska* 2,3.

Anonymous. 1977. Skagway Residents Reassess New Park. *Southeast Alaska Empire* November 7(1).

Bearss, Edwin C. 1970. *Proposed Klondike Gold Rush National Historic Park: Historic Resource Study*. National Park Service, Washington, D.C.

Berton, Pierre. 1958. *The Klondike River: The Life and Death of the Last Great Stampede*. Alfred Knopf, New York.

Bond, David L. 1972. Skagway: Gateway to History, *Seattle Post-Intelligence*, May 7.

Burdge, Rabel J. 1987. The Social Impact Assessment Model and the Planning Process. *Environmental Impact Assessment Review*, 7 (2): 141-150.

Burnett, Frederick J. 1972. The Village of Skagway, Alaska, Which Was Once Gateway to the Land of Gold. *Sunset*, 62, 24-26.

Carson, Sir Edward. 1903. Statement of October 2, 1903, *Proceedings of the Alaska Boundary Tribunal, Volume VII*. Senate Document 162, 58th Congress 2nd Session. U.S. Government Printing Office, Washington, D.C., 728-29.

Dixon, Mim. 1978. *What Happened to Fairbanks? The Effects of the Trans-Alaska Oil Pipeline on the Community of Fairbanks, Alaska*. Boulder, Co.: Westview Press.

Field, Donald R., R. Clark and B. Koth. 1985. Cruise ship Travel in Alaska: A Profile of Passengers. *Journal of Travel Research*, 16(2).

Freudenburg, William R. and K.M. Keating. 1982. Increasing the Impact of Sociology on Social Impact Assessment: Toward Ending the Inattention. *The American Sociologist*, 17: 71-80.

Kaufman, Harold F. (1959) Toward an Interactional Concept of Community. *Social Forces*, 38, (October) 8-17.

Lotz, J. 1970. *Northern Realities: The Future of Northern Development in Canada*. New Press, Toronto.
MacBride, W.D. 1954. The White Pass Route, *Beaver*, Autumn: 18-23.

Smith, K.L. 1980. The Most Wonderful Railroad of the North. *Scientific American*, 98 (January): 29-30.

Stanton, W.J. 1953. Analysis of Alaska Travel: With Special Reference to Tourists, June 1 through September 30, 1952. Part one, Volume 2, National Park Service, Alaska Recreation Survey. National Park Service, Washington, D.C.

U.S. Department of Interior. 1945. *Alaska.* U.S. Department of Interior, Washington, D.C.

Wade, R.C. 1964. *The Urban Frontier: Pioneer Life in Early Pittsburgh, Cincinnati, Lexington, Louisville, and St. Louis.* University of Chicago Press, Chicago.

Warren, Roland L. 1978. *The Community in America.* Rand McNally, Chicago.

Wells, Stephen R. 1982. *Skagway Costal Management Plan.* CASA, 5180 Northeast Sullivan Rd., Bainbridge, WA 98110.

Wilkinson, Kenneth P., James G. Thompson, Robert R. Reynolds, Jr. and Lawrence M. Ostresh. 1982a. Local Social Disruption and Western Energy Development. *Pacific Sociological Review*, 25 (July): 275-96.

Wilkinson, Kenneth P., Robert R. Reynolds, Jr., James G. Thompson, and Lawrence M. Ostresh. 1982b. Response, *Pacific Sociological Review*, 25 (July): 367-76.

Chapter 12

AN EX-POST FACTO ANALYSIS OF THE ECONOMIC AND SOCIAL IMPACTS OF RESERVOIR CONSTRUCTION[1]

Rabel J. Burdge

This chapter reports selected economic and social impacts of construction and operation/maintenance ten years after a reservoir project was completed. The case example is Lake Shelbyville, a multi-purpose impoundment planned, built and operated by the U.S. Army Corp of Engineers in east central Illinois. Data on agricultural land use patterns, private sector expenditures, community infrastructure development, perceptions and attitudes toward the project as well as community organization were obtained prior to and during construction and at selected times since operation and maintenance of the reservoir began. The major conclusions of the economic and sociological components of the study are reviewed by asking the question *what has been the impact of the reservoir?* Furthermore, have the expectations raised by a federal water project been realized? Each portion of the chapter responds from the standpoint of the people, institution or organization that was impacted. I conclude with important recommendations for state agencies that may be asked to support federal water projects in the future.

A Short History of the Lake Shelbyville Reservoir

In the pre-impoundment setting, both Shelby and Moultrie counties were typical prairie areas devoted to agricultural production. The population was declining as farms increased in size due to mechanization. Young people lacking farming opportunities, either moved into the service sector or commuted to jobs in distant urban centers. The flat prairie was ideally suited to energy intensive agricultural production. Labor could easily be replaced by machines. Employment in the region reflected the emphasis on agricultural and related services.

The Kaskaskia River which was dammed to form Lake Shelbyville flowed from North-to-South through both counties. Although the river flooded on occasion, the losses were greater downstream than in these two counties. The Kaskaskia drained most of Shelby County in an adequate manner, with some flooding in the upper ends of the Moultrie County. Figure 12.1 provides a chronology of events leading to the operation stage of the Lake Shelbyville reservoir.

The Army Corps of Engineers attempted to develop a comprehensive plan to control flooding in the entire Kaskaskia Basin. The Lake Shelbyville reservoir were

[1]Abridged from the original. Rabel J. Burdge. 1987. An Ex Post Facto Analysis of the Economic and Social Impacts of Reservoir Construction. in Audit and Evaluation in *Environmental Assessment and Management: Canadian and International Experience.* Barry Sadler, ed. The Banff Centre: Alberta, Canada, Vol. II, p. 701-728. Reproduced here with permission of the author and the publisher.

Figure 12.1
The Pre-Operation Period of the Shelbyville Reservoir Project, 1958 - 1973

Lake Shelbyville	Related Projects	Activity
1958		Construction of Lake Shelbyville approved by Congress
1962 (Oct.)		First construction contract approved by Congress
	1963(Oct.)	Navigation project downstream approved by Congress
1963 (Apr.)		First construction contract approved
1963 (May)		Ground broken for first construction at Shelbyville
	1964 (June)	Shelby County hospital adds new wing
	1966 (June)	Work begins on canal excavation
1966-67		Shelbyville construction runs into problems of old mine shafts below river and a layer of bad shale
	1967 (Apr.)	Carlyle Reservoir begins operation
1970 (Sept)		Dedication Day for Lake Shelbyville
	1973 (May)	Kaskaskia Canal ready for barge traffic

one component, but also included was Carlyle Reservoir and Kaskaskia Canal (both completed) and numerous levees (never build).

Interest groups who saw benefits from the reservoir include downstream industrial interests, downstream farmers, upstream business and commercial interests, recreationists, and upstream farmers, upstream business and commercial interests, recreationists, and upstream landowners. Some of the interest groups that were active in obtaining the Shelbyville reservoir are now opposed to the way it operates - particularly downstream farmers. Since operation began, the fluctuating lake level has reduced the number of recreational visits.

During normal weather, all users of Lake Shelbyville within the Kaskaskia Basin, can be satisfied — water for the recreationists, slow release of water for the barge canal, some space in the reservoir for flood control and downstream flood protection for farmers. But abnormal weather brings conflicts among users that were compounded by the Corps' underestimation of channel capacity and what to do with the runoff that would normally be absorbed by tributaries. The Lake Shelbyville reservoir is smaller relative to the real watershed it must handle. By over-designing such projects in the future, these tensions between social groups could be alleviated. As it now stands, water for recreation and the barge canal conflicts seriously with flood control/farm protection during the rainy periods. Construction of planned levees might have helped, but they are expensive and would do little to help the tile drainage due to a full river.

ECONOMIC IMPACTS OF THE RESERVOIR

Changes in Agriculture Income

Findings from this section, as shown in Table 12.1, indicate that a decline in agricultural revenues did occur because of the removal of land from production upstream from the impoundment. The lands removed from production included those lands flooded for the reservoir itself and those adjacent to the reservoir that underwent a change in use.

While it was found that a loss in net agricultural income did occur, the magnitude of that loss is still uncertain. The uncertainty regarding the magnitude of the loss has two sources: the lack of knowledge of production costs on the land removed from agriculture, and the restriction of this study to effects upstream from the dam. Those areas south of Shelbyville were frequently flooded before the dam was built and represent one of the justifications for building the reservoir. However, Corps engineers anticipate that downstream flooding will continue until a levee system is developed locally to help with the flood control (U.S. Army Corps of Engineers, 1975). These effects therefore should be evaluated carefully to increase the accuracy of total effects of the entire reservoir project.

Future reservoir development by all U.S. Federal agencies will be subjected to *Principles and Standards* with support by extensive and accurate evidence of agricultural benefits and costs. Indeed, the regulations specifically disallow casual estimates or consideration of less than the whole benefit-cost picture of a given set of objectives. In the area of agriculture income effects of future natural resource projects, it will be very important for state and regional decision-makers to protect the interest of the state or region, since *Principles and Standards* use a National Economic Development stance to examine the economic feasibility of projects. Since Illinois is heavily agricultural in economic makeup, care must be taken to ensure that the agricultural benefits of federal projects do, in fact, equal or exceed the costs. In the case of Lake Shelbyville that was not supported by research.

Changes in Tax Base for the Reservoir Counties

The tax base portion of the Lake Shelbyville study was divided between impacts on property tax and those on other revenue sources (lease income, sales tax, and fines). In general, it was found that the land area included in the property tax base declined due to the appropriation of land by the Federal Government. This decline in land area is for the most part offset by an increase in land valuation and tax rates. The effect of the land appropriation and attempts to offset it were not uniform between the two counties. While both Moultrie and Shelby counties saw a general increase in revenues from property taxes, some townships in Shelby County experienced losses and the magnitude of revenue increases in that county was smaller on an average than those in Moultrie County.

The revenue from lease income is peculiar to a reservoir and although initially high in the two counties, will decline over time. Moultrie County receives more of these funds than does Shelby County. Both counties experienced an increase in revenues from fines with Shelby County receiving the largest share. This increase in fines in a reflection of the lake development. Finally, there was some sales tax revenue increases from restaurant and gasoline sales, which probably reflect the impact of the

Table 12.1
Estimated Direct Effects and Total Effects for the Study Area (Units: Dollars)

Year	Direct loss due to water impoundment (agri. sector)[a]			Total losses due to water impoundment (agri. sector)[b]		
	Moultrie Co.	Shelby Co.	Total	Moultrie Co.	Shelby Co.	Total
1969	608 667	369 931	978 598	1932 222	818 884	2751 106
1970	708 653	426 670	1135 323	2249 629	944 482	3194 111
1971	643 386	391 837	1035 223	2042 438	867 375	2909 813
1972	901 064	539 481	1440 545	2860 440	1194 202	4054 642
1973	1332 410	788 472	2120 882	4229 754	1745 372	5975 126
1974	1496 010	884 134	2380 144	4749 105	1957 131	6706 236
1975	1276 160	767 857	2044 017	4051 188	1699 738	5750 926
1976	1433 330	863 912	2297 142	4550 126	1912 145	6462 271

[a] Direct losses associated with basic level management from Table 7-5 were used here (Burdge and Opryszek 1982: 110).
[b] Total loses were calculated by considering the income multiplier effects for the two counties.

reservoir. However, Moultrie County's share of sales tax increased faster than the average for Southern Illinois counties while Shelby County's increase in revenues from this tax lagged behind the average.

Because farmland values increased rapidly during the study period at both the regional and national levels the increased valuation in land in the two counties may reflect this trend rather than any lake related impact. By 1985, agricultural land values had declined to a pre-impoundment level, reflecting the continuing decline in demand for farm ground.

Changes in Employment and Income

I now turn to the impact of the Lake Shelbyville Reservoir on employment and personal income. Two types of models were employed. In the first of these models, classical economic base theory was used to look at basic impacts (income brought in from outside the local area) and induced impacts (multiplier effects from the re-spending of the income brought in) from the reservoir. The other model was a shift-share model which analyzes changes in employment or income between economic sectors within a study area.

According to the adjusted estimates, the patterns and the magnitudes of the lake impact on employment in both counties were very similar. Except for the first few years of the project's construction, both counties appeared to be similarly impacted by the lake in terms of employment.

In terms of personal income, the adjusted estimates of lake impact are greater in real values than the original estimates since 1970 in Moultrie County's analysis and since 1969 in Shelby County's analysis.

The adjusted estimates indicate that the lake had negative effects on Moultrie County's economy in 1968, 1969, 1971, and 1973 with the greatest negative impact equivalent to a loss of about 1.25 million dollars in 1971. The loss constituted only 2.57 percent of the total income. Positive impact equivalent to more than 4.5 percent of income in the county occurred in 1970, 1974, and 1975.

Changes in Business and Government Expenditures

The shift-share model developed for use on changes in employment and income was applied to business sales and government expenditures. In the business portion of the study, the model was applied to three small communities (Windsor, Bethany, and Findlay) and two large communities (Sullivan and Shelbyville) in Moultrie and Shelby counties. The analysis showed that the reservoir had negligible impacts on the smaller communities and more observable impacts on the larger ones. The actual impact of sales on the larger communities was understated by the analysis because during the reservoir construction period both Sullivan and Shelbyville were suffering from a decline in their manufacturing sector.

In the government expenditure section of the analysis, two conclusions stand out. First, nearly three quarters of the expenditures (other than the construction costs) made by the U.S. Army Corps of Engineers during the construction of the project were retained locally. Secondly, local government expenditures tripled over the period of analysis. These increased expenditures occurred in those areas (roads, law enforcement, and planning and zoning) where lake impacts would be anticipated.

Changes in Business and Industrial Development

Over the 1965-1974 period, there were three major economic events that occurred simultaneously in the two-county area.

The recession which started in the late 1960s, and apparently ended in 1973 in Moultrie County, went on for at least two more years in Shelby County. Manufacturing was the sector most affected. Between the two counties, other situations being equal, Shelby County seemed to be more affected by the recession and took longer time to recover from it (Table 12.1).

Farm prices dropped in the second half of the 1960s and then began to rise in the early 1970s. The effects of this fluctuation were initially felt in the agriculture sector, but the overall effects on the entire economy were great, especially in areas where agriculture was the leading source of income and employment. In this respect, Shelby County which was more heavily dependent on agriculture may be expected to be more affected by the price fluctuation than Moultrie County.

The Lake Shelbyville development had mixed effects on the economies of both countries. Among its negative effects, as reported in a previous section, was the loss of farmland which led to a decline in farm income and tax revenue; the dislocation of families in the project area that might result in a loss in population which ultimately means an economic loss to the area; and, perhaps, the temporary jobs generated by the lake might indirectly lead to losses of or delay the development of more permanent employment sources in the area. Among its positive effects on the economies were the impacts of the construction, of operation and maintenance of the lake, of the lake visitors' expenditures in the area, and of the limited commercial development brought about by the lake.

The predictions of rapid and continuous growth upon which Lake Shelbyville was authorization — proved to be quite exaggerated. Unfortunately, the original benefit-cost analysis was done on a regional basis and did not provide detailed figures for the two county impacted area (U.S. Army Corps of Engineers 1975).

SOCIAL IMPACTS OF THE RESERVOIR

Changes in Land Use and Zoning

The land acquired by the Corps for construction and operation of the reservoir changed the land from traditional agricultural uses to recreation. Most of the acquired land was previously used for pasture, timber or row cropping.

Based on a detailed study of Shelby County over the past 10 years, we concluded that the lake has induced a considerable number of land use changes both in the anticipation of its completion and during operation (Table 12.2). These changes have been in close physical proximity to the lake. Almost all these changes have been away from traditional agricultural use and toward business and residential use.

The Corps of Engineers recognized that both counties needed zoning and land use laws and were instrumental in securing adoption. Although spot zoning changes did occur in Shelby County they were quite small. No doubt the presence of zoning laws deterred what might have been haphazard development in the reservoir area. As pointed out, both counties had zoning laws when construction began; however, no large developments were proposed that might test enforcement. As shown in Table 12.2, most zoning changes occurred during construction and the initial operation phase of the reservoir. Almost all zoning changes that occurred for the two county area were adjacent to the lake.

Table 12.2
Distribution of Zoning Changes by Year

Year	No. of Changes	Year	No. of Changes
1965	1	1971	9
1966	3	1972	6
1967	7	1973	10
1968	3	1974	5
1969	2	1975	3
1970	4		

Community Response to Reservoir Development

The major community problems that occurred were increased vehicle traffic that produced congestion and deterioration of roads designed for intermittent agricultural traffic. Increased traffic meant more traffic citations (Table 12.3). In addition, demand for emergency and hospital facilities increased sharply. The presence of the lake did not increase the permanent population in the area, but probably slowed down the out-migration pattern common to rural areas (Table 12.4). No change was noted in the employment patterns of the two county area. In a separate study, it was found that persons visiting the area for recreation were most dissatisfied with the conditions of local roads (Table 12.5). An expansion of police, fire, health and sewage facilities and services was required to meet the needs of the recreation population (Burdge *et al* 1979).

Adjustment of Shelby and Moultrie County
Residents Relocated Due to the Reservoir

The research reported in Illinois and verified in both Kentucky and Ohio found that property owners, older individuals, smaller households, and people with strong ties to the area, were the most severely impacted by relocation (Chapter 3). Data for Shelby and Moultrie Counties come from interviews with a sample of relocated persons (mainly household heads) who returned a questionnaire delivered to their home.

In the two county area, most people sought a new residence which was close in kind and location to the place where they previously lived. Most carried on similar occupational and family household positions after relocation, the important exception being that most of those forced out of farming either retired or changed from part-time to full-time industrial employment. Most displaced families improved their material comforts after relocation, but complained of unhappiness in the family, separation from friends and relatives and higher costs at their new locations (Table 12.6). The respondents were unanimous in their dislike of the U.S. Army Corps of Engineers and felt that they were not treated properly during the acquisition and relocation phase.

Table 12.3

Showing Comparison of Percentage Change in Traffic Counts for the Lake Shelbyville Area and the Control Area Paris - Edgar County, 1966-1973.

Year	Lake Shelbyville Area Percent Change	Paris-Edgar Co. Comparison Area Percent Change
1966-1967	+1.8	-2.9
1967-1969	+17.0	+15.8
1969-1971	+32.5	-3.4
1971-1973	-12.6	+9.7
1966-1973	+37.8	+19.2
	+37.8 Lake Shelbyville Area +19.2 Control Area +18.6 Traffic Increase Attributed to the Lake	

Table 12.4

Selected Population Characteristics for Shelby and Moultrie Counties

County	No. of Families 1970	Population Size					Net Migrants 1970-1975
		1960	1970	1980	1990[a]	2000[a]	
Shelby	6,151	23,404	22,589	21,291	20,854	21,830	100 (+4%)
Moultrie	3,558	13,635	13,263	12,746	13,619	14,749	100 (+0.7%)

[a]Estimated

Table 12.5

Percent of Recreationists Dissatisfied or Very Dissatisfied With Selected Local Government Services

Service	Percent Dissatisfied or Very Dissatisfied
Roads	17
Directional Signs	7
Police Security	8

Table 12.6
Perception of Changes in Life Situation After
Displacement by Shelbyville Reservoir

Situation	Negative Difference[a]	Situation	Difference[1]
Taxes	-18	Quality of schools	1
Cost of home	-13	Radio reception	1
Amount of land	-9	T.V. reception	1
Happiness in household	-9	Access to newspapers	2
Time of leisure	-8	Quality of roads	4
Indebtedness	-7	Distance to work	5
Distance to family	-4	Distance to shop	6
Economic security	-4	Distance to medical	
Job satisfaction	-4	facilities	6
Distance to friends	0	Size of home	8

[a]Refers to the absolute difference between the number of households reporting improvement in situation and the number reporting a worsening in situation.

Social Effects of Land Acquisition

Information presented in this section comes from detailed ethnographic studies of individuals and families that had been impacted by land acquisition and relocation. Many of the families were centered in Okaw Township, just north of the town of Shelbyville. Field data were collected in 1982.

Land acquisition disrupts social networks upon which families, relocated or not, are dependent for financial and social resources. The resiliency of large groupings of interlocked families was reduced when constituent units lost land or were forced to relocate. A farm family business is not the product of a single generation, or single family. It is intimately tied to the intergenerational land transfer process among many interconnected families. Thus, the time perspective in examining changes wrought by land acquisition and relocation must be extended if the full range of impacts is to be represented. Area-wide changes in land availability and land prices made the already tough task of establishing a land base and family farm even harder for some, as indicated in the case studies of several families. Acquisition of marginal farms served to decrease the economic and cultural diversity of the townships studied, concentrating farmland in even fewer hands. The Army Corps of Engineers was felt to have misrepresented the lake project as an economic stimulus to the region. Expected revenues had *not* been realized and flood control management was perceived as poor.

Recreational Visitation Patterns at Lake Shelbyville

Lake Shelbyville is the most important water-based recreational facility in the east central Illinois region. However, when one moves outside the 100 mile circle of the reservoir, other recreation facilities can be found that are comparable to Lake Shelbyville. It seems unlikely that Lake Shelbyville will continue to expand its drawing power much beyond its present limits, especially when an increase in transportation costs from farther regions is taken into account. Even so, regional demand for the recreation opportunities provided by Lake Shelbyville will probably remain stable, if not decline over the next decade.

Competing facilities are being developed near Lake Shelbyville that may draw off some of its visitation, just as Shelbyville drew off visitation from other areas when it opened. Although only half the size of Lake Shelbyville and with less developed camping facilities, Clinton reservoir in DeWitt County is likely to siphon off some visitation — for two reasons. First, since it is a new reservoir, the fishing at Clinton is likely to be better than that at Shelbyville. Second, the Clinton reservoir is located about as far north of the city of Decatur as Lake Shelbyville is south. Decatur was the residence for the single largest group of 1978 Lake Shelbyville visitors (13.9 percent).

In all probability, Lake Shelbyville will continue to receive the heavy amount of recreational use it currently does (Table 12.7). Declines in visitation, stemming from competing facilities in the region and reduced visits from more distant points, will be offset somewhat by increased local demand for water-based recreation, caused in part by many east central Illinoisans seeking recreational opportunities closer to home (Table 12.8).

Local Economic Impact of Recreation Expenditures

Overall, the impact of recreation expenditures on personal income in Shelby and Moultrie counties has been slight when compared with other sources such as agriculture. It has been much less than the optimistic expectations of early civic boosters of the project. It has also been far below the forecasts of Army Corps of Engineers' planners. One reason for this shortfall is that reservoir visitation has never reached the levels anticipated, but additional factors can be cited. The figure of 15.9 million in expenditures used in early planning documents was an estimate of gross sales to recreationists, rather than a projection of net earnings from these sales. Also included in the total were sales to local residents using the reservoir. However, expenditures by these visitors represent a recirculation of money already in the local economy. Both practices inflated the magnitude of the projected impact over and above the contributions to personal income that can be uniquely attributed to Lake Shelbyville.

Undoubtedly, the impact of visitor expenditures in communities immediately adjacent to the reservoir represented a somewhat higher proportion of total personal income than in Shelby and Moultrie counties as a whole (Table 12.9).

Table 12.7
Annual Lake Shelbyville Visitation[a]

Year	Number of Visitor-Days	Year	Number of Visitor-Days
1970	1 192 726	1975	3 076 594
1971	2 627 697	1976	2 997 238
1972[b]	3 900 834	1977	3 577 883
1973	2 803 458	1978	2 937 241
1974	2 827 970	1979	2 640 415

[a] Source: U.S. Army Corps of Engineers, 1975.
[b] First full year of recreation operation.

Table 12.8
Distance Travelled as a Percentage of Lake Shelbyville
Visitors in 1973, 1978 and 1979

Distance Traveled	Percent of Visitors		
	1973[a]	1978[b]	1979[a]
1-25 miles	45%	25%	28%
26-50 miles	26%	26%	32%
51-100 miles	14%	23%	13%
100 + miles	15%	26%	27%

[a]Source: U.S. Army Corps of Engineers, 1975.
[b]Source: Burdge et al. 1979.

Table 12.9
Amount and Location of Trip-Specific[a] Expenditures
at Lake Shelbyville (May-October, 1978)

	Nonresidents	Residents
Average Expenditures per Trip:		
- At Home	$19.62 (29.1%)	-
- En Route	$8.70 (12.9%)	-
- In Vicinity	$38.99 (57.9%)	$31.95 (100%)
- Total per group	$67.31 (100%)	$31.95 (100%)
Expenditure per Visitor-Day	$10.94	$11.31

[a]Includes gas and oil for cars and recreational vehicles, groceries and beverages, entrance fees, restaurant meals, and models.

However, the manner in which economic data are typically aggregated did not allow for an examination of impacts at anything less than the county level. Nevertheless, even if the *micro-impact* in areas immediately surrounding the reservoir was extremely heavy (and the low level of retail and service development in the area makes this seem unlikely), it is a weak primary justification for a development of the magnitude of Lake Shelbyville. Future claims arguing that recreation expenditures occasioned by reservoir construction will provide a substantial stimulus to local economics should be weighed against other potential costs and benefits of the project, as well as against the contrary findings of this chapter (Table 12.10).

Weekend Residents: Taking Without Caring
This section reports on social interactions between the local residents and the recreationists that came to use reservoir facilities. Most of our interviewers were concentrated in the south end of the lake, which has the most access points. The varied

impacts reported here are neglected in most social projections of user-impact on recreation areas. Many of the impacts are attitudinal and negative toward outsiders in general. Not to be neglected, however, are the quantifiable financial impacts such as equipment damage, litter costs associated with cleaning up the roadsides, damaged fences and crops, and increased risks due to road hazards. Even the inability to complete road repairs without risking contempt of the recreation user population is an impact.

As an example, Okaw Township residents perceive the influx of recreationists as severely taxing limited emergency and law enforcement services, as well as degrading the lake access roads. Until very recently, the voters of this township steadfastly refused to increase their own tax burden to maintain the roads. Current costs of providing the minimal level of maintenance to one mile of road are about $5,500. With 35 miles of road to maintain, the total is well over $190,000. However, only $60,000 in 1981 had been budgeted for road repair. While the state and federal governments have spent many thousands of dollars on select roads within the township, theirs was a one-time contribution.

Table 12.10
Total Basic and Induced Impact of Visitor Expenditures in
Shelby and Moultrie Counties, May-October, 1978

Type of Expenditure	Direct	Direct and Indirect	Induced Impact	Total Income Impact	Personal Income
Nonresident[a] Trip-Specific Expenditures	$1,367,000	$1,529,000	$627,000	$2,156,000	0.84%
Nonresident[b] Seasonal Expenditures	$172,000	$209,000	$85,000	$294,000	0.11%
Combined	$1,539,000	$1,738,000	$712,000	$2,450,000	0.95%

[a]Includes purchases of gas and oil for cars and recreation vehicles, groceries and beverages, restaurant meals, motels, and entrance fees.
[b]Includes purchases of sporting licenses, repairs to cars and boats, and purchase and repair of miscellaneous other equipment.

The County and Corps administrators seem to feel that the local populace's reluctance to increase their tax rate for road maintenance was an evasion of legitimate fiscal responsibility. Locals do want good roads for everyone; however, they do not feel it fair that the township must continue to pay for what they do not tear up. An insignificant amount of monies is received from recreationists to help alleviate the user costs. Thus, the residents view the township's attempt to put the financial burden back onto the county, state and federal government as a just way of regaining control usurped when their communities were developed by an outside agency. These attempts help locals maintain self-respect in spite of having little choice but to host weekend residents who *take without caring*.

OBSERVATIONS ON THE IMPACTS OF LAKE SHELBYVILLE

What really happened at Lake Shelbyville? The project was hatched in the post World War II era where large federal projects were seen as the solution to a variety of problems. Everybody was seen to benefit from flood control: improved water quality, a steady supply of downstream water, recreation benefits for an area that had none and, of course, help for a local economy that was dependent upon a declining agricultural industry.

•The recreation opportunities materialized as predicted, although not as many people came as was hoped. Those who did come were mostly locals and what they spend cannot be counted as an economic contribution. Except for the marinas and grocery stores, the recreation related business has never boomed. Probably 75 percent of the benefits to the area come from reservoir related recreation. If the Corps were in the business of providing recreation, then they did a good job.

•The miscalculation on the downstream carrying capacity of the Kaskaskia has antagonized an early support group, namely downstream farmers. Anticipating some of the side effects of the downstream flooding problems would have provided a better picture of project costs.

•The loss of agricultural income has never been replaced because the reservoir sponsored no new development to take its place. While some compensation is being made to the tax base for land taken by the project, those payments will diminish with each passing year.

•The problem of roads and road maintenance likely will never be solved. Township governments do not have the taxing capacity to maintain roads for recreational travel. That problem could have been dealt with in pre-project arrangements.

•Population increases have never materialized and the lack of lake related development has not generated new employment opportunities. The lake has probably slowed down an out-migration that would be normal for an agricultural area that was experiencing farm consolidation due to mechanization. Farmers displaced through acquisition probably forced a temporary increase in the price of farmland as they sought new holdings. However, the continued depression in agriculture has led to even lower land prices.

•Local communities did increase the size of law enforcement agencies as a result of the lake. In addition, the size of search and rescue operations increased and the capacity of the local hospital was expanded.

•Based on the analysis presented in this paper we can say that the Lake Shelbyville project never met its expectations. However, the most serious impact that the lake brought was the arrival of a new, very big and powerful neighbor to Shelby and Moultrie counties. The new neighbor is a government agency represented by the U.S. Army Corps of Engineers. The neighbor was not like the others, because it played by rules established in Congress, the district headquarters in St. Louis and the Illinois legislature. The norms by which the Corps operated were those of a large bureaucracy and not those of small rural communities like Shelbyville or Sullivan. People still talk about mistreatment during land acquisition. They blame the Corps for the bad roads and the weekend traffic. Most of all they feel the Corps is not sensitive to their needs because the Corps has no reason to be responsive to local interests. The lake manager at Shelbyville at the time of the study was seen as a good person, but he was also seen as someone charged with carrying out Corp's directives.

Probably the best summary of local attitudes towards the reservoir comes from one farmer:

To me, all these lake projects that are put in, no matter where...those sponsors of the project are not explaining the full facts to these people that have to live in the area after it goes in—the people who have to live with it year-after-year. If these sponsors would explain the facts to the residents and all the trouble with taxes, roads, outsiders and so forth, fewer lakes would be approved. At least we would know what to expect and carve out a more equitable arrangement.

CONSIDERATIONS IN FUTURE RESERVOIR DECISIONS

•Development projects often take decades for planning and implementation. As such, the persons who make the initial decision may no longer be involved and regulations governing the activity may no longer apply. Furthermore, records can be lost. In the case of Lake Shelbyville, this was a problem for the State of Illinois. Some errors were made as in the underestimate of the size of the channel below the dam and failure to take into account the capacity of upstream tributaries during high water. The Corps did not respond to repeated requests for detailed information to verify and analyze their cost-benefit ratio.

•The decision agency (in this case, the State of Illinois) should develop a computerized record system for storing and receiving relevant project data. The development agency (in this case, the Corps) should not be relied upon to maintain project records.

•The decision agency must not assume that the development agency has total expertise and the best interests of the local population at heart. The continued disruption of the local transportation system by visitor use of the reservoirs and errors by the Corps in the boundary surveys suggests that state and provincial governments must be more active in protecting local interests.

•The history of the Lake Shelbyville project suggests that an appropriate relationship between state government and federal agencies could be an employer-employee relationship, with the state as the *employer*. The state would give more attention to project demands on its locality; require data sharing as part of the price of participation; verification of a particular agencies; *references* by inquiring about competence and cooperation in recently completed projects in other states; *auditing* the agencies' technical competence on selected critical points (especially where an agency has a history of failure); rejection of funding when project execution is incompatible with state goals; inclusion of penalty, lawsuit, and damage clauses in federal-state contracts and agreements to provide the state with recourse for federal failure, ready recourse to lawsuits as the last resort; and finally, withdrawal of state approval by the Executive Branch and the Illinois Congressional Delegation.

•Federal agencies differ in technical and administrative capabilities. Furthermore, considerable variation in quality exists between departments in federal agencies. Decision agencies at the state and local level should not be intimidated by the size of the federal bureaucracies, realizing that each is made up of small pieces-some good, others not so good.

•Decision agencies should remember that the serious and long run negative impacts of a project will only hurt the state and its local populations. The development agency (in this case the Corps) is neither responsible nor accountable to the local community.

•The decision agency should adopt a more supervisory and skeptical (aloof) attitude toward execution of federal projects. Precedent is available from the Constitution of the State of Illinois, *The public policy of the state and the duty of each person is to provide and maintain a healthful environment for the benefit of this and future generations* (Article XI, Section 1).

•The decision agency should promote a local citizen's advisory board which would provide feedback to the public and state government regarding the development agencies' activities. That advisory board should remain in place after the project has been developed. In the case of Lake Shelbyville, the Kaskaskia Valley Association disbanded after the project was built. Had that organization remained, people in the two county area would have retained a legitimate platform from which to respond to the Corps' activities.

•Lake Shelbyville should not be abandoned as a study area. Baseline data have been obtained and much is known about the area. The urgency of water resource development has receded but other resource development planning has taken its place, e.g., energy (coal). The study remains timely although the impact setting has shifted.

•The Lake Shelbyville study points out that an institution-building job is needed at the state level to exercise oversight on federal (and private) development planning proposals. State institutional capability for responding to such development to these is needed as part of a large effort towards comprehensive project review.

Prologue

Despite evidence that financial success is not likely, attempts to salvage some economic benefits from the Lake Shelbyville Reservoir continue. The State of Illinois Department of Conservation has appropriated funds for the construction of a resort style hotel-motel complex within the present State Park. The hope being that such a resort will attract convention trade and enhance tourism development in the region. The decision to proceed was made despite a slow decline in the region's population, the decline in recreation related receipts since 1980, and the continued deterioration in the fishery of the lake. Local residents complain that the issue of who pays for the maintenance of the access roads has never been solved to their satisfaction.

REFERENCES

Burdge, Rabel J., James H. Gramann and Thomas Buchanan. 1979. *Lake Shelbyville Recreation Study*. Urbana, Il: University of Illinois, Institute for Environmental Studies, Research Report No. 5 UILU-IES 79 0005.

Burdge, Rabel J. and Paul Opryszek. 1981. *Coping With Change: An Interdisciplinary Assessment of the Lake Shelbyville Reservoir*. University of Illinois at Urbana-Champaign, IES Research Report No. 8, p. 386, (UILU-IES 81-0008).

Dwyer, John, and Robert Espeseth. 1977. *Improved Local Planning for Reservoir-Oriented Recreation Opportunities*. Urbana, Illinois: University of Illinois, Water Resource Center Research Report No. 123.

Korsching, Peter F., Joseph F. Donnermeyer and Rabel J. Burdge. 1980. Perception of Housing and Property Settlement Among Displaced Persons. *Human Organization*, 39: 332-338.

U.S. Army Corps of Engineers. 1969. *Estimating Initial Reservoir Use Technical Report No. 2*. Washington, D.C.: Office of Chief of Engineers.

U.S. Army Corps of Engineers. 1975. *Environmental Impact Statement of Operation and Maintenance of Lake Shelbyville, Illinois: Vol. 1*. (St. Louis, MO.)

Chapter 13

ON MIXING APPLES AND ORANGES: THE SOCIOLOGIST DOES IMPACT ASSESSMENT WITH BIOLOGISTS AND ECONOMISTS[1]

Rabel J. Burdge and Paul Opryszek

INTRODUCTION

Lake Shelbyville, located in Eastern Illinois, is a typical Corps of Engineers flood-control reservoir. It was planned in the early 1930s and completed in 1970. This chapter details the administrative problems of an interdisciplinary university research effort to examine the *real* environmental impacts of the reservoir ten years after it had begun operation. The project titled *Ex Post Reservoir Study: The Case of Lake Shelbyville* was housed in the Institute for Environmental Studies at the University of Illinois, and headed by Rabel J. Burdge, a rural sociologist (Burdge and Opryszek 1981). Our experience in project administration illustrates some of the problems in doing interdisciplinary team assessment, which are here shared. While not implying that **Apples** and **Oranges** don't mix, problems do result when we try to bring together a group of disciplinary researchers. We write this chapter in the hope that environmental impact assessment will remain interdisciplinary. Indeed, one of the reasons we are in this "environmental fix" is the singleness of our disciplinary perspectives.

Measuring and understanding the intricate impacts of a flood-control reservoir on the natural and human environment requires the combined expertise of researchers from varied disciplines. A truly interdisciplinary effort is needed to arrive at a comprehensive view of the impacted physical and social environments, yet *interdisciplinary* can easily become a false label. If the principal investigator and researchers are not attentive to project administration on a day-to-day basis, the end product reflects the practice of integrating findings *with a staple*. Among the obstacles to doing a truly interdisciplinary research project:

- Establishment of budget sub-allocations;
- Data compatibility;
- Developing an effective decision-making structure;
- Working at the interfaces between discipline and project segments; and

[1]Abridged from the original. Rabel J. Burdge and Paul Opryszek. 1983. On Mixing Apples and Oranges: The Sociologist Does Impact Assessment with Biologists and Economists. in *Integrated Impact Assessment*. F. A. Rossini and A. L. Porter eds., Boulder, Co: Westview Press pp. 107-117.

•Enforcement of understandings between participants.

Failure to successfully meet these challenges is likely to produce a series of miniature discipline-based projects and a final report which mirrors the list of university departments. Although the lure of funding produces comfortable platitudes to the contrary, the realities of day-to-day research soon demonstrate that academic communities have not been successful in producing truly interdisciplinary research. Unfortunately, with the continuing contraction of many university budgets has come a hardening of the already formidable barriers to interdisciplinary work.

Among useful insights gained from the Lake Shelbyville Reservoir Project were an acid test of some organizational theories and a gradual awareness of realistic procedures for interdisciplinary project management. Problem areas in this type of work can, and for us did, occur in data collection, personnel retention, and budget management. Some intriguing, but impractical, approaches tried at Lake Shelbyville were:

- Survey-based, local level input-output analysis (Suwanamalik 1980; Tuan and Scott 1980);
- Collective project decision making;
- The use of graduate students in supervisory roles;
- The *shotgun* approach to social inventories; and
- The assumption that *altruism,* while rarely found in the real world, might be present in academia.

PROJECT ADMINISTRATION

Proposal Formulation

As in all research, interdisciplinary work begins with the proposal. Commonly, one person writes a proposal and then seeks interest from others. In such an approach the discipline of the principal investigator is presented in a very sophisticated and knowledgeable manner, while less familiar disciplines are treated in a very general way. The Shelbyville project did not permit total formulation of the final interdisciplinary proposal by one individual or from the orientation of one discipline.

The leadership of the Shelbyville project circulated a call for ideas and interested researchers, based on the general problem to be studied. Disciplinary specialists were then urged to identify their point of entry. Two types of responses were received. First, there was the identification of persons interested in the project, and second, a list of topical research areas. Collectively, these diverse responses produced a much wider assortment of approaches and insights than any one researcher could have devised. Diverse input is important in the formulation of an environmental impact assessment research program, because what is included under the rubric of impact is only now being established within the literature (Finsterbusch and Wolf 1977).

Not all persons who expressed an interest in the project wanted to become directly involved in the actual research. However, from either personal curiosity or a sense of collegial responsibility they were willing to lend their expertise in a non-paid consultant role. The informal evolution of such a process did in fact benefit the Shelbyville project, leading to a formalization of the position of *advisory board* members. One outcome of the advisory board was that graduate research assistants could have access to an advisor, even though the student, and not the advisor, was paid from the project.

Multidisciplinary Versus Interdisciplinary Funding

Alternatives for funding the Shelbyville research ranged from total centralization of expenditures, as in a task force concept, to subcontracting with investigators for specific project components. The disaggregation of funding into individual grants led to a fragmentation of the effort into a multidisciplinary rather than interdisciplinary study of reservoir impacts.

It was eventually decided that four teams would be set up—social, economic, biological, and integrative. Faculty members and their students from several disciplines would make up each team. One person was designated to lead each team, with the principal investigator assuming overall project responsibility. Initially, funds were allocated by the collective body to disciplinary teams.

After the project was funded and sub-allocations began to be passed to each research team, the hidden agendas of each discipline and their faculty began to surface. We found that hidden objectives constantly threatened to subvert those portions of the project that were permitted to be excessively independent. Hidden agendas took various forms. Researchers covertly sought funding for work they wanted done as part of another project. If these private goals were close enough to project objectives, there was no conflict. The most common problem was that separate research agendas were quietly pursued, gradually sidetracking important areas of the project. One result of this problem was that one team acquired data it wanted, but failed to submit the analysis that was the end product and in turn needed by other teams.

The distribution of research funds from a central source can minimize the tendency of a project to fragment, and through the use of funding supervision, to hold the various teams to a set of research objectives. Jealously independent faculty clearly dislike any administrative structure whose demands they see as capricious and needlessly intrusive. Such individual traits are reinforced by the traditionally decentralized university structure which houses faculty by discipline. Based on the Shelbyville experience — **we suggest that the more centralized the administrative control, the more likely an impact assessment project is to remain interdisciplinary**.

DISCIPLINARY CHAUVINISM

Any effort to combine the resources of different disciplines will be hindered by the fact that faculty careers are advanced by touching disciplinary chords. Specialists, by definition, are persons who know one subject area in great depth (generally the exclusion of breadth). Interdisciplinary projects would benefit by screening out those researchers so narrowly specialized that they are incapable of collaborating with others.

Outside of the need to take the time to find out what another person does, the most basic obstacle to integrated research is that one discipline does not understand what it costs another to do research. For example, the collection of quality ethnographic data by a trained anthropologist takes months and often years. Therefore, salary costs are high. The collection of water quality data requires little human labor, but much equipment. The biologist could not see spending $6,000 for an anthropologist to live in Shelbyville, but would quickly spend four times that for a piece of equipment. Busy researchers do not want to take the time to become familiar with data collection costs for other disciplines. After the Shelbyville project budgeted a large amount for one team, the implied question from the others was... what is it that you *guys* in x-ology really do to use all that money? Such was the predominant attitude of the biological sciences toward the social sciences. The biologists were reliant on expensive technology to gather data. Assaying, analyzing, and measuring were seen as technical problems. For the social scientist, the quality of the data depended to a large extent upon the relationship with the local population (Burch 1971). What it boils down to is that each of the major teams (biophysical, economic, and sociology-anthropology-geography-planning) wanted two-thirds of the total funding for data collection, at the same time they were unwilling to understand the data collection procedures of other disciplines. Of course, the principal investigator or project coordinator must make a decision on the division of funding. Perhaps this would be easier if group budget proposals were submitted for ranges of data acquisition with corresponding levels of funding.

DATA COMPATIBILITY

Aside from an unwillingness to learn about data collection costs, the divergent nature of the data bases used by economists, biologists, and sociologists complicated well meaning efforts at cooperation.

Economists

National level, annual statistics are the strongest of the economic data bases. On the other hand, local data bases are frequently incomplete or nonexistent. Monthly, even quarterly, statistics are unobtainable for some series. For example, in Shelby County there was only one major manufacturer that produced farm implements. To protect the proprietary rights of that firm, its gross sales could not be reported unless there were three other manufacturers present in Shelby County for that category of information.

While regional data such as sales, regional imports, and regional exports are available (commonly used in regional input-output models), these models frequently are for overlapping geographical areas. Each study may adopt different numbers and content of categories, and studies are not compiled for identical points in time. They rarely reach down to the non-metropolitan county level and are also expensive. Economist are quick to point out that a survey based table may cost ten times as much and take eight times as long to prepare as a secondary data table (Richardson 1972:85). Local level economic data are therefore often limited to the bare essentials of employment figures by occupation (or type of employer) and sales tax receipts (perhaps broken down into broad categories for each type of business). In the Shelbyville study we tried to interview small businessmen in the two county area to obtain figures on type and amount of expenditures, income, and employment, among others. However, the questionnaires used to obtain data for the input-output table were lengthy and cumbersome. What little information we got was incomplete. Such an approach is therefore useless for small rural counties. Finally we found that graduate students in economics were not trained to collect reliable and valid survey data.

Biologists

The biologists did an excellent job of compiling a myriad of detailed measures for air and water quality as well as type and distribution of fauna and flora. The problem in relating to other disciplines stems from the extremely localized nature of their findings. Descriptions vary drastically even for sites located side-by-side. Furthermore, interpretation was needed before non-technicians could interpret their results as normal and abnormal. The experience at Shelbyville was that the biologists spent too much of the allocated funds in the collection of data that was of local interest and had little generalizability. A particular excess was raw data on chemical concentrations and fish counts.

The ability of biochemical scientists to make ecological generalizations is growing, but this capacity is in the formative stages. The importance of ecological generalization and analysis came to light in an Illinois controversy over the proposed Oakley-Springer Reservoir (Harris 1978). The decision not to build the project revolved almost exclusively around conflicting biological analyses of the effects of the impoundment on an ecosystem near the proposed reservoir's headwaters. Ecological generalizations concerning national level problems like pesticide accumulation are, however, of limited utility for a project studying a wide range of problems on a vastly smaller ecosystem. Our experience indicates that impact work needs scientifically derived biological statements at the project and regional level.

Sociologist

The social scientists in the Shelbyville study collected data on daytime recreation users, overnight campers, census data on control and comparison counties, historical records, life histories, and observational as well as census demographic information. Like the biologist, we found the applied sociologist was so deep in data that the level of analytical sophistication never exceeded tabular and descriptive analysis. In the case of the social impact portions of the project, the theory for analyzing and integrating the vast amount of information was weak. Lacking theoretical justification or guidance for targeting in on important impact variables, the sociologists dissipated much effort in a "shotgun" approach to impact assessment. Laundry lists of potentially impacted variables have been developed that would put even a descriptive biologist to shame (Burdge and Johnson 1977).

The identification of relevant impact variables was a particular problem when interfacing the biophysical and the social scientists. Lack of familiarity with the others' data needs made it difficult for one specialist to prepare data for another specialist doing different but related work. The mechanics of disciplinary interdependence takes place through exchange of data and analysis. The only resolution to this problem is for team members to take the time to understand the basic unit of analysis for each discipline and how impacts in one might affect the other.

COMBATTING DISCIPLINARY CHAUVINISM

Role of Principal Investigator

Disciplinary specialists need to be grouped together for day-to-day work, yet the project must be governed and coordinated effectively. Four alternatives for administration of the Lake Shelbyville project were originally discussed:

- The principal investigator makes decisions based on advice from all participants.
- A committee of participants makes decisions based on majority opinion.
- Each participant would have a veto on changes in direction or budget affecting their research.
- Unanimous consent of project participants would be required for changes in budget and research direction.

Although we sought harmony, the fourth alternative requires too much time, even when attainable. The problem with the second approach became apparent when one large team with a big budget was represented by only a team leader at project meetings, while other teams, with less budget and less responsibility, were equally or even more heavily represented by faculty. We never resolved the problem of allocating votes. The third alternative represents a valuable safeguard for the problem of disparity in the size of the budget and responsibility, but nobody wanted to give up part of their program for others. Therefore, it was difficult to shift resources from one team to another even though it was necessary.

We found that if the principal investigator made a point to be sensitive to the needs of the research team, as well as remain conscious of the research objectives, the first alternative was most practical. The more communication among participants and with the principal investigator concerning research direction and overlapping data needs—the better.

Our experience, in short, indicated a simple organizational scheme, plenty of communication, and a strong but sensitive principal investigator. That person was held responsible for overall coordination of the research effort, monitoring the budget and preparation of reports. The principal investigator must, therefore, set the general policy for the research teams and make the necessary budget *sub-grants* after a thorough discussion with the participants. Placing both final report obligations and final authority in one spot apparently is the only realistic way to ensure that interdisciplinary research achieves its goal.

Interfaces Between Disciplines

Working on an interdisciplinary project means a willingness to negotiate and to be held to specific performance targets, especially in providing data that can be used by other research teams. In the case of the Lake Shelbyville project, the centrifugal forces tugging at research teams created the need for written agreements concerning what data would be exchanged between disciplines. The enforcement of these subcontracts means coming up with the agreed product in a timely fashion. When one teams lets down another, frustrated expectations become a major cause of persons leaving the project or retreating into the disciplinary shell.

Data Manager

Environmental impact assessment needs high quality, valid data from a variety of disciplines that can be scientifically defended and justified before nontechnical funding agencies. Detailing the procedures for collecting quality data represents the crucial item in the decision on whether a project is funded. We found it necessary to have someone supervise data management to insure the collection of data in near-parallel form by the different research teams. Only then was it possible for the information to be used by more than one team. The data manager can assure that the agreed products are in on time and distributed to project users.

A data inventory form was distributed to all Shelbyville project participants. These forms were to be completed for all data sets, copied and periodically distributed as a "directory" of data availability. In this way everyone would know what was available and whom to contact. Redundancy would be eliminated and gaps in desired information become more readily apparent.

The attempt to develop the position of data manager on the Shelbyville project was only partially successful, in that only graduate students were available for the position. As we found in the case with the principal investigator, the data manager must possess persuasive talents to deal with a variety of personalities and disciplines.

The ideal data manager is a full-time non-faculty person with masters level training. Besides an effective work personality and interpersonal skills, data managers must have a technical background. That person also needs a flexible mind and the ability to intuitively grasp technical methods and results produced by biologists, economists, and sociologists. The administrative assistant position worked quite well for another Institute for Environmental Studies project, *Illinois, Today and Tomorrow* (Burdge and Kelly 1978). The manager of that project was able to keep faculty to agreed-upon deadlines by unobtrusive prodding.

Finally, even the best administrative arrangements can be frustrated by team participants who do not work cooperatively. Individuals making up each team must have the ability and willingness to collect and interpret data that can be understood by other teams. Conversely, they must be willing to recognize how data from others teams fit their projects.

Role of Graduate Students

We found that the graduate students were among the most dedicated members of the project teams. The completion of the project likely meant the successful completion of their thesis. However, their effectiveness as project participants depends upon:

- Carving out a well-defined portion of the project for their participation, which ideally can also serve as a thesis.
- Students must not be put in a position of having to remind a truant faculty member that a contribution is behind schedule.
- Developing a written agreement between the research team and the student as to exactly what is expected and for how long.
- Minimizing the use of graduate students as a stand-in for faculty members. It is a good idea to have them observe and take notes on the project meetings—but that is all. At a future date they must perform, and eventually direct interdisciplinary research.

CONCLUSION

Interdisciplinary research creates its own set of operational necessities. Informal communication and decentralized decision-making may represent a comfortable work climate for the isolated scholar, however, academic insulation will defeat the goal of integrated impact assessment. An uncommon spirit of cooperation is demanded of all participants, along with an acceptance of the need to make explicit agreements with colleagues. The Lake Shelbyville project was marginally successful in meeting the recommendations outlined in this chapter. Data management represented our biggest failure. The experiences shared here are offered not to endorse the authoritarian nature of the principal investigator, but to underscore the central characteristic of interdisciplinary research—the need to fit disciplinary parts together in such a manner that a more complete scientific picture can be presented.

REFERENCES

Burch, William R., Jr. 1971. *Daydreams and Nightmare: A Sociological Essay on the American Environment*. New York: Harper and Row.

Burdge, Rabel and Johnson, Sue. 1977. The Socio-Cultural Aspects of the Effects of Resource Development. In *Handbook for Environmental Planning: The Social Consequences of Environmental Change*. James McEvoy III and Thomas Dietz eds., New York: John Wiley, pp. 241-279.

Burdge, Rabel J. and Ruth M. Kelly. 1978. Citizen and State Agency Response to University Research on Public Policy: The Case of Illinois: Today and Tomorrow. In *State Policy Affairs*, Samuel K. Grove and Richard A. Follinger eds. Urbana: University of Illinois Press, pp. 65-75.

Burdge, Rabel J. and Paul Opryszek. 1981. *Coping With Change: An Interdisciplinary Assessment of the Lake Shelbyville Reservoir*. Urbana: University of Illinois, Institute for Environmental Studies. IES Research Report No. 8, IULU-IES-81 008.

Finsterbusch, Kurt and C.P. Wolf eds. 1978. *Methodology of Social Impact Assessment*. Stroudsburg, Pennsylvania: Dowden, Hutchinson, and Ross.

Harris, Britta B. 1978. *The Oakley Reservoir Mirage: A Case Study in Water Resource Decision Making*. Urbana, Illinois: University of Illinois, Institute for Environmental Studies.

Richardson, Harry W. 1972. *Input-Output and Regional Economics*. New York: Wiley.

Suwanamalik, Nuntana. 1981. Changes in Employment and Income for Moultrie and Shelby Counties. in Rabel J. Burdge and Paul Opryszek pp 142-158. *op. cit.*

Tuan, Francis C., and John T. Scott, Jr. 1978. Impact of the Shelbyville Reservoir on the Agricultural Sector. Illinois Agricultural Economics Staff Paper, No. 78E-45. Urbana, Illinois: Department of Agricultural Economics, University of Illinois.

PUBLIC INVOLVEMENT AND SOCIAL IMPACT ASSESSMENT

Chapter 14

SOCIAL IMPACT ASSESSMENT AND THE PUBLIC INVOLVEMENT PROCESS[1]

Rabel J. Burdge and Robert A. Robertson

BACKGROUND

The purpose of this chapter is to clarify the distinction between Social Impact Assessment (SIA) and the Public Involvement (PI) process and make the case for the PI process as an integral part of SIA. PI is seen as a process in and of itself but one that also provides the social impact assessor with a means to measure and obtain information regarding social impact variables.

The requirement for public involvement first began to appear in the early '60s in the federal legislation which launched the war on poverty. By the late '60s and into the '70s the U.S. Congress had attached public involvement requirements to every significant piece of environmental legislation to include the National Environmental Policy Act of 1969 (NEPA).

NEPA is the federal statute that requires, among other things, public participation within the federal environmental decision making process. In 1978 the U.S. Council on Environmental Quality issued the final regulations implementing this law. It requires a *scoping* process (much of which is public involvement) to be held prior to the preparation of a full scale Environmental Impact Statement.

Scoping is defined procedurally..."there shall be an early and open process for determining the scope of issues to be addressed and for identifying the significant issues related to the proposed action." Significant issues are to be identified and insignificant issues are to be eliminated from the detailed study, through consultation with all interested parties. Public hearings are required (usually within 45 days) following the publication of the draft EIS. The information gained through these hearings is to be incorporated to the final EIS (Jeffery 1983; Taylor 1984).

Social Impact Assessment (SIA), as practiced in North America (Finsterbusch 1985), arose out of the same statutes (NEPA 1969, CEQ 1973 and 1978), that required Federal agencies to prepare an EIS before beginning any action which has a *significant* impact on the natural or human environment.

The utilization and implementation of SIA procedures has moved forward in an uneven manner among U.S. federal agencies, even though EIS statements are required by law to make *integrated use* of social science expertise (Llewellyn and Freudenburg 1989 and Wilke and Cain 1977). While the original NEPA legislation required that

[1]Abridged from the original. Rabel J. Burdge and Robert A. Robertson. 1990. Social Impact Assessment and the Public Involvement Process. *Environmental Impact Assessment Review,* 10(1/2): 81-90. Reproduced here with permission of the authors and the publisher.

social (human) impacts be considered, the 1973 and 1978 Council on Environmental Quality (CEQ) guidelines do not specifically mandate it. The regulations do state that EISs are to *consider* all relevant "ecological ... aesthetic, historic, cultural, economic social or health" effects, whether they are "direct, indirect or cumulative" (Freudenburg and Keating 1982).

Many agencies in developing their own NEPA implementation procedures have recognized the need for social impact assessment and have included specific requirements in their manuals and handbooks (Branch, *et al.* 1983 and USFS 1982). However in 1985, Freudenburg and Keating concluded that environmental impact statements have generally failed to make an "integrated use" of such data. The numbers of environmental impact statements completed by agencies beyond the initial environmental assessment have greatly diminished during the '80s and many of those completed do not include SIAs (Burdge 1987). Neither sociological findings nor social science methods could be found in 86 percent of the EIS reviewed by Culhane and colleagues (1987).

The practice of SIA at the federal level has been hindered further by the unfortunate equating of SIA with public participation and public involvement (Garcia 1983a and Garcia and Daneke 1983). Selected PI techniques have been well developed (Creighton 1981) and are utilized by the U.S. Federal land management agencies that prepare large numbers of EIS statements (Hanchey 1975). Unfortunately, administrators tend to think that doing PI also meets the requirements for SIA. In accepting such a fallacy they fail to recognize the critical difference between gauging public opinion and understanding the social impacts of development. A proposed development will alter individual and family lives as well as the course of community events (Freudenburg and Olsen 1983).

THE DISTINCTION BETWEEN SOCIAL IMPACT ASSESSMENT AND PUBLIC INVOLVEMENT

The SIA Process

SIA has no single, universally accepted definition. However, content and subject matter consist of distinguishable components that consistently appear when the SIA process is implemented. Based on the writings of several SIA practitioners (Wolf 1974; Bowles 1981; Waiten 1981; Burdge 1983; Wildman and Baker 1985; and Dietz 1987), we have identified five features characteristic of the SIA process.

- SIA is a *systematic effort to identify*, *analyze*, and *evaluate* social impacts of a proposed project or policy change on the individual, social groups within a community, or an entire community . . . *in advance of the decision making process* . . . in order that the information derived from the SIA can actually influence decisions.
- SIA is a means for *developing alternatives* to the proposed course of action and *determining the full range of consequences* for each alternative.
- SIA *increases knowledge* on the part of the project proponent and the impacted community.

- SIA *raises consciousness* and the *level of understanding* of the community and *puts the residents in a better position to understand the broader implication of the proposed action*.
- SIA includes within it a process *to mitigate* or *alleviate* the social impacts likely to occur if that action is desired by the impacted community.

Part of the problem project proponents have in understanding and utilizing SIA is that they rarely see the full potential of a properly executed social impact assessment. Of the many completed EISs, only a few have addressed social assessment issues (Culhane *et al.* 1987). Many U.S. government agencies suffer from too narrow a definition or understanding of the SIA process. For the most part, SIAs that have been completed can be categorized as infrastructure and demographic in their focus (Canter, 1977 and Canter and Hill 1979). The goal of a properly executed SIA is to identify and understand the consequences of the change for human populations given different impact events (Burdge 1987).

The Public Involvement Process

Public Involvement has the potential to benefit both the project proponent and the community in several ways. Drawing from the writings of Tester and Mykes (1980), Burdge (1983), Daneke (1983), Freudenburg (1983), and Sproul (1986) we identify the following uses for PI.

- It functions as a means of *educating the impacted community* as to the potential benefits and costs of the proposed action, alternative courses of action, and their respective consequences.
- It serves as a means for the community or larger society to provide <u>input</u> to a proposed project *before a final decision* is reached. In effect, the public becomes part of the planning and decision-making process.
- PI may function as a catalyst behind *community self-evaluation and analysis leading to assessments and situations with regard to how communities cope with change*.
- It functions as an *on-going data gathering tool for social impact variables*. The process may supply factual information regarding population impacts, community/institutional arrangements, conflicts between local residents and newcomers, individual as well as family level impacts, and community infrastructure needs (Burdge 1987).
- PI may be a way of *proposing alternatives to a suggested plan or cause of action*. The *key* assumption being that persons know their community better than outsiders.

We see public involvement as occurring continuously throughout the entire planning and development process. It begins as a means to inform and educate the impacted population as well as the project proponent about the proposed action before and after development decisions have been made. It can assist in the identification of problems associated with the proposed projects, as well as the needs and values of the impacted population. The PI process can beneficially *publicize costs*, especially those external to the project sponsors that might otherwise be overlook. It can also act as a means of increasing the proponent's credibility and lessening public resistance to change by providing them a *voice* in the decision-making process.

PUBLIC INVOLVEMENT IN THE SOCIAL
IMPACT ASSESSMENT PROCESS

PI is a continuous process in project development. It occurs in the initial planning stages, during project implementation or construction, during operation, and during abandonment or closure. SIA first appears in the early planning stages of a project and always prior to a decision to go ahead. PI within the context of SIA is primarily utilized to collect data on social impact variables. The social assessor may obtain information on social impact variables while engaging in the PI process.

Burdge (1983) identifies seven general categories of public involvement techniques which used either singularly or in combination fit within the SIA process:

1) Key Informants; 2) Advisory Groups; 3) Community Forums; 4) the Nominal Group Process; 5) the Delphi Technique; 6) Questionnaire surveys (including community surveys, community leader studies, community-regional independent surveys and synchronized policy issue studies (see chapters 15 and 16); and 7) Jury Panels.

Each of the techniques, except jury panels, increases the breadth of representativeness of the community or region under study (Butler and Howell 1980). These techniques also become progressively more complex while providing different and more in depth analysis of the community. Many may be used in combination to provide the social assessor opportunities for measuring one of the a social impact variables outlined in Chapter 5 (Burdge 1990a).

A wide range of public involvement techniques were utilized, as part of the social impact assessment process required by the National Forest Management Planning Act of 1976 (NFMA), in the development of the Coronado National Forests Management Plan. The information gathered from their carefully designed public involvement program was utilized to identify and to better understand the role the National Forest played in the surrounding populations value system and lifestyle, as well as the local populations goals for forest management (Garcia, 1983b). Blahna and Shepherd (1989) studied ten National Forest plans developed under the mandates of NEPA. It was found that planning teams who initiated the public involvement process early and often were able to implement a plan with the aid of local communities. Many of the forest supervisors who did not implement public involvement have yet to implement a plan.

The PI technique(s) selected by the assessor depend upon the nature of the information or data required *from* and *about* the community. It also depends on the resources available to include time, money, and professional and technical assistance (Burdge 1990b). Lastly, the expertise of the assessor must be taken into account because evaluation and understanding of data obtained through PI techniques are complex tasks. If not done properly, they can result in misleading information which in turn can lead to negative consequences for both the project proponent and the impacted community. These may include under-representation or no representation from individuals and interest groups from part of or all of the impacted community, loss of credibility of the project proponent, loss of potentially "positive benefits" to a community, and misconceptions about the proposed project which lead to unnecessary time delays, increased expenses, and losses to all involved.

As a team project, for the course, *Public Involvement in Natural Resource Management and Planning*, graduate students at the University of Illinois at Urbana-Champaign completed an evaluation of the public involvement component of the Champaign County landfill siting process. It was concluded that the public involvement techniques utilized (primarily public hearings and public meetings) raised serious questions with respect to their representativeness. The techniques were also criticized for maintaining existing community authority patterns. The evaluation concluded by observing that the spectrum of the quality and quantity of the public involvement within the Champaign County landfill siting process would have been greatly enhanced if other techniques such as public surveys, community appointed advisory boards, or nominal group idea generating procedures had been utilized (Vining 1988).

THE SOCIAL IMPACT ASSESSMENT PROCESS

Precisely how SIA is carried out and what steps or stages are emphasized vary depending on the nature and scope of the proposed action, the publics perception of the agency or organization promoting the project, the size and scale of the affected area and the time, resources, and expertise of the social impact assessor. Most practitioners recognize eight stages in the social impact assessment process. These are scoping, formulation of alternatives, profiling, projection, assessment, evaluation, mitigation, and monitoring (Wolf 1980; Waiten 1981; Finsterbusch and Wolf 1981).

Suggestions for How PI Fits into SIA

PI techniques are necessary to proceed through many of the stages of the SIA process. In some stages PI is essential while in other stages of the planning process it plays a minor role. Following is a list of the SIA stages, what happens in each stage of planning that is relevant to the PI process, and how the PI process might be used in that stage (adapted from Wolf 1980).

•**Scoping** - In this stage the social impact assessor identifies the potentially impacted public and their concerns in an attempt to determine if a full scale social impact assessment is needed. A community needs assessment may be part of that determination. At this stage secondary information and agency records are useful. The assessor is likely to identify key informants and establish contact with the community. Burdge (1983) provides detailed suggestions on how to evaluate community needs through PI techniques. Adequate needs assessed is a likely combination of two or more techniques depending upon the size of the project. For example a combination of key informants and synchronized policy and issue surveys, has been used to establish agreement between leaders and the general public on the likely impacts of proposed projects (Garkovich 1979).

•**Formulation of Alternatives** - A set of "reasonable" alternatives to the proposed project, reflective of the impacted community's concerns and needs is developed. The assessor may utilize the nominal group process with advisory groups, tasks forces, and community forums to *brainstorm* a large list of alternatives based on input from representatives of the impacted community.

•**Profiling** - In this stage the assessor determines which social impact variables are relevant to the SIA, measures them, and complies a social profile. The social impact variables to be measured will dictate what PI technique, if any, should be used. In chapter five, Burdge (1987 and 1990a) identifies and defines 26 social impact assessment variables, provides detailed reasons why each variable is important, and suggests how each variable might be measured and interpreted within the context of the planning process. Secondary information and agency records are used to measure the variables in all but three cases; formulation of attitudes toward the project, interest group activity, and perceptions of public health and safety. Methods of collecting data on these variables through the required public involvement processes is demonstrated.

•**Projection** - Here the assessor must evaluate the data and information gathered, through numerous public involvement techniques including surveys and interviews, and make projections about what is likely to occur (changes in the social environment) both with and without project implementation. By describing a number of these projections (scenarios), decision makers and potentially affected parties can be informed of possible costs and benefits of the proposed action. Suggestions for preventing potential consequences can also be made during this stage (Finsterbusch 1985).

•**Assessment** - In the assessment stage the social assessor attempts to determine what *difference* do the changes really make. The assessor may use key informants, advisory groups, community forums or the Delphi Process in order to develop a better understanding of the significant impacts. The social assessor needs community feedback on the various projected outcomes to know which impacts are relevant to all persons in the community.

•**Evaluation** - In this stage, who benefits, who pays and how much by whom is assessed. The assessor attempts to analyze the tradeoffs and identify the preferred alternative. Advisory groups and community forums are convenient ways to present the SIA findings to the community leaders as well as the impacted population and to obtain their immediate feedback. Preferred alternatives can be based on not only who gains and who loses but how groups and individuals feel about *how much* they are gaining or losing.

•**Mitigation** - If the impacts are significant and the community is interested, PI techniques can be used to begin the mitigation process. By simply being aware of the changes likely to occur the community and its leaders will be better able to cope with change. Community forums may work to enhance the sense of community identity and speed infrastructure development necessary to benefit from significant changes (Burdge *et al.* 1989).

•**Monitoring** - This stage involves measuring the actual versus the predicted impacts as well as how the community as a whole and the individual residents have adapted to change. The use of key informants, community leader surveys, and questionnaire surveys are three methods the assessor could use to determine the accuracy of pre-project analysis. Monitoring can also provide data to be incorporated into the feedback process by government agencies to keep policies, decisions and programs responsive to unforeseen changes in the impacted community (Carley 1986).

CONCLUSION

Social impact assessment is not the same as the public involvement process.

SIA is a systematic process that attempts to determine the impacts on the day-to-day quality of life of persons whose environment is affected by physical development or policy change. SIAs begin with a description of the current situation and then outline the likely future situation in order to estimate the impact on the community, once the project or policy is operational. SIA is important in monitoring and measuring the actual versus the predicted social impacts.

Public Involvement refers to the process whereby the community or larger society provides systematic input to a proposed policy or project through social impact assessment. The PI process continues for the entire life of a project. It serves as a means to educate the community about potential benefits and costs (hazards) of the proposed project. For the impacted population it provides input before a final decision is made; and leads to heightened community awareness with regard to its present situation and aspirations for the future. In addition, the public involvement process can serve as a means of collecting valuable data on specific social impact assessment variables.

PI is a vital component of the SIA, which cannot be done without input from the potentially impacted community. However, it is important to remember that public involvement is just one of many approaches used to gather information within the social impact assessment process.

As is the case with the Social Impact Assessment Process, Public Involvement is a means to an end, not an end in and of itself.

REFERENCES

Blahna, Dale J. and Susan Yonts-Shepherd. 1989. Public Involvement in Resource Planning: Toward Bridging the Gap Between Policy and Implementation. *Society and Natural Resources*, 2(3): 209-227.

Bowles, Roy T. 1981. *Social Impact Assessment in Small Communities*. Toronto: Butterworths.

Branch, Kristi, Douglas A. Hooper, James Thompson and James C. Creighton. 1983. *Guide to Social Impact Assessment: A Framework for Assessing Social Change*. Boulder, CO: Westview Press.

Burdge, Rabel J. 1983. Community Needs Assessment and Techniques. In *Social Impact Assessment Methods*. Kurt Finsterbusch, L.G. Llewellyn, and C.P. Wolf eds. Sage Publications, Inc. pp. 191-193.

Burdge, Rabel J. 1987. Social Impact Assessment Model and the Planning Process. *Environmental Impact Assessment Review* 7:2: 141-150.

Burdge, Rabel J. 1990a. Utilizing Social Impact Assessment Variables in the Planning Model. *Impact Assessment Bulletin,* 8(1/2): 85-99.

Burdge, Rabel J. 1990b. The Benefits of Social Impact Assessment in Third World Development. *Environmental Impact Assessment Review,* 10(1/2): 123-134.

Burdge, Rabel J., Donald R. Field and Stephen R. Wells. 1989. Utilizing Social History to Identify Impacts of Resource Development on Isolated Communities: The Case of Skagway Alaska. *Impact Assessment Bulletin,* 6(2): 37-54.

Butler, Lorna and Robert E. Howell. 1980. *Coping With Growth: Community Needs Assessment Techniques.* Corvallis, OR: Western Rural Development Center, Oregon State University, WREP 44.

Canter, Larry W. 1977. *Environmental Impact Assessment.* New York, NY: McGraw Hill.

Canter, Larry W. and Loren G. Hill. 1979. *Handbook of Variables for Environmental Impact Assessment.* Ann Arbor, MI: Ann Arbor Science Publishers.

Carley, Michael S. 1986. A Policy Approach to Technology Assessment: Values and the Future. In *Science and Public Policy,* 13(2).

Creighton, James L. 1981. *The Public Involvement Manual.* Cambridge, MA: ABT Books.

Culhane, Paul J., H. Paul Friesema and Janice A. Beecher. 1987. *Forecasts and Environmental Decisionmaking: The Content and Predictive Accuracy of Environmental Impact Statements.* Boulder, CO: Westview Press.

Daneke, G.A. 1983. Public Involvement: What, Why, How. In *Public Involvement and Social Impact Assessment* G. A. Daneke, M.W. Garcia and J.D. Priscoli, eds. Boulder, CO: Westview Press, pp. 11-34.

Dietz, Thomas. 1987. Theory and Method in Social Impact Assessment. *Sociological Inquiry* 57(Winter): 55-69.

Finsterbusch, Kurt. 1985. State of the Art in Social Impact Assessment. *Environmental and Behavior* 17(2): 193-222.

Finsterbusch, Kurt and C.P. Wolf, eds. 1981. *Methodology of Social Impact Assessment,* 2nd edition. Stroudsburg, PA: Hutchinson Ross.

Freudenburg, William R. and Kenneth M. Keating. 1982. Increasing the Impact of Sociology on Social Impact Assessment: Toward Ending the Inattention. *The American Sociologist,* 17: 71-79.

Freudenburg, William R. and Kenneth M. Keating. 1985. Applying Sociology to Policy: Social Science and the Environmental Impact Statement. *Rural Sociology,* 50 (4): 579-605.

Freudenburg, William R. and Darryll Olsen. 1983. Public Interest and Political Abuse: Public Participation in Social Impact Assessment. *Journal of the Community Development Society,* 14 (2): 67-82.

Freudenburg, William R. 1983. The Promise and Peril of Public Participation in Social Impact Assessment. In *Public Involvement and Social Impact Assessment.* G. A. Daneke, M.W. Garcia and J.D. Priscoli, eds. Boulder, CO: Westview Press, pp. 227-234.

Garcia, M.W. 1983a. The Future of Social Impact Assessment and Public Involvement. In *Public Involvement and Social Impact Assessment,* G. A. Daneke, M.W. Garcia and J.D. Priscoli, eds. Boulder, CO: Westview Press, pp. 283-297.

Garcia, M.W. 1983b. Public Involvement and Social Impact Assessment: A Case History of the Coronado National Forest. In *Public Involvement and Social Impact Assessment.* Daneke, G.A., M.W. Garcia and J.D. Priscoli, eds. Boulder, CO: Westview Press, pp. 283-297.

Garcia, M.W. and G.A. Daneke. 1983. The Role of Public Involvement in Social Impact Assessment: Problems and Prospects. In *Public Involvement and Social Impact Assessment.* G. A. Daneke, M.W. Garcia and J.D. Priscoli eds. Boulder, CO: Westview Press, pp. 161-176.

Garkovich, L. 1979. What Comes After the Survey? A Practical Application of the Synchronized Survey Model in Community Development. *Journal of the Community Development Society* 10 (1):29-38.

Hanchey, James R. 1975. *Public Involvement in the Corps of Engineers Planning Process.* Fort Belvoir, VA: Institute for Water Resources. IWR Research for Report 75-R4.

Jeffery, Michael I. 1983. Public Participation Along Alaskan's Coast: Reaching Out to the Villages. In *Alaska Symposium on Social, Economic, and Cultural Impacts of Natural Resource Development.* Sally Yarie, ed. Fairbanks: University of Alaska, pp 135-143.

Llewellyn, Lynn G. and William R. Freudenburg. 1989. Legal Requirements for Social Impact Assessment: Assessing the Social Science Fallout from Three Mile Island. *Society and Natural Resources,* 2(3): 193-208.

Sproul, Christopher A. 1986. Public Participation in the Point Conception LNG Controversy: Energy Wasted or Energy Well Spent? *Ecology Law Quarterly,* 13:51.

Taylor, Serge. 1984. *Making Bureaucracies Think the Environmental Impact Statement Strategy of Administrative Reform.* Stanford: Stanford University Press.

Tester, Frank J. and William Mykes. 1980. *Social Impact Assessment Theory, Method and Practices.* Calgary, Alberta, Canada: Detseling Enterprises Ltd., 6147 Dalmarnock Circle N.W.

U.S. Forest Service. 1982. Guidelines for Economic and Social Analysis of Programs, Resource Plans and Projects: Final Policy. *Federal Register*, Vol. 47, No. 80, Monday, April 26, pp. 17940-17954.

Vining, Joanne *guest ed.* 1988. Public Involvement in Natural Resource Management. *Society and Natural Resources,* 1(4) entire issue.

Waiten, C.M. 1981. *A Guide to Social Impact Assessment.* Prepared for the Research Branch Corporate Policy, Department of Indian and Northern Affairs Parks, Ottawa, Canada K1A 0H4.

Wildman, Paul and Geoffrey Baker. 1985. *The Social Impact Assessment Handbook.* Lindfield, New South Wales, Australia: Social Impact Publications.

Wilke, Arthur S. and Harvey R. Cain. 1977. Social Impact Assessment Under NEPA: The State of the Field. *Western Sociological Review* 8: 105-108.

Wolf, C.P. ed. 1974. *Social Impact Assessment*: *EDRA 5.* Environmental Design Research Associates, Inc., Box 23120, Washington, DC 20024.

Wolf, C.P. 1980. Getting Social Impact Assessment into the Policy Arena. *Environmental Impact Assessment Review,* 1(1): 27-36.

Chapter 15

NEEDS ASSESSMENT SURVEYS FOR DECISION MAKERS[1]

Rabel J. Burdge

INTRODUCTION

The first county agents, school superintendents, and community nurses asked their client groups what major problems they faced. Based on these assessments, programs were designed and implemented to address the clients' preferences, concerns, and needs. Historically, needs assessment was as casual as a "windshield survey" or as systematic as careful consultation with identified community leaders (Beal and Hobbs 1964) and was generally satisfactory. However, beginning in the 1960s many legislative and regulatory statutes in transportation, health, and land use planning, as well as in extension programs, require that the needs of the client or community be determined. The requirement for systematic public input provided the impetus for social scientists and managers of public programs to modify and adapt the methods of survey research to needs assessment surveys.

Surveys were initiated when it was found that representativeness and thoroughness were important for making sure that the true needs of the client population were identified. Armed with information on public perception of problems and secondary needs assessment data on standards and indicators, policy makers and program planners ideally could design programs or modify existing ones in line with expressed public need.

Planning standards, such as acres of park land or number of hospital beds per thousand population, is a traditional form of needs assessment. Needs may also be inferred through secondary indicators, such as number of students per classroom teacher, incidents of violent crime, or persons admitted to mental institutions. More police or teachers may be added or subtracted depending upon the direction of the needs assessment indicators. This chapter deals only with surveys as a method of needs assessment.

FIVE TYPES OF SURVEYS

Needs assessment research usually operates on the assumption that people can verbalize their problems or preferences on a given issue, that they can respond to a questionnaire, and that programs based on citizen input will be better received by the

---

[1]Abridged from the original. Rabel J. Burdge. 1982. Needs Assessment Surveys for Decision Makers. in *Rural Society in the U.S.: Research Issues for the 1980s*. Don A. Dillman and Daryl J. Hobbs eds. Westview Press: Boulder, CO, pp. 273-283. Reproduced here with permission of the author and the publisher.

public. Many of the techniques used in needs assessment are applicable in obtaining public participation and citizen input into governmental decision making (Koneya 1978).

For analytical purposes, we identify the following five approaches to needs assessment surveys: **1) citizen-developed community surveys**; **2) standardized community surveys**; **3) community leader surveys**: **4) regional/statewide independent surveys**; and **5) synchronized policy surveys**.

The bases for differentiating five approaches to needs assessment surveys are the following seven dimensions:

•Focus of the survey (Cohen *et. al.* 1977): Will the questionnaire deal with limited issues, such as mental health or education, or will it be "omnibus" in nature, including all community problems?

•Use of the information (Blake *et.al.* 1977): Will the information be used for decision making, to identify priorities for action, to identify the preferences of key organizations or categories of people, to identify support for a particular program, or to enhance a sense of community?

•Who decides what goes into the questionnaire (Goudy 1975; Goudy and Weprecht 1977): Will the questions be developed by local citizens, a collection of local leaders, a community development professional, or an outside consultant such as a rural sociologist?

•The geographical boundaries: Will the needs assessment effort be limited to one neighborhood, an area of a community, an entire city, a county, a sub-state region, or an entire state?

•Who is to be interviewed? Will the sample frame be restricted to persons who have received a service, such as former mental patients? Will it be limited to formal community leaders or will a sample be drawn from the general population?

•The survey technique (Dillman, 1978): Will personal interviews, telephone interviews, mail questionnaires, or some combination of these techniques be used?

•Extent of involvement by professionals: Will the rural sociologist or community development specialist assume total responsibility for all phases of the needs assessment survey or, at the other extreme, only act as an occasional consultant?

Citizen-Developed Community Surveys

Surveys initiated by the local community members are used to identify individual and organizational support for projects such as schools, health delivery and sanitation, or to improve a sense of community (Wells *et.al.* 1980) The boundaries of the study are the local community, and full participation of community members is an essential objective. Therefore, contacting all community members with a questionnaire may be as important or even more important than obtaining a representative sample. Face-to-face interviews are often preferred because they increase contact among community members.

In some settings, a rural sociologist or other professional may be available to work with the community on the survey research process. In the case of the citizen-developed survey, the process is almost as important as the results, for proposed solutions may flow from a heightened sense of community awareness and involvement (Blake *et al* 1977).

However, preparing a questionnaire, interviewing, and recording the results is a time consuming and difficult task that may discourage many communities. Further, the local community survey may be criticized on methodological grounds unless expert help is available. Finally, unless the action alternatives are well specified in advance, nothing may come from the study.

Standardized Community Surveys

The first step in this type of community survey is for the community development specialist, rural sociologist, or other consultant to meet with community leaders to help identify problems to be studied. The rural sociologist may provide technical assistance in many ways (e.g., standardized questionnaires, sampling techniques, interviewer training, data analysis and write-up (Hobbs 1977; Ryan 1980). Local people generally do the interviewing, either using a personal interview or dropping off a questionnaire with an explanation of the need for it. Representativeness is crucial because results will be used to determine needs, evaluate programs, or develop an agenda for community action. This approach may be a part of the synchronized policy issue surveys described later (Garkovich 1979).

Local community surveys using standardized formats have the appearance of being locally initiated because the community decides what questions are to be used and community volunteers collect the data. The rural sociologist can use the latest technology in data collection, thereby improving turnaround time and minimizing the possibility of breakdown in the survey process. The results of community needs assessment apply only to the local situation, and may suffer from the criticism of being *just another study* unless some connection is established between needs identification and action programs.

Community Leader Surveys

Community leader surveys focus on elected, appointed, professional, and/or volunteer-informal leaders of political, social, business, and professional organizations. Leader surveys are often based on the hope that those who are surveyed will take action on problems they identify (Basson 1970).

The community development specialist, regional planner, or extension agent may initiate the study with outside technical assistance. The telephone or mail technique is generally used because the numbers and geographical limits of the sample are known. Interviews with leaders could be a first step in developing either the statewide independent survey or the synchronized policy issue survey.

Needs assessment surveys of leaders may be used to identify opposition and support for proposed community development programs. In addition, leaders may be better informed about community issues and therefore in a better position to respond to a complex policy issue on a questionnaire. However, needs assessments that survey only leaders may be open to the charge that the real needs of the population are not being identified. Substantial research by rural sociologists has demonstrated that leaders differ from the general population in their perception of community needs (Miller 1953).

Regional and Statewide Independent Surveys

Needs assessment information from independent regional and statewide surveys generally includes many issues of concern to state and local governments. Results are used for identifying, prioritizing, and comparing problem areas. Items selected for regional/statewide surveys come from consultation with state agencies, legislators, planning groups, and research and extension professionals. However, the final decision on questionnaire content is usually made by the research organization. Because of the expense incurred in contacting large numbers of people, data gathering is often limited to some combination of the telephone and mailed questionnaire approach (Dillman *et al*. 1974). Advances in survey technology have produced response rates between 68 and 75 percent for mail questionnaires and up to 85 percent for telephone interviews. Except for checking with local and state leaders on question selection, the entire research process is usually administered by the university rural sociologist. Successful statewide/regional surveys have recently been completed by rural sociologists in Arizona, Colorado, Florida, Indiana, Illinois, Michigan, Kentucky, North Carolina, Pennsylvania, and Washington (see Burdge *et al*. 1978; Burdge and Warner 1975; Beaulieu and Korsching 1979; Moore and Ishler 1980; and Dillman *et al*. 1974).

The statewide/regional survey has the advantage of providing reliable information on needs assessment in a short time. Because samples are large, comparisons are possible among counties and communities (Christenson 1976). If funds are available, the study can be repeated at frequent intervals to identify shifts in priorities and preferences.

At the community level, the independent survey is useful only in comparing preferences and problems among communities. It provides no indication of citizen acceptance of specific policies or goals (Blake *et al*. 1977). A major complaint about independent surveys is that citizens do not have enough information about the variety of problems facing a community to make intelligent responses (Dillman 1977). Furthermore, they sometimes fail to provide information specific to the needs of individual communities.

Synchronized Policy Issue Surveys

Elements of the independent and leader surveys have been combined into an approach called *synchronized policy issue surveys* in an attempt to make needs assessment surveys an integral part of the policy process (Dillman 1977; Wardwell and Dillman 1975). The approach involves obtaining information on problem areas, goals, or preferences from an audience of leaders or community representatives similar to the leader survey described earlier (Garkovich 1979; Cohen *et al*. 1977; Goudy and Wepprecht 1977). Information obtained from leaders is then used as the basis for developing an independent survey for a general population. The community leaders (task force members, extension committee, planning board, etc.) then modify and finalize policy recommendations based on their evaluation of the citizen answers to the independent survey. If time allows, reformulated policies and goals could again be put before the citizen population through another survey.

The procedure could be applied to one community, as reported by Garkovich (1979) in the case of Jessamine County, Kentucky, or used for a State, as in the case of *Alternatives for Washington*, as outlined by Wardwell and Dillman (1975). Improvements in the telephone and mail questionnaire techniques allow rural sociologists to provide decision makers with quality evaluation of policy alternatives within a short time.

Synchronized policy issue surveys require both a financial commitment on the part of the sponsoring organization and willingness on the part of the rural sociologist to become involved in the policy process. However, this approach combines the strengths of the community leader surveys with the representativeness of regional/statewide independent surveys.

· RESEARCH ISSUES IN NEEDS ASSESSMENT

Uses of Needs Assessment Surveys
Research is needed to identify the appropriate problem areas and decision settings for which needs assessment surveys can be most effectively used. Few decisions should be made solely on the basis of public surveys, but better decisions could be made if more information were available on preferences of the general population. Research needs to identify the best timing, setting, and content of surveys. Decision makers in Illinois reported the following uses of information from a statewide independent needs assessment survey: a topic of discussion with other people, legitimization for development of new programs and discontinuance of old programs, the expansion or constriction of current programs, support for agency positions and legislative proposals, general background reading about the state of Illinois, justification for political lobbying efforts, programming materials for community affairs activity, and, finally, to refute or support other public opinion surveys (Safman and Burdge 1980).

Legislated Programs
Research is needed to identify state and federal legislated programs that require needs assessments as a form of citizen input. Programs in social services, health care delivery, social and environmental impact assessment, among others, require that the congruity between needs of the clients and proposed or ongoing programs be specified. However, the methods for obtaining public *needs* are seldom specified. For example, in the case of environmental impact assessment, the laws simply say that the impacted human population be consulted about possible consequences. Nothing is said about techniques or content of the assessment or who is to be consulted. Previews of federal and state legislation with an eye to providing the most appropriate form of needs assessment input is needed.

Appropriate Types of Surveys
Research must identify the appropriate policy use for each of the five types of needs assessment surveys outlined in the first part of this chapter. The statewide independent survey is excellent for providing information on problem area priorities in subgroups of the population. However, this approach does not provide an evaluation of policy alternatives. Community leader surveys adequately describe the perceived needs of the persons that are most likely to implement a program, but leader views may not be those of the general population. Standardized community surveys identify possible directions for social action, but only within geographic-specific areas. The synchronized policy issue survey approach may be useful for combining the strengths of the community leader survey and the regional independent surveys when specific

issues or goals are decided. By case study, the benefits of each survey approach must be linked to the appropriate needs assessment setting.

Differences Between Leader and Citizen

Research is needed on the similarities and differences between leader and citizen perceptions of needs. Except for citizen-initiated surveys, leaders either partially or totally decide what needs assessment items are to be included in the questionnaire. Research needs to document the assumption that community and state leaders are more likely to use the results of needs assessment surveys as a basis for policy formulation if they have been a part of the needs assessment process. Which leads to a second question — do state and local leaders, whether elected or appointed, perceive needs the same as the general population?

Standardized Procedures

*Research is needed on developing components of a **needs assessment** survey package for use in a variety of policy and geographic settings.* The successful implementation of needs assessment surveys during the 1970s suggest that decision makers, program planners, and "average" citizens find the results of the studies useful (Safman and Burdge 1980). However, consolidation is needed to bring together a consistent and comparable list of questions, formats, sampling plans, and other procedures that, with appropriate alterations, could be used in a variety of settings. Hobbs (1977) and Ryan (1980) have developed materials on survey procedures that can be implemented by local communities. However, recent advances in mail and telephone techniques (Dillman 1978) and methods of formatting and tabulating the regional/statewide independent and community leader surveys are not widely available. With validated survey technology at hand, the researcher would be better able to make needs assessment surveys in integral part of the policy process.

Results From Different Procedures

Research is needed on which type of questionnaire and sampling framework works best for the five approaches to needs assessment surveys and the degree to which each survey technique yields the same quality of response. The basic research question is to what degree the mail, telephone, or personal interview yields similar quality responses (Dillman and Mason 1979). If responses are the same regardless of the type of questionnaire, then research may address the issue of what combination of techniques works best for each of the five approaches to needs assessment.

Sources of names for sample selection include telephone books, city directories, professional listing services, voter registration lists, motor vehicle registration lists, and lists of licensed drivers (Warner *et al.* 1977). Each source has different characteristics in terms of cost, availability, accessibility, representativeness, and provision of background information on sample respondents. Research should specify which sample source works best for each of the five types of needs assessment surveys.

Relationship to Secondary Information Sources

Research is needed on the relationship between responses to needs assessment surveys and available census counts and other secondary statistics. The approaches to needs assessment surveys outlined in this chapter represent a primary input to needs assessment. However, survey data would be more valuable if it could build upon available information in the form of data on standards, census counts, and regularly accumulated evaluation statistics. An independent survey showing that health care is a major community problem might be supported by county health statistics showing unmet standards (e.g., too few doctors and inadequate hospital space).

WHO WILL CONDUCT NEEDS ASSESSMENT SURVEYS IN THE 1980s

Two developments in the 1970s elevated needs assessment surveys to widespread importance for citizens and public officials. The first was advances in the mail and telephone techniques. The other was recognition by policy makers that citizen input to government programs was necessary. Impetus for this turn of events came from three sources: the availability of funds under the Rural Development Act of 1972 to land grant colleges for the study of rural communities, the increased costs of personal interviews, and the availability of state and federal funds for planning in such areas as social services, health delivery, and community and regional planning. Social scientists, particularly rural sociologists, at land grant universities are in a position to continue advances in needs assessment surveys if the research program outlined in this chapter is followed.

As society becomes more complex, citizen involvement becomes more important, both for maintaining a sense of community and to ensure that government programs remain in tune with the needs of the citizens. The research program outlined here could help meet this crucial need and, at the same time, strengthens the tie between the university researcher and decision makers at the community, state, and federal levels.

REFERENCES

Basson, Priscilla. 1970. Planning and perception of needs in five upstate New York counties. *Journal of the Community Development Society* 1(2):23-29.

Beal, George M. and Daryl J. Hobbs. 1964. *The Process of Social Action in Community and Area Development*. Ames, Iowa: Cooperative Extension Service, Iowa State University Publication 16.

Beaulieu, Lionel J. and Peter F. Korsching eds. 1979. *Focus on Florida: The Citizens' Viewpoint*. Gainesville, Florida: Center for Community and Rural Development - IFAS, University of Florida, Special Series 1.

Blake, Brian F., Ned Kalb and Vernon Ryan. 1977. Citizen opinion surveys and effective CD effects. *Journal of the Community Development Society* 8(2):92-104.

Burdge, Rabel J., Ruth M. Kelly and Harvey J. Schweitzer. 1978. *Illinois: Today and Tomorrow*. Urbana: University of Illinois, Cooperative Extension Service, Special Series 1.

Burdge, Rabel J. and Paul D. Warner. 1975. *Issues Facing Kentucky*, Lexington, Kentucky: University of Kentucky, Cooperative Extension Service.

Butler, Lorna Michael and Robert E. Howell. 1980. *Coping With Growth: Community Needs Assessment Techniques*. Corvallis, Oregon: Western Rural Development Center, Oregon State University, WREP 44.

Christenson, James A. 1976. Public Input For Program Planning And Policy Formation. *Journal of the Community Development Society*, 7(Spring):33-39.

Cohen, Mark W., Grayce M. Sills and Andrew I. Schwebel. 1977. A two-stage Process For Surveying Community Needs. *Journal of the Community Development Society*, 8(1):54-61.

Dillman, Don A. 1977. Preference Surveys and Policy Decisions: Our New Tools Need Not be Used in the Same Old Way. *Journal of the Community Development Society,* 8(1):30-43.

Dillman, Don A. 1978. *Mail and Telephone Surveys: The Total Design Method*. New York: Wiley-Interscience Publications.

Dillman, Don A., James A. Christenson, Edwin H. Carpenter, and Ralph M. Brooks. 1974. Increasing Mail Questionnaire Response: A Four-State Comparison. *American Sociological Review*, 29:744-756.

Dillman, Don A. and Robert Mason. 1979. The use of face-to-face, telephone, and mail surveys in state, substate, and community needs assessment efforts. Proposal submitted to the Western Rural Development Center, Oregon State University, Corvallis, Oregon.

Garkovich, Lorraine and Jerome M. Stam. 1980. Research on selected issues in community development. In *Community Development in America*. James A. Christenson and Jerry W. Robinson, Jr. eds., Ames, Iowa: Iowa State University Press.

Goudy, Willis. 1975. *Studying Your Community: Community Summaries*. Ames, Iowa: Department of Sociology, Iowa State University, Sociology Report 128B.

Goudy, Willis J. and Frederick E. Wepprecht. 1977. Local/regional programs developed from residents' evaluations. *Journal of the Community Development Society*, 8(1):44-52.

Hobbs, Daryl. 1977. *Surveying Community Attitudes: A Technical and Procedural Manual for Communities*. Columbia, Missouri: Division of Community Development, University of Missouri, Manual 108.

Koneya, Mele. 1978. Citizen participation is not community development. *Journal of the Community Development Society*, 9(2):23-29.

Miller, Paul A. 1953. *Community Health Action*. East Lansing, Michigan: Michigan State University Press.

Moore, Dan E. and Anne S. Ishler. 1980. *Pennsylvania: The Citizens' Viewpoint*, University Park, Pennsylvania: Agricultural Experiment Station, Pennsylvania State University.

Ryan, Vernon. 1980. *CD-DIAL*, Ames, Iowa: Department of Sociology and Cooperative Extension Service, Iowa State University.

Safman, Phyllis and Rabel J. Burdge. 1980. Taking the last step: Reporting the influence of community problem studies on government policy making and program development. Presented at the meeting of the Rural Sociological Society, Ithaca, New York. (August)

Wardwell, John A. and Don A. Dillman. 1975. *Alternatives for Washington: The Final Report, Volume 6*. Olympia, Washington: Office of Program Planning and Fiscal Management, State of Washington.

Warner, Paul D., Susan D. Hoffman and Rabel J. Burdge. 1977. Drivers license list as a sampling frame. *Public Data Use*, 5(September):3-10.

Wells, Betty, Arthur H. Johnson and John L. Tait. 1980. Citizen involvement in local action: Much work for little-but sufficient-gain. *Newsline* (Rural Sociological Society), 9(November):40-44.

Chapter 16

COMMUNITY NEEDS ASSESSMENT AND TECHNIQUES[1]

Rabel J. Burdge

INTRODUCTION

The purposes of this chapter are 1) to provide the reader with an understanding of exactly what needs assessment is; 2) to illustrate the process and the techniques for collecting needs assessment information at the community level; 3) to show how needs assessment information may be interpreted; 4) to discuss how needs assessment information fits into the EIA-SIA process and other planning activities; and 5) to provide an example outline of a needs assessment report. Information in this chapter is needed by social impact assessors, community and regional planners, professional and lay community leaders, extension advisers, and others who wish to understand social impacts and planning at the community and regional levels.

A Short History of Needs Assessment Studies

The formal process of determining what people needed was originally developed by local teachers and school superintendents as an aid in planning curricula for elementary and secondary schools. Soon county agents, forest rangers, nurses, public health workers, and others, upon arrival in a new community, first asked their client groups what major problems they faced. Based on the professionals' assessment of the needs of the local population, programs were designed and implemented in line with concerns of the client group. Historically, *needs assessment* was as casual as a *windshield survey* or as systematic as careful consultations with identified community leaders and important government workers (Beal and Hobbs 1964). The assessment by the field professional was satisfactory in the absence of clear legislative direction. However, beginning in the 1960s, regulatory statutes in transportation, health, and land-use planning, as well as the federal land management agencies, required that the expressed needs of the clients, the community, or the impact area be considered. The directive for agencies to include local as well as national interests in the needs assessment process provided the impetus for social scientists to develop innovative methodologies for gaining public input. As the methods to tap needs became increasingly sophisticated, the requirement of including needs assessment as a step in the planning process became established. The National Environmental Policy Act (NEPA) specifically mandates needs assessment both in the initial environmental assessment and the subsequent full-scale Environmental Impact Statement.

---

[1]Abridged from the original. Rabel J. Burdge. 1983. Community Needs Assessment and Techniques, in *Social Impact Assessment Methods*. Kurt Finsterbusch, Lynn G. Llewellyn and C.P. Wolf eds. Beverly Hills, CA: Sage Publications pp. 191-213. Reproduced here with permission of the author and the publisher.

Defining Needs Assessment Activity

As a tool in the planning process, public assessment activities provide an initial look at the thinking of a client population about a problem area. Put another way, assessing needs means finding out what people think they need, want, or desire in a particular program area. The planner or the change agent then sets about to design that program, or at least to modify existing ones, in line with expressed public input. In the case of social impact assessment, the question is whether the proposed project or change in policy will meet the needs identified by the affected population.

When available, planning standards, such as the acres of park land or number of hospital beds per thousand population, represent a way of determining the difference between "haves" and "needs". For example, information on changes in the number of students per classroom teacher, incidents of violent crime, or persons admitted to mental institutions indicate changing needs. More police or teachers may be added or subtracted depending upon the direction of the indicated needs. Needs assessment activity provides a systematic way to account for the needs of different client groups during the planning process.

DEVELOPING A NEEDS ASSESSMENT REPORT: GENERAL STEPS

From our definition, a needs assessment program is a research and planning activity designed to determine a community's needs and utilization patterns in a variety of service areas (Warheit *et.al.* 1977:4). The purpose of social impact studies is to answer the following question: will there be a measurable difference in the quality of life in the community as a result of what the proposed project is doing or might do in the future?

A careful examination of these research and planning activities shows how needs assessment and social impact assessment are interrelated not only by law, but by planning necessity. It is not possible to conduct impact studies without first gathering baseline data on the community—to include needs and utilization patterns of a wide variety of services of those living in the area. Table 16.1 provides a schematic overview of the needs assessment process.

The Community Overview

A description of the community is the first step in a comprehensive community needs assessment analysis. The purposes of this phase are first, to obtain information on the sociological, demographic, economic, and geographic patterns of persons living in the area where the likely impacts will occur, and secondly, to secure historical data on the network of federal, state, and local agencies in the community that might provide help in identifying community needs.

The needs assessor will first identify the data sources available, their format, accessibility, and the costs of procurement and analysis. This step is very important since the nature, availability, and costs of securing, analyzing, and presenting the data are important factors in deciding on the extent of the needs assessment effort. Much useful information is available from a variety of sources at minimal costs. Table 16.2 lists some suggested starting points.

Specifically, information ought to be gathered on community needs from the sociological and demographic characteristics of the community (often labeled *secondary data).* Data on age, race, sex, ethnicity, family income, per capita income, marital status, family structure, housing characteristics, population density, mobility, migration and distribution, labor force characteristics, and educational levels can be obtained from census reports. The 1990 U.S. Census has a *neighborhood* feature, which allows summary tabulations on clusters of census blocks and tracts. These special runs are available at nominal cost from regional census centers. Vital statistics can provide information on morbidity, mortality, and incidents of decease. Some local and regional planning councils can supply information on land use and population changes. Next, the needs assessor must match needs or standards to available supply as reported by various agencies and business. However, in developing "secondary data" for the community overview, considerable sociological detective work is required. A list of human service agencies operation in the community can be obtained from local directories and knowledgeable informants. The objective is to develop an overall profile of community needs based on information other persons and agencies have collected about specific needs.

OBTAINING COMMUNITY INPUT
IN THE NEEDS ASSESSMENT PROCESS

As summarized in Table 16.2, it may be necessary to go beyond census data and agency records to assess the needs and concerns of the community, particularly under the conditions of anticipated rapid change associated with either growth or decline. Seven approaches that may be used in combinations, jointly, or in the suggested sequential pattern are described. The various approaches are outlined and a review and critique of their design is offered. The references at the end of the chapter list sources on implementation and interpretation. The seven ways to obtaining direct public input are through **key informants, advisory groups, community forums, the normal group process, the delphi technique, questionnaire surveys** (*including community surveys, community leader studies, community-regional independent surveys and synchronized policy issue studies*), and lastly **jury panels.**

Each of the following approaches, except jury panels, requires increased amounts of time, provides more details as to the amount of different needs, and requires increased cost as measured by both professional and volunteer time but is more representative of community sentiment. The community overview study provides the foundation for applying each of these techniques. Many may be used in combination to provide a better view of a community's perceived needs.

Key Informants and Expert Input

Experts or *key informants* are persons from both the public and private sectors having knowledge of the community under study. They are selected by the needs assessor because they have broad knowledge of the community, its services, and most of all its history. Other ways of using expert opinion, discussed later in this section, are through the *nominal group process* and the *Delphi technique*. Expert input can also be institutionalized by establishing formal task forces or advisory groups (Cohen *et al.* 1977; Warheit *et al.*, 1977:20-22). Expert input can be helpful in some of the following ways:

- identifying issues for community or general population surveys;
- building awareness and understanding of community problems;
- helping the needs assessor to discover populations and organizations that should be involved in planning;
- building support for program implementation;
- evaluation of proposed solutions to community problems;
- assisting the needs assessor in establishing priorities among program alternatives.

Table 16.1
Summary View of the Needs Assessment Process[a]

Community Overview Studies

> *Focus*: The sociological-demographic characteristics of the community or area to be affected:
> - ✓ the community's population characteristics, such as age, race, gender, income, employment, housing, migration, and education;
> - ✓ available historical information on the sociological, demographic, economic, and geographic characteristics of the total community prior to the impact event.

Needs Assessment

> *Focus*: Determine the specific needs of the community:
> - ✓ the needs and service patterns of specific populations and socio-demographic groups in the community;
> - ✓ comparative analysis of the goals, activities, and client patterns of local agencies with the needs and service patterns of those in the community;
> - ✓ obtaining citizen views of the impact event;
> - ✓ utilizing needs assessment in planning and mitigating the effects of the impact event.

Social Impact Studies

> *Focus*: Specific sub-categories within the community, such as age, race, gender, ethnic, and occupational grouping, who are likely to be affected:
> - ✓ data for comparative analysis of needs and service utilization of subgroups in the community;
> - ✓ monitoring the general socio-demographic, economic, and sociological changes in the community during the impact event;
> - ✓ data on changing conditions provided by local health and social service agencies

[a] Adapted and modified from Warheit *et.al.* (1977:8-10).

Table 16.2
Census of the Population, Agency Records, and Secondary Sources for Needs Assessment Data[a]

Census and Agency Records
- public libraries
- offices of city, county, or regional planning commissions
- county extension offices
- school district offices
- college or university departments (sociology, anthropology, education, planning, public health, library)
- financial institutions
- utility companies
- chambers of commerce
- agencies and organizations responsible for health, rehabilitation, law enforcement and protection, and recording vital statistics

Secondary Sources
- museums, libraries, and church records
- newspaper archives
- county offices that record land tenure changes, titles, sales, marriages, divorces, deaths, criminal offenses, and employment
- school and hospital registers and files
- planning commissions
- political institutions and organizations
- utility companies
- financial institutions
- businesses
- community organizations with special interests
- individuals' photography albums, diaries, and collections
- family clippings, obituaries, and mementos

[a] Adapted from Butler and Howell (1980:6-7) and Burdge and Johnson (1977:257-274).

By way of caution, key informants may represent only personal and local interests, and not those of the general population. However, with careful planning, the quality of this type of needs assessment approach can be quite good. Key informants are easy to use and are the least expensive of any of the alternatives.

Advisory Groups and Task Forces

It is often useful for a project to have a formal advisory group selected by the needs assessor from among members of voluntary, service, business, and conservation organizations within a community or region. The advisory group can be chosen from some of the following organizations and groups:

(1) *Service organizations*: Civic clubs, such as Rotary or the Kiwanis, provide a place to present a proposed development or management plan. Because these organizations include individuals from different parts of the community, they provide a good "first reaction" as to problems a proposed development will likely face in a community.

(2) *Business organizations*: Groups such as the chamber of commerce and the board of realtors can provide information on how they see their community being affected by changes in business activity brought about by the proposed development.

(3) *Conservation organizations*: Groups such as the Issak Walton League, rod and gun clubs, the Audubon Society, Boy Scouts of America, and others provide clues as to important environmental and aesthetic impacts.

The selection of persons to make up task forces or advisory groups requires that diverse views be represented. Those selected are asked to meet together and can be useful in some of the following ways:

(1) identifying methods for conducting a needs assessment
(2) identifying various population and organizational groups that should be involved in a community needs assessment
(3) assessing potential impacts of a development
(4) collecting information
(5) evaluating a community program or policy
(6) giving technical assistance or advise (Butler and Howell, 1980:12)

Community Forum

A community forum is based on one or more public meetings to which people are invited to express their opinions about a proposed project, management plan, redesignation of resource utilization, or a listing of the major problems facing the community (a needs assessment). The community forum is an offshoot of the idealized New England town meeting, where everyone knew everyone else and most were unafraid to express their opinions in public.

Community forums differ from public hearings in that a deliberate attempt is made to tap all segments of a community and the organizer of the community forum always distributes information in advance. Strengths of the community forum as a way of obtaining needs assessment information include the following:

(1) Much information can be obtained about citizen and community viewpoints in a short time and at minimal expense.

(2) Community forums can be useful in identifying problems, locating needs, or suggesting issues that were not uncovered by experts or the advisory groups.

(3) In the absence of a full-scale needs assessment survey, it does give all citizens an opportunity to be heard.

(4) It provides visibility to the proposed environmental impact through pre- and post-community forum media exposure.

Nominal Group Process

The nominal group process is a structured problem-solving or ideal-generating strategy in which individuals meet in a face-to-face non-threatening group situation. First, the leader presents the topic or issue to the group and instructs members to write as many responses or ideas as possible. Next, in a round robin all ideas and issues are listed and then are clarified and discussed. A secret vote allows the ideas to be ranked in importance. The nominal group process assures a balanced input from all participants and takes advantage of each person's knowledge and experience. In the needs assessment setting, it is useful for generating and clarifying ideas, reaching consensus, setting priorities, and choosing among proposed actions. Most important, it allows individual generation of ideas without undue influence by a dominant group member (for further discussion of this process, see Delbecq *et al.*, 1975: Butler and Howell, 1980).

The needs assessor might be the nominal group technique in the meeting of a community advisory group or task force. A possible agenda would be (1) to determine what community problems are of greatest immediate concern; (2) to decide on a needs assessment strategy for dealing with identified problems; and (3) to design improved community services or programs.

Delphi Technique

The Delphi technique is another way of obtaining group input for ideas and problems solving. Unlike the nominal group process, the Delphi technique does not require face-to-face participation. The approach utilizes a series of carefully designed questionnaires interspersed with information summaries and feedback from preceding responses. A panel of respondents is chosen that best represents the views of the community (Delbecq *et.al.*, 1975).

The process begins with the initial development of a questionnaire focusing on suggested needs in a specified area. Each panel member then responds to the questionnaire independently and returns it. The initiators of the questionnaire summarize responses, develop a feedback summary, and submit a second questionnaire to the panel. After reviewing the feedback summary, panel members independently list priorities in needs assessment areas in the second questionnaire. Sometimes a third round is conducted and, on rare occasions, a fourth. The final summary represents the ranking of community needs.

In assessing community needs, the Delphi technique could be used for many of the same tasks as the nominal group process-determining and ranking community problems, setting goals, designing needs assessment strategies, planning a conference or community forum, developing improved community services, or evaluating alternative plans for community development. However, because most of the people in a community will be together geographically, it may simply be easier to call a meeting.

The Delphi technique has the advantage of allowing people to assess possible community needs under less time pressures, and, most important, so seek out information before responding. The Delphi technique allows the inclusions of responses of persons who do not live in the area. The procedures are detailed in Delbecq et.al. (1975) and the advantages and disadvantages in Butler and Howell (1980:17).

Questionnaire Surveys

Questionnaires are very good at finding out what people think are important community needs and problems. They may also be designed to supply information on attitudes, beliefs, behaviors, and attributes in response to specific questions. Some examples of needs assessment information obtained through questionnaire surveys are: (1) alternative solutions to community problems (2) community and area reaction to problems and, most important, proposals for action; (3) information on citizen knowledge, attitudes, opinions, and beliefs in order to identify and rank community needs; (4) citizen awareness of community problems; (5) changes in the community's position on a variety of community issues; and (6) citizen attitudes or reactions to alternative community development proposals.

Surveys have the advantage of providing representative input by reaching all affected populations. Furthermore, trends established through surveys can be compared to other data bases, such as the U.S. Census. However, cost may be a problem because experts may be needed to develop the survey instruments, train interviewers, conduct interviews, and analyze results. Fortunately, the use of community volunteers can reduce the costs of questionnaire surveys and legitimize the use of the results by local persons. Research has demonstrated that development initiatives that include citizen participation have a better chance of being adopted (Koneya, 1978).

Propose five types of surveys, to obtain public input to needs assessment and community problems. They are (1) community surveys using citizen-developed needs assessment agendas, (2) community surveys using standardized needs assessment agendas, (3) community leader needs assessment surveys, (4) community-regional independent needs assessment surveys, and (5) synchronized policy issue studies. Chapter 15 discusses each approach in depth.

Community surveys using citizen-developed needs assessment agendas - Community surveys are studies of all or a sample of persons in a community. In the case of citizen-developed agendas, community volunteers do the entire needs assessment, from questionnaire formulating through report writing. The local needs assessor could assist the community in developing agenda items and in designing the research process. Obtaining information on perceived needs from as many members of the community as possible is an important as obtaining a representative sample. Face-to-face interviews are preferred because they increase contact among community members. Here the research process is almost as important as the results, for solutions to problems may flow from a heightened sense of community awareness and involvement (Blake et al. 1977).

Community studies using standardized needs assessment agendas - Sometimes a community will want a needs assessment study, but will not have time to conduct the process. In such cases, university or agency sociologists may be brought in to provide technical assistance in some or all phases of the questionnaire survey. Rural sociologists have developed standardized needs assessment questionnaires and are knowledgeable in sampling techniques, interviewer training, data analysis, and write-up (Hobbs 1977; Ryan 1980). Local people could do the interviewing, using either the face-to-face format or "drop-off" questionnaires. When a needs assessment study is initiated locally, the sample must be representative because the results will be presumed to reflect the needs of the entire community.

Local community studies utilizing standardized need assessment questionnaires have the advantage of being locally initiated because the community decides that problems are to be addressed and local people actually collect the information. The needs assessor can utilize the latest technology in data collection, thereby improving turn-around time and minimizing the possibility of breakdown in the research process.

Community leader needs assessment surveys - The community leader approach to needs assessment determination focuses on the elected, appointed, professional, or volunteer positions in a community or region. Either a sample or all of the community leaders might be chosen. Issues dealing with the needs assessment, the environmental impacts of a proposed development, or other community problems are formalized in a survey research instrument. The needs assessor may initiate the study with technical assistance available from a research sociologist associated with an agency, or local college or university. Telephone or self-administered questionnaires or face-to-face interviews are used, depending upon the numbers and the geographical limits of the study. This approach has the advantage of obtaining uniform responses to needs assessment questions, and it can be done with standardized surveys and may not require the presence of the needs assessor in the community. Information from community leaders may be used as a way to identify opposition and support for proposed development (Basson 1970). In addition, leaders may be informed about environmental impact issues and thus may be in a position to respond knowledgeably to the complex issues that go together to make policy. However, research efforts that focus only on leaders may be open to the charge that the *real* needs and preferences of the general populations are not being identified. Substantial research by community sociologists has demonstrated that community leaders differ from the general population in their perception of what should be done in the community (Miller 1953).

Interviews with community leaders could be a first step in gaining public input to needs assessment alternatives prior to either the community-regional independent survey or the synchronized policy issue survey described in this section.

Community-regional independent needs assessment surveys - Community-regional independent surveys differ from community questionnaire surveys only in that the studies are conducted independently of community input. They are similar to public opinion-type polls, but include needs assessment topics.

The format of independent, community, and multi-county surveys can include questions on any number of issues. The results may be used for identifying, comparing, and ranking problem areas. Topics selected for inclusion in these surveys may not always be applicable to each local community. Because of the expense incurred in contacting large numbers of people, data gathering is limited to some combination of the telephone and mailed questionnaire approaches (Dillman 1978). Successful independent surveys dealing with needs assessment priorities for program development and government spending have been completed by rural sociologists in the states of Washington, Arizona, Colorado, Indiana, Illinois, Michigan, Kentucky, Pennsylvania, North Carolina, and Florida (for example, see Burdge *et. al.* 1978;

Burdge and Warner 1975; Beaulieu and Korsching 1979; Moore and Ishler 1980; Dillman *et al.* 1974).

The community-regional independent survey has the advantage or providing reliable information on a variety of needs assessment issues in a short time. Because the samples are large, comparisons are possible with other communities, counties, and even states (Christenson 1976). In states and regions where large needs assessment surveys have been completed, the social assessor will have a broad view of area priorities.

At the community level, the independent survey is useful in comparing and identifying problems and establishing needs assessment preferences. It can provide an indication as to citizen attitudes toward development projects in general. However, a common complaint about questionnaire surveys (public opinion-type polls) is that citizens do not have enough information about the variety of alternatives to make intelligent responses (Dillman 1977).

Synchronized policy issue studies - Two rural sociologists (Dillman 1977; Wardwell and Dillman, 1975) have combined elements of the nominal group technique and community surveys into an approach called "synchronized policy issue studies." Their objective was to make information obtained from questionnaire surveys an integral part of the planning process. Briefly put, the approach involves obtaining information on problem areas, program alternatives, or preferences from community leaders through the use of the nominal group technique or through interviews with community leaders (Garkovich 1979; Cohen *et al* 1977; Goudy and Wepprecht 1977). Information obtained from the leaders is then used as the basis for developing items to be included in a needs assessment questionnaire survey of the general population. After the information from the survey has been gathered and tabulated, the policymaking group (community leaders, task force members, council representatives, planning boards, or the like) modifies and finalizes policy recommendations based on its evaluation of the public's response to the questionnaire survey. If time allows, reformulated policies based upon the nominal or delphi techniques could again be put before the general population through another questionnaire survey.

This back-and-forth procedure can be applied at the community level, as reported by Garkovich (1979) in the case of Jessamine County, Kentucky. It has also been used at the state level, as reported by Wardwell and Dillman (1975). The improvements in administering and coding telephone and self-administered questionnaire allows need assessors to analyze citizen responses to policy alternatives within a short time.

Synchronized policy issue surveys require both financial and time commitments on the part of the sponsor and a sociologist to work closely with leaders in translating the needs assessment issues into the questionnaire format. The approach combines the specialized knowledge of the community leader (experts) study with the representativeness of a community-regional independent survey.

Jury Panels

The final needs assessment technique discussed here is an experimental one labeled the *jury panel* (Herberlein 1976). It combines random selections of persons from the community with techniques in group decision making. First, a random sample of the adult population in a community or region is chosen. Using the sequential random sampling techniques, each person receives a priority, as in the call to jury duty. Persons are phoned in turn until the required number of "jurors" have agreed to participate. The *respondents* agreeing to participate in the needs assessment project receive a modest honorarium and expenses in return for two days of hearing about a proposed government action and providing information to the researchers on how they see the proposals affecting the community. At the end of the period they are asked to give their "verdict" on what they see as major community impacts or needs. Since selection is random, it may be assumed that all class positions in the community are represented. The jury panel is an excellent way to obtain representative public input, at acceptable costs, and in timely manner.

The *jury panel* technique has the disadvantage of requiring considerable advanced planning and a facilitator who is trained in group dynamics (Butler and Howell 1980). This needs assessment technique has been tried at the Shawnee National Forest in southern Illinois and the Wisconsin Department of Natural Resources (Heberlein 1976). The approach is promising but needs more test cases in order to be properly evaluated.

ASSESSING THE STRENGTHS AND WEAKNESS OF NEEDS ASSESSMENT TECHNIQUES

The previous section has introduced the reader to a variety of ways to obtain needs assessment information. Some needs assessment situations require secondary information only — others may require and use input from a variety of sources. The major constraints are the availability of time and the amount of detail contained in the needs assessment requirements. Table 16.3 represents an attempt to summarize, in a very general way, the overall strengths and weakness of each of the techniques. The techniques are ordered in the table according to the ease in obtaining the information. If time permits, questionnaire surveys of the community population are the best source of information, but they require the knowledge of a well-trained sociologists for interpretation. Nevertheless, a creative combination of the techniques provides an excellent picture of actual needs for the community under study.

Writing the Needs Assessment Report
A report of the needs assessment activity that provides a ranking of the major needs of the community will be required. At a minimum, the following five topics should be include.

✓ *Purpose of the needs assessment study* - Emphasis would be on the type of planning activity that mandated that the study by conducted, for example, social impact assessment.
✓ *Background of the study* - Any historical or legislative requirements may be included here, along with justifications for conducting the needs assessment research.
✓ *Design of the study* - This section should provide enough detail on the needs assessment techniques utilized to enable replication of the process.

✓ *Presentation of the findings* - This section presents the data and the analysis, using graphics and tables for effective communications.

✓ *Listing priorities and recommendations* - Recommendations, naturally, would flow from the purposes and findings of the needs assessment study. To be of maximum value, the list of needs assessment recommendations ought to (1) be based on facts derived form the data; (2) be rank ordered in terms of a time-cost priority; (3) be achievable — some objectives at once, others over time, and (4) reflect the best interests of the persons in the community.

There is no guarantee that the needs assessment information will be used creatively for program and development evaluation, even when the data are presented graphically, dramatically, and powerfully. Neither is there certainty that the recommendations that logically follow from carefully designed data analysis will be adapted. But if data are analyzed and presented poorly, and if recommendations are carelessly and thoughtlessly prepared, the probability of effecting any decision regarding whether or not the project is to be built is greatly diminished.

Using Needs Assessment Information in the Social Impact Assessment Process

As mandated in the NEPA process, public input must be obtained *up front*, before decisions have been made. If the scoping process, as outlined in the 1978 CEQ guidelines, is followed, a positive result may be the acceptance of the proposed action. Programs in social services, health care delivery, and environmental alteration, among others, require that the congruity between needs of the clients and proposed or ongoing programs be considered. However, the methods for establishing congruity with public needs are not well specified. In the case of environmental impact assessment, the laws simply say that the affected human population be consulted about possible consequences. That statement was part of the initial EIS legislation (NEPA, 1969), but since the Council on Environmental Quality (CEQ) guidelines were issued in 1978, that relationship has been specified in more detail. In the initial problem identification and scoping processes (sometimes called "pre-assessment"), the social assessment member of the EIS team must determine whether or not the proposed development will have any real *environmental impact*.

If it has been determined that a full-scale environmental impact statement is needed, then at the baseline data collection stage (sometimes called the "profiling" stage) a more detailed needs assessment survey is conducted. The requirement for public involvement also enters into the SIA process. Many of the needs assessment techniques outlined here may come under the category of public involvement and may be used in the stages where the persons who are affected will have a say in which of the alternatives are chosen.

A community needs assessments is an excellent means of involving the public in problem solving and developing local goals. There is a tendency for people to resist change — frequently because they have inadequate information, or because they have not been involved in making decisions. A needs assessment can therefore be reviewed as a process of citizen involvement whereby people not only learn more about the situation, but also feel that they have had a voice in the outcome.

Table 16.3
Summary of Strengths and Weaknesses of Needs Assessment Techniques

Needs Assessment Technique	Major Strengths	Major Weaknesses
Secondary information	Can be obtained quickly, with little time spend in the local community	Does not include input from the impact population and requires good sociological detective work
Agency records	Can be obtained quickly, but requires time in community	Does not include input from the impact population and requires good sociological detective work
Key informant (expert input)	Can be obtained quickly and provides contact with the community	May not be representative of community and produces limited perspective
Advisory groups (task forces)	Includes representative input of community leadership	May not be representative of community and requires regular meetings
Community forums	Can include all segments of population and large amounts of input in short periods	Requires careful planning and may not be representative of minority viewpoints
Nominal group process	Generates a large amount of ideas in short time	Requires expert leadership and may be best as a consensus-seeking technique
Delphi technique	Helps achieve consensus on community needs, best for technical issues	Requires expert leadership and time-consuming questionnaire preparation
Questionnaire Surveys		
- Community studies (citizen-developed needs assessment agendas)	Involves citizens in the needs assessment process	Very time consuming; citizens may lose interest
- Community studies (standardized needs assessment agendas)	Involves citizens in some of the needs assessment process but eliminates technical drudgery	Time consuming; citizens may think experts have major input
- Community leader surveys	Ensures representation of all community leaders; does not require face-to-face meeting	Not representative of entire community and time consuming
- Community-regional independent surveys	Good for comparing community needs with adjacent areas; is representative	Very expensive and requires highly trained research staff
- Synchronized policy and issue surveys	Combines the nominal group process with questionnaire surveys	Requires cooperation between policymakers and experts in survey research
Jury Panels	Chooses an advisory group by random selection from the general population	Requires experience in group dynamics and survey research; an untested technique.

REFERENCES

Bailey, K.D. 1978. *Methods of Social Research.* New York: Macmillan.

Basson, P. 1970. Planning and perception of needs in five Upstate New York counties. *Journal of the Community Development Society,* 1(2):23-29.

Beal, G.M. and D.J. Hobbs. 1964. *The Process of Social Action in Community and Area Development.* Ames: Iowa State University Cooperative Extension Service.

Beaulieu, L.J. and P.F. Korsching. eds. 1979. *Focus on Florida: The Citizens' Viewpoint.* Gainsville: Center for Community and Rural Development IFAS, University of Florida.

Blake, B.F., N.Kalb, and V. Ryan. 1977. Citizen opinion surveys and effective CD efforts. *Journal of the Community Development Society,* 8(2):92-104.

Burdge, R.J. 1982. Needs assessment surveys for decision makers, in *Rural Society in the U.S.: Research Issues for the 1980's.* D.A. Dillman and D.J. Hobbs eds. Boulder, CO: Westview, pp. 273-283

Burdge, R.J. and S. Johnson. 1977. Sociocultural Aspects of the Effects of Resource Development. in *Handbook for Environmental Planning.* J. McEvoy III and T. Dietz eds. New York: John Wiley. pp. 241-278.

Burdge, R.J. and P.D. Warner. 1975. *Issues facing Kentucky.* Lexington, KY: University of Kentucky, Department of Sociology, Cooperative Extension Service.

Burdge, R.J. and R.M. Kelly, and H.J. Schweitzer. 1978. *Illinois: Today and Tomorrow.* Urbana: University of Illinois Cooperative Extension Special Series No. 1.

Butler, L.M. and R.E. Howell. 1980. *Coping with Growth: Community Needs Assessment Techniques.* Corvallis, OR: Western Rural Development Center, WRFP 44.

Christenson, J.A. 1976. Public Input for Program Planning and Policy Formation. *Journal of the Community Development Society,* 7(Spring): 33-39.

Cohen, M.W., G.M. Sills, and A.I. Schwebel. 1977. A two stage process for surveying community needs. *Journal of the Community Development Society,* 8(1):54-61.

Delbecq, A., A. Van De Ven, and D. Gustafson. 1975. *Group Techniques for Program Planning: A Guide to Nominal Group and Delphi Processes.* Glenview, IL: Scott, Foresman.

Dillman, D.A. 1978. *Mail and Telephone Surveys: The Total Design Method.* New York: John Wiley.

Dillman, D.A. 1977. Our new tools need not be used in the same old way. *Journal of the Community Development Society,* 8(1): 30-43.

Dillman, D.A., J.A.Christenson, E.H. Carpenter, and R.M. Brooks. 1974. Increasing mail questionnaire response a four-state comparison. *American Sociological Review,* 29:744-756.

Ferber, R.E. 1980. *How to Do Surveys.* Washington, DC: American Statistical Association.

Garkovich, L. 1979. What comes after the survey? A practical application of the synchronized survey model in community development. *Journal of the Community Development Society,* 10(1):29-38.

Garkovich, L. and J.M. Stam. 1980. Research on selected issues in community development. in *Community Development in America.* J.A. Christenson and J.W. Robinson, Jr. eds. Ames:Iowa State University Press. pp. 155-186

Goudy, W. J. and F.E. Wepprecht. 1977. Local, Regional Programs Developed from Residents' Evaluation. *Journal of the Community Development Society,* 9(1):44-52.

Heberlein, T.A. 1976. Some observations on alternatives mechanisms for public involvement: the hearing, public opinion poll, the workshop and the quasi-experiment. *Natural Resources Journal,* 16 (1):197-213.

Hendee, J.C., R.N. Clark, and G.H. Stankey. 1974. A framework for agency use of public input in resource decision making. *Journal of Soil and Water Conservation,* 29(2):60-66.

Hobbs, D. 1977. Surveying community attitudes: a technical manual for communities. Missouri Division of Community Development, Columbia: University of Missouri. Manual 108,

Koneya, M. 1978. Citizen Participation is Not Community Development. *Journal of the Community Development Society,* 9(2):23-29.

Miller, P.A. 1953. *Community Health Action.* East Lansing: Michigan University Press.

Moore, D.E. and A.S. Ishler. 1980. Pennsylvania: the citizens' viewpoint. University Park, PA: Cooperative Extension Service, College of Agriculture, Pennsylvania State University.

Ryan, V. 1980. *CD-Dial* Ames: Iowa State University Cooperative Extension Service.

Schatzman, L. and A.D. Strauss. 1973. *Field Research Strategies for a Natural Sociology*. Englewood Cliffs, N J: Prentice-Hall.

U.S. Bureau of the Census. 1975. *Census Data for Community Action*. Washington, D.C.: Government Printing Office.

---(continuing dates) *Census Reports and Current Population Reports* (various topics). Washington, DC: Government Printing Office.
---(continuing dates) *City and County Data Books* (various topics). Washington, DC: Government Printing Office.

Wardwell, J.A. and D.A. Dillman. 1975. *Alternatives for Washington: The Final Report*, Vol. 6. Olympia, WA: Office of Program Planning and Fiscal Management.

Warheit, G.J., R.A. Bell, and J.J. Schwab. 1977. *Needs Assessment Approaches: Concepts and Methods*. Rockville, MD: National Institute of Mental Health.

Webb, K. and H. Hatry. 1973. *Obtaining Citizen Feedback: Application of Citizen Surveys to Local Government*. Washington, DC: Urban Institute.

Chapter 17

GETTING AND STAYING IN TOUCH: SOCIOLOGICAL TECHNIQUES FOR EVALUATION OF RANGE MANAGEMENT DECISION ALTERNATIVES[1]

Rabel J. Burdge

INTRODUCTION

The purpose of this chapter is to review the utility of various approaches to obtaining public input to the planning process through the use of various data collection processes. The example is the Bureau of Land Management's (BLM) Resource Management Plans and Environmental Impact Statements. These public involvement activities are outlined against a backdrop of *one situation* and *one constraint*. The *situation* being a bi-polar view of how to use public lands; best described as development versus conservation/preservation makes compromise in land use and long-range planning difficult. The *constraint* is Office of Management and Budget (OMB) Circular A-40 which places limits on the use of survey instruments to obtain information from general population surveys. That constraint means that considerable justification must be gathered to do *public opinion* type surveys.

Importance of Public Assessment Activity

As a tool in the planning process, public assessment activities provide an initial look at the thinking of a client population about a problem area. Put another way, assessing needs means finding out what people think they need, want or desire in a particular program area and then setting about to design that program, or at least modifying existing ones in line with expressed public input.

When available, planning standards, such as the acres of park land or number of hospital beds per thousand population, are a traditional form of determining needs. For example, information such as number of students per classroom teacher, incidents of violent crime, or persons admitted to mental institutions may be used as a form of needs assessment. More police or teachers may be added or subtracted depending upon the direction of the indicated needs. Range managers go through somewhat the same process in establishing grazing limits. After determining the carrying capacity of land,

---

[1]Abridged from the original. Rabel J. Burdge. 1984. *Getting and Staying in Touch: Sociological Techniques for Evaluation of Range Management Decision Alternatives*, in *Developing Strategies for Rangeland Management*. National Research Council eds. Boulder, CO; Westview Press, pp. 1638-1652. Reproduced here with permission of the author and the publisher.

a decision on whether or not to issue grazing permits could be made. However, other factors may be important — to include the long-run maintenance of the resource, the aesthetic quality of the region, and the needs of different users. Needs assessment activity provides a systematic way to account for the needs of different client groups during the planning process. The development of specific standards is a possible outcome as well as expressed preferences and opinions. The next section explores various ways of obtaining public input to policy alternatives.

OBTAINING PUBLIC INPUT TO POLICY
AND PLANNING ALTERNATIVES

This section discusses six ways of obtaining pubic input to a management plan during formulation, implementation and operation: 1) **general population surveys**; 2) **expert input**; 3) **community forums**; 4) **letters from the public**; 5) **interest group viewpoints**; and 6) **organization and association input**. Each approach provides a different type of input, is representative of different publics, and has different cost requirements.

General Population Surveys

These types of studies take many forms and various combinations of approaches. Surveys may be designed to supply information on attitudes, beliefs, behavior and attributes in response to specific questions. Some examples of information gotten from general population surveys that might be applied to range management situations include:

- To search for alternative solutions to management problems.
- To solicit community and area reaction to problems and, most importantly, proposals for action.
- To gather information on citizen knowledge, attitudes, opinions, and beliefs in order to identify and prioritized management goals.
- To solicit opinions regarding management goals.
- As a device to make citizens aware of agency problems.
- To measure changes in client's position on range management policies.
- To obtain client attitudes or reactions to alternative spending and pricing proposals.

The details as to the strengths and weaknesses of surveys as a policy-making tool are discussed in Chapter 16 (Heberlein 1976). General population surveys have the advantage of providing representative input by reaching all affected populations. Furthermore, trends established through survey research can be compared with other surveys such as the census. However, expense may be a problem because experts are needed to develop the survey, train interviewers, conduct interviews and analyze results. As mentioned previously, certain types of general population surveys done for U.S. Federal Agencies may require approval of the Office of Management and Budget.

Expert Input

Experts are persons from both the public and private sectors having knowledge of the management alternatives under consideration. They may be lay people as well as professionals. Expert input could be institutionalized to the point of establishing formal task forces or advisory groups (Cohen *et.al.* 1977). On the other hand, a group of experts could be designated to consult with a manager on an *ad hoc* basis. Other ways of using expert opinion are through the *nominal group process* and the *delphi technique*. The nominal group process puts experts together in a face-to-face setting and then asks them to identify problems and then prioritized them. The delphi technique seeks consensus among the experts on program priorities through a series of repeated mailings (Delbecq *et al* 1975). In dealing with range management planning, expert input could be helpful in some of the following:

- Identifying issues from community or general population surveys.
- Building awareness and understanding of management alternatives.
- Helping the agency to discover populations and organizations that should be involved in planning.
- Building support for program implementation.
- Giving technical assistance and advice.
- Evaluation of proposed management alternatives.
- Assisting the agency in prioritizing program alternatives.

Expert input, whether it be from formally designated local advisory boards or from *ad hoc* collection of individuals, should be regarded as only one form of public input. Experts may represent only personal and local interests, and not those of the general population. Furthermore, experts may not be representative of all local interest groups.

The use of experts to obtain planning input requires some training in group problem solving techniques or several problems could arise. First, they will not stay in the expert advisory role long unless some evidence is presented that their advice is being followed. Secondly, even the experts will have to be educated as to proposed management alternatives.

Community Forum

A community forum is based on one or more public meetings to which people are invited to express their opinions about a proposed project, management plan or redesignation of resource utilization. If planned wisely, community forums have some of the following advantages:

- Much information can be obtained about citizen and community viewpoints in a short time and at minimal expense.
- Community forums can be useful in identifying problems, assessing needs, or suggesting issues which were not uncovered by experts.
- In the absence of a needs assessment survey, it does give the local citizens an opportunity to be heard.
- Provides visibility to the management alternatives through pre- and post-community forum media exposure.

The idea for a community forum was taken from New England town meetings, where everyone knew everyone else and most were unafraid to express their opinion in public. Not so with the modern day equivalent. Persons that conduct public hearings for U.S. Federal Agencies seldom are trained in the procedures to conduct community forms. One study in Wisconsin found that hearings on changes in hunting laws were conducted between 8 a.m. and 5 p.m. weekdays. The very time when working class hunters were on the job (Heberlein 1976). Furthermore, vocal special interest views often dominate at the expense of majority viewpoints or those of native populations. Delivering an oral summary of a position on a management plan is not the usual experience—even for very educated persons.

Letters from the Public

Written input can take the form of letters to the agency, letters to editors or newspapers, and written statements submitted at public hearings. Newspaper editorials and articles may also be a form of public input to the extent that they represent the opinion of local residents. Letters from the public must be subjected to a content analysis and provide the following type of input to the planning process (Webb *et al.* 1966):

- Information on changes over time in attitudes toward the implementation of a particular project.
- Provides clues to reasons for public satisfaction or dissatisfaction with a particular issue or program.

Letters from the public always represents one viewpoint and often accentuate the negative. The U.S. Forest Service has developed a program called CODINVOLVE, which provides a research technique to systematically organize and evaluate the content of letters from the public (Clark *et al.* 1974). Agency personnel must be on the lookout for orchestrated letter writing campaigns from special interest viewpoints rather than those which represent the general public. On the other hand, letter writing provides input from persons who might otherwise be hesitant to express their views in public.

Interest Group Viewpoints

Pressure groups or political lobbying organizations are made up of individuals who have special interests and will likely profit from implementation of a particular policy or program. A case in point would be the *Sagebrush Rebellion*, which seeks to transfer certain federal lands to state ownership. On the other hand, environmental organizations may seek reclassification of publicly owned grazing land to different uses. Regardless of how they side on a particular issue, interest group input to decision making can legitimate and be useful in the following ways:

- Interest groups help the management agency to identify who will benefit and who will loose by a change in management policy.
- Interest groups often take the time to do much legal and economic impact assessment work for which the agency does not have the time and resources. However, that information may *not* have a disinterested perspective.

- The presence of pressure groups helps identify the relevant political actors who may challenge the agency's final decision.

Pressure groups represent an important input to the public decision-making process and provide the agency with information that might not otherwise be obtained. However, pressure groups are made up of individuals who will benefit from a particular policy alternative. The reconciliation of opposing interest groups may be difficult if little *ground* is available for compromise.

Community Organizations

This category of public input seeks to identify the views of voluntary, service or business organizations within a community or region. The individuals within these organizations represent a variety of viewpoints and generally have the good of the local community in mind. In essence, a microcosm of the larger population. Resource management agencies will find input from voluntary and services organizations useful in the following ways:

- Service organizations, like civic clubs, Rotary or the Kiwanis, provide a place to present the agency's proposed management plans. Because community service organizations include individuals from different parts of the community, they provide a good *first reaction* as to how the general public might later respond.
- Business organizations such as the Chamber of Commerce and the Board of Realtors provide information on how they see their communities being impacted by changes in business activity brought about by a proposed management plan.

If community organizations support a particular management alternative, they might act as a legitimizer to the larger community. However, not all leaders are represented in community organizations, and these organizations do not necessarily represent the general population. Business organizations often ignore the consequences of a decision on governmental services and tax structure in a region. Some voluntary organizations like Scouts, nature clubs, etc., may be similar in membership to special interest organizations.

APPROACHES TO COLLECTING NEEDS ASSESSMENT INFORMATION

This section reviews the traditional methods of collecting information from general population surveys; 1) *the mailed, self-administered form*; 2) *the telephone survey*; and 3) *the personal face-to-face interview*. The next section of the chapter outlines recent advancements in questionnaire technology that have improved response rates leading to more useful input to the evaluation of policy alternatives. The American Statistical Association publishes an excellent book for the educated audience on how to interpret public opinion type surveys (Feber 1980).

Mailed, Self-Administered Forms

The mailed survey requires a source of names to which a questionnaire is sent to be completed by a designated respondent and then returned. Some of the **advantages** of the mailed approach are:

✓ It can be completed at the convenience of the respondent, with no pressure from a person at the door or on the phone. As such candid, thoughtful and valid results can be obtained.
✓ It is quite cheap.
✓ The amount of information obtained is limited only by the patience of the respondent.

Some of the **disadvantages** of mailed surveys are:

✓ Response rates have traditionally been low but changes in administrative procedures developed by social scientists and, in particular, rural sociologists have removed that disadvantage (Burdge *et al.* 1978).
✓ Reading and comprehension skills are required to complete self-administered questionnaires. As such, populations with minimal formal education may not be able to respond.
✓ Respondents must see some benefit from the completion of the questionnaire, *i.e.*, topics of interest to them or an opportunity to express an opinion about an issue.
✓ The questionnaire must be properly worded to avoid double meanings, and the layout must avoid confusion. In short, considerable up-front work is required to develop a valid self-administered survey instrument.
✓ If structured, requires OMB approval.

The Telephone Interview

The telephone interview requires contacting a person by phone and then obtaining and transcribing answers to a pre-set series of questions. **Advantages are**:

✓ It does not require extensive pretesting and formation; therefore, information may be obtained very quickly.
✓ The cost is not as great as a face-to-face interview, but remains high compared to self-administered forms.
✓ Although trained interviewers are best, office personnel may be used at times when work is slack.

Some disadvantages are:

✓ Only limited amounts of information can be obtained. Respondents on the average will talk for 15 minutes. However, longer interviews have been successful when the respondent was interested in the topic of the study.
✓ Good telephone interviewers must be selectively recruited and well trained.
✓ Households that do not have telephones cannot be contacted. Families without telephones tend to be concentrated in the low-income areas of cities and in

sparsely populated areas of the Appalachian Mountains, the Western Great Plains and the mountain and desert West. The introduction of the random digit dialing technique has eliminated the unlisted number problem.

✓ OMB approval is not required, unless the questions are structured.

The Face-To-Face Interview

This approach requires catching the respondent at a convenient time and convincing them to spend time answering questions. **Advantages are**:

✓ It is flexible in that the interviewer can establish rapport with the potential respondent, thus cutting down on refusals.

✓ Often, answers to sensitive and complicated questions can only be obtained by personal interview.

✓ Audio and visual materials may be used and, of course, the interviewer is always present to rephrase and interpret questions for respondents.

✓ Allows for in-depth and detailed responses to policy issues.

✓ OMB approval is not required unless the number of topics exceeds fifteen.

Some of the disadvantages include:

✓ It is expensive. Except for marketing research, group interviews and in-depth studies of special populations, the personal interview is beyond the financial limits of most universities and agencies.

✓ The high response rate, once characteristic of face-to-face interviews, may be diminishing. People are more afraid to talk to interviewers for fear of fraud, robbery or assault; or simply because they see the interviewer as an invasion of their privacy.

The combination of the three approaches to data collection are discussed in Chapter 15. A self-administered form with a telephone follow-up combines the advantage of length and at minimal cost with the encouragement of a person on the phone. A mailed questionnaire provides advanced information prior to a face-to-face interview. Resource managers wanting detailed input, yet not having the time for extensive personal interviews, might use the *drop-off* approach. After a few brief instructions about the importance of the study, the questionnaire is left along with a return envelope.

ADVANCES IN INTERVIEW TECHNOLOGY

During the 1960s and 1970s, sociologist made considerable advances in the areas of questionnaire design, sampling frameworks, improving response rates to interviews and in developing formats for presenting information on social relations. The introduction of the computer allowed for rapid data tabulation and analysis.

Questionnaire Design

Led by the work of the Census Bureau and survey research labs, interview formats were developed for standardizing measures of behavioral, attitudinal and demographic indicators. The self-administered questionnaire increased in popularity because electronic sensors could code and tabulate the results instantly. The questionnaire design, once restricted to written materials, now includes elaborate visuals and even accompanying audio explanation. Sophisticated recording and transcription capabilities allow questions and answers to be exchanged in a relaxed conversational setting.

Sample Selection

To do a study, one must have a list of persons from which to sample. At one time, face-to-face interviews required detailed maps showing either homesteads or city blocks. Using an agreed upon sampling procedure, the interviewer could usually find persons to interview. However, with the storage capacity of computers, it is now possible to access such lists as:

- ✓ Licensed drivers (some states even issue identification cards for non-drivers).
- ✓ Owners of motor vehicles.
- ✓ Voter registration lists.
- ✓ Property owners and tax records.
- ✓ Utility users.
- ✓ Telephone customers.

If special populations are to be studied, computer sampling programs can be designed to control for any number of demographic characteristics.

Improved Response Rates

For samples of the general adult population, rural sociologists (Dillman 1978; Warner *et al* 1978; Burdge *et al* 1978 and Moore 1980), have consistently obtained response rates to mail surveys of 70 to 80 percent by using repeated mailings to include certified letters. Mailed questionnaires to homogenous samples with a telephone follow-up have produced response rates close to 90 percent.

Data Tabulation, Analysis, and Formatting

With improved questionnaire layout and electronic scanning devices, coupled with advances in layout and printing, the time from interviewing to final report may be short. In addition to statistical procedures available in standard packages, the computer, through video display procedures, can now provide a variety of tables, charts, graphs, and map overlays. Word processing facilities speed up final report writing and distribution. Currently, the application of computer technology to the analysis and collection of information is limited only by the imagination of the researcher.

Although unrelated to technology, one of the major changes in the last two decades is that people have come to accept the necessity to be interviewed. While being interviewed is seen by some as an invasion of privacy, decision makers do look at the *polls*. People who do not take the time to be interviewed will miss out on a chance to be counted.

CRITICISMS OF USING SURVEYS OF THE GENERAL POPULATION AS A DECISION MAKING TOOL

The use of surveys as a form of public input to decision making is favored by social scientists, and in particular, sociologists who use public opinion surveys as a major research tool. Being a democratic society, we must listen to the people we serve. One way for the people to speak, albeit in an anonymous manner, is through needs assessment type surveys of the general public. One example of obtaining input is to list a series of problems and then have people rank each item according to the perceived degree of seriousness. The items that surface will be the most serious problems.

If policy makers attempt to implement policy that is unpopular, *i.e.*, prohibition, a ban on hunting on BLM lands, or school busing, it is likely to be resisted, thereby leading to enforcement problems and possible hostility toward the affected agency. The likelihood of public acceptance in advance is a powerful need on the part of federal agencies. On the other hand, the decision makers, which usually means Congress, state legislators, and local officials, as well as members of state and federal agencies, have powerful arguments against the use of public preference in decision making. That are follows:

The general population is not well enough informed about a pending decision to make a knowledgeable response.

If people are familiar with an issue, they respond only on the basis of self interest. As a November 1979 BLM report correctly points out...how could a small rancher who sees the quality of his permit land deteriorate, voluntarily cut the herd that represents his livelihood? People will respond based on their own interests, even though they may understand the larger *tragedy of the commons*.

A third argument is that people's preference statements on issues are changeable and therefore, superficial. In the case of range management, where decades of careful conservation may be required to make up for past abuses, ephemeral preferences are a flimsy basis for making long-range policy.

The results of public preference studies are often unrelated to the recommendation of the social scientist. For example, research may identify a rise in alcoholism in a given community. The report may recommend more and better recreation facilities - not that alcoholism programs be introduced.

An earlier version of this chapter included a detailed discussion of the populations and techniques that can be used to obtain input to alternatives for land management agencies as well as a short list of criteria to be used to select these alternatives. These approaches are detailed in Chapter 15.

THE CURRENT USE OF PUBLIC INPUT BY THE BUREAU OF LAND MANAGEMENT

The Bureau of Land Management utilizes advisory panels, coordination with other federal agencies, and the viewpoints of special interest organizations as major sources of input to management alternatives. Sociologists working with the agency have used public hearings, expert panels and face-to-face interviews as a way of obtaining public input. BLM is in the process of preparing Environmental Impact Statements covering all lands grazed by domestic livestock.

Advisory Councils

Following a tradition started by the Soil Conservation Service (SCS), BLM has established *District Multiple Use Advisory Councils*. Much the same as with SCS, the *Advisory Councils* have no formal control over BLM policy or the district manager. Nevertheless, they can be quite valuable if the members are serious about their positions and if the district managers are properly trained in techniques for utilizing advisors' viewpoints.

Research on Soil Conservation Districts by rural sociologists has shown that two problems could face advisory councils:

- The manager must insure that council members do not become advocates for BLM policies and therefore are not representing the audience of clients.
- The managers will have to demonstrate to the councils that their advice is being utilized. Otherwise, attendance at the meetings will decline and communication between the managers and the council will be one-way.

Interest Group Viewpoints

Conservation organizations such as the Izzak Walton League and the Audubon Society are sympathetic to Soil Conservation Service and, therefore, willing to represent its views before legislation. Other land management agencies such as the U.S. Forest Service have organizations which support its interests. Special interest input can be helpful us long as it is balanced. The Bureau of Land Management may have particular difficulties in deciding what input to accept from which special interest group.

The Social Impact Assessment (SIA) Process

The collection of writings in this book emphasizes the importance of the SIA process in the evaluating of Resource Management Plans. As we pointed out, public input must be obtained *up front* before final decisions are made. If the scoping process, as outlined in the 1978 CEQ guidelines, is followed, a positive result to the agency may be the acceptance of the final management plan on the part of the local community.

SUGGESTIONS FOR THE BUREAU OF LAND MANAGEMENT IN THE IMPLEMENTATION OF STUDIES ON THE EVALUATION OF POLICY ALTERNATIVES

Deciding on which of the seven approaches to public involvement to use to obtain response to management alternatives requires preliminary analysis of each policy setting. For example, a one-time, large, independent survey of one or two states would provide a good *first response* to policy alternatives. A follow-up study with selected community leaders or a jury panel would provide modifications in policies for local application. Sociologists within the agency could develop monitoring systems to evaluate changes in public attitudes toward the implementation policy using content analysis techniques. In short, all of the techniques have some utility once the nature of the policy setting is understood. The following suggestions may help the agency obtain and use public input:

1. Through the state or regional Cooperative Extension Office, develop in-service training programs on one or more of the following topics:
   - techniques for identifying community leaders,
   - handling conflict in a group setting, and
   - understanding social group processes.

2. Petition the Office of Management and Budget to lift the ban on structured questionnaires. If the ban cannot be lifted, at least request a modification that will allow repeated use of the same research instrument.

3. Develop an interdisciplinary longitudinal study design, which allows for the evaluation of impacts of management plans, during and after implementation.

4. Encourage the sociologists within the agency to adapt the CODINVOLVE system developed by the U.S. Forest Service for monitoring letters and messages received about BLM policies.

5. Explore ways of using data collected from permits and other registration sources as a device to better understand the users of BLM policy settings.

6. Develop an *in-house* publication or newsletter series for reporting information from data monitoring systems and for the dissemination of research developed from other agencies and universities that might deal with BLM problems.

7. Continually review the public involvement programs of other state and federal land management agencies.

8. Continue in-service training programs with district and area managers on the use of public involvement within the social impact assessment process.

9. Where possible, at the county or area level, locate offices in the same building as other agencies like Cooperative Extension, SCS, and the Forest Service. Not only will it allow one stop shopping, but it will permit agency people to exchange ideas on common problems.

10. Using evaluation research procedures, determine what public involvement techniques work best in which settings. The study approaches should be restricted to methods which do not use survey research.

CONCLUSIONS

This chapter has dealt with approaches to obtaining public input in the evaluation of resource management alternatives. Recommendations have been presented under the constraint that little additional time, money and personnel will be available for analyzing public response. As such, most of the suggestions focus on in-service training of present BLM personnel. In addition, the sociological research capability within the agency may have to be redirected.

A further constraint is that the *bread and butter* of sociology - the structured survey research instrument - may not be permitted. Fortunately, most of the techniques suggested here avoid the necessity for clearance by the U.S. Office of Management and the Budget.

Finally, the bi-polar nature of the client groups of BLM makes the implementation of long-range management policy difficult. Being a *good neighbor*, which all public land management agencies wish to be, may not always allow adherence to the overall mission of the agency.

REFERENCES[2]

Alexander, Chauncey A. and Charles McCann. 1956. The Concept of Representation in Community Organization. *Social Work* 1(1):48-52.

Beal, G.M. and D.J. Hobbs. 1964. *The Process of Social Action in Community and Area Development.* Ames, IA: Iowa State University Cooperative Extension Publication 16.

Bureau of Land Management. 1979. Managing the Public Range Lands--Public Review Draft. November. U.S. Department of the Interior, Washington, D.C.

Christenson, J.A. 1976. Public Input for Program Planning and Policy Formation. *Journal of the Community Development Society,* 7 (Spring):33-39.

Clark, R.N., G.H. Stankey and J.C. Hendee. 1974. *An Introduction to CODINVOLVE: A System for Analyzing, Storing, and Returning Public Input to Resource Decisions.* PNW-223, Pacific N.W. Forest and Range Experiment Station, Portland, Oregon.

Delbecq, A., A. Van de Ven and D. Gustafson. 1975. *Group Techniques for Program Planning: A Guide to Nominal Group and Delphi Processes.* Glenview, Il: Scott, Foresman, and Company.

Dillman, D.A. 1978. *Mail and Telephone Surveys: The Total Design Method.* New York: Wiley-Interscience.

U.S. Department of Transportation 1976. Washington, D.C. Federal Highway Administration, Socio-Economic Studies Division, A catalog of techniques, *Effective Citizen Participation in Transportation Planning Vol. II.* pp. 240-279.

---

[2]The text citations not found here appear in Chapter 16.

Garkovich, L. and J. M. Stam. 1980. Research on Selected Issues in Community Development. in *Community Development in America*. J.A. Christenson and J. W. Robinson, Jr., eds. Ames: Iowa State University Press, pp. 155-186.

Hendee, J.C., R.N. Clark and G.H. Stankey. 1974. A Framework for Agency Use of Public Input in Resource Decision Making. *Journal of Soil and Water Conservation*; 29(2):60-66.

Safman, P. and R.J. Burdge. 1980. *Taking the Last Step: Reporting the Influence of Community Problem Studies on Government Policy Making and Program Development*. Presented at the annual meeting of the Rural Sociological Society, Cornell University, Ithaca, New York, (August).

Warheit, G.J., R.A. Bell, and John J. Schwab. 1977. *Needs Assessment Approaches: Concepts and Methods*. Rockville, Maryland: National Institute of Mental Health, pp. 34-39.

Webb, E.J., D.T. Campbell, R.D. Schweatz and L. Sechaest. 1966. *Unobtrusive Measures: Non-reactive Research in the Social Sciences*. Chicago, Illinois: Rand McNally.

Webb, K. and H. Hatry. 1973. *Obtaining Citizen Feedback: Application of Citizen Surveys to Local Government*. Washington, D.C.: Urban Institute.

SOCIAL IMPACT ASSESSMENT IN AN INTERNATIONAL CONTEXT

INSTITUTIONAL CONSTRAINTS TO ADOPTION OF SOCIAL IMPACT ASSESSMENT AS A DECISION-MAKING AND PLANNING TOOL[1]

Roy E. Rickson, Rabel J. Burdge, Tor Hundloe, and Geoffrey T. McDonald

The Cultural and Institutional Context of Social Impact Assessment

Even though most national governments and international donor agencies accept social impact assessment (SIA) as necessary, it is often partially, rather than fully, applied to development projects. Its adoption of planning and decision making is problematic, because some of its basic assumptions can contradict sociocultural and political traditions. A principle of modern SIA is that publics potentially affected by development should participate in assessing consequences. Because SIA models are heavily influenced by Western social liberal traditions about public participation, for instance, they are often incompatible with the established cultural, religions, social and political institutions of Third World countries. Bureaucratic rigidity and disciplinary inertia are two potential barriers to adoption of SIA. Rancorous conflict, extreme poverty, and ignorance are also factors affecting how SIA is used in an international setting. Barriers to using impact assessment techniques are being overcome by attempts to integrate SIA with the general planning process. SIA therefore assumes a positive role in development planning-to be integrated with economics and natural environment considerations.

Adoption of Impact Assessment Models

SIA, as part of general environmental impact assessment, is now required by most national governments and international donor and development agencies. However, there are important institutional factors limiting its effectiveness as a decision-making and planning tool. We refer to both the range of projects for which social impact assessment procedures may be used and whether they are seen by decision makers as an integral part of planning and development. Although assessments may be required by law and policy, government decision-makers and responsible agencies are selective as to which projects will be subject to social impact assessment. Burdge (1990) and Henry (1990) point to limited financial resources and lack of trained personnel as

---

[1]Abridged from the original. Roy E. Rickson, Rabel J. Burdge, Geoffrey T. McDonald, and Tor Hundloe. 1990. Institutional Constraints to Adoption of Social Impact Assessment As a Decision-Making and Planning Tool. *Environmental Impact Assessment Review*, 10(1/2): 233-43. Reproduced here with permission of the authors and the publisher.

affecting how these decisions are made as well as political pressure and public mobilization.

Secondly, governments may nominally accept social impact assessment as necessary, but fail to fully apply all aspects of the SIA model (Burdge 1987). The basic model, as broadly outlined in previous sections of this book includes scoping, assessment or prediction of potential impacts, mitigation of impacts, and long-term monitoring. It is increasingly recognized that impact assessment should also include education-especially where levels of public education are low, or there is a lack of skilled personnel to design and conduct impact assessments. Impact assessment is an educational and learning process rather than only a management tool. Governments and developers may fund research to predict impacts and consider implementation of mitigation procedures, but then ignore long-term monitoring.

Significant problems arise when impact assessment procedures are only partially or ineffectively used. One is that neither unanticipated impacts, cumulative impacts (those emerging over time but not initially present), nor those that were predicted but fail to emerge will be detected. Mitigation programs are also sharply diminished in effectiveness. Adoption of impact assessment models and procedures is therefore a complex process. Even though there are comparatively few outright barriers to the use of social impact assessment, there are sociocultural, political, and economic constraints to the adoption of social impact assessment. A discussion of constraints on adoption of social impact assessment by both national and local community leaders is the focus of this chapter.

Institutional Constraints

The constraints we refer to are *institutional*; that is, they are patterns of behavior, values, and beliefs that have been established over time and are associated with the most critical dimensions of societies and communities. Included are the distribution of prestige, power, and equity (government, law, politics, and decision making), the provision of goods and services (the economy), transmission of knowledge and inquiry (education and science), and the practice of religion. Social institutions are inherently resistant to change—but do change over time.

Institutionalized patterns of behavior and belief are supported by organizations such as government agencies, business and industry, universities and research organizations, and the judiciary. That is, who participates and how people should participate in decisions about development depend upon cultural definitions of appropriate behavior among people of different socio-economic, religious, or perhaps ethnic status. Bureaucracies are conservative and slow to change. They respond reluctantly to new ideas such as social impact assessment. Furthermore, how bureaucrats treat their clients is related to the same set of cultural factors. Social impact assessment, to the extent it is seen as presuming a Western style of public participation and involvement, is unacceptable in many Third World countries (Burdge and Robertson 1990).

Acceptance of impact assessment as a planning and decision tool presumes interdisciplinary relationships and a sharing of influence across disciplines that have varying professional status. Since most professionals have been trained in universities that are organized around disciplinary departments, and professional associations are primarily based on disciplines, planning techniques promoting the necessity of interdisciplinary relationships will meet some resistance. Economists, for example, are accustomed to having primary influence in development agencies and are unlikely to be sympathetic to decision making or evaluative methods that challenge the primacy of economic concepts.

Public Involvement, Public Participation

Government planning often assumes that local people will adjust to new technology or policies, and the consideration of local customs, knowledge, and attitudes is irrelevant to the long-term success of projects and plans (Corbett 1985). The problem is intensified when politicians and program administrators assume they know all the answers to problems and how to achieve objectives defined by them (Derman and Whiteford 1985). A common view is that local institutions can be changed through either persuasion or force to fit project plans. Decision makers and technical professionals often fail to distinguish sociocultural or institutional parameters from purely physical ones (Wisner 1985). They fail because they do not know where to look to find social institutions (Burdge 1987).

There is a continuum of public involvement in development decisions, and the public can be involved in several different ways. Many countries are willing to allow involvement (to inform people, meet with local representatives, or even request opinions from local people) but refuse to delegate actual decision making to local representatives. Participatory democracy is atypical in the global political scene. A source of resistance to SIA by leaders of some Third-World countries is that it presumes a Western style participatory democracy, which they see as incompatible with their cultural traditions and the realities of power. Others note that the very poor and uneducated cannot participate in a manner assumed by Western SIA scholars (Berger 1983).

Conversely, Western scholars critical of SIA and assuming that it should be used as "means for political reforms" have suggested that modern social assessors are usually more concerned with measurement and data collection, rather than real issues of justice and equity. It is politically safer to define participation or involvement in technical terms - as responses by individuals to statistical surveys -rather than for community workers to encourage participation and risk some transfer of political power from central governments to the local community. In reality, social impact assessors approach participation in a variety of ways. It can be defined broadly as direct involvement by people in the design and implementation of development projects (Derman and Whiteford 1983) or more narrowly in terms of the measurement of local attitudes about projects and potential impacts (Daneke *et.al.* 1983).

Participation in development decisions varies across several different social and cultural groups, and there are differences as to who participates, how they participate in what types of issues, and how often. Milbrath and Rickson (1989) conclude that lack of involvement by Taiwanese villagers in decisions about siting of noxious chemical plants led them to believe that their government did not care about their welfare. Secondly, because government planning agencies had not measured local opinion, they could not estimate what people were willing to accept and support.

All communities have a general conception of what constitutes the good life, how "things" should be, and what should or should not be changed. However, categories of the population vary as to their power to express their beliefs and influence decision making. All governments ranging from Western liberal democracies, explicit dictatorships, Second-World socialist systems, to guided democracies respond cautiously to vocal and highly mobilized interest groups. Aside from institutional biases or power relationships, there is variety of factors inhibiting public participation by members of local communities. Poverty and ignorance are two. The very poor have little time to consider the future and therefore are often reluctant to speak or lack mobilization, knowledge, and confidence to participate in plans for development (Burdge and Robertson 1990).

At the other end of the scale, governments sometimes prefer to instigate change through force before local populations can mobilize and resist change. Also, participation at local levels may be dominated by elite community groups working for themselves rather than the general community good. All these conditions affect relationships among local communities, political leaders, and agency administrators and how each party responds to a social impact assessment of development programs.

Public Bureaucracy and State-Federal Relations

Government agencies or public bureaucracies have a key role in development decisions and substantially influence decisions and implementation of projects. In Third World countries, introduction of large-scale projects in general has been accompanied by an expansion of the role of the state and the assumption by it of new roles including paternalistic supervision and control rather than just public service. Government, in most nations, has the primary responsibility for supervising and regulating development initiatives whether they originate in the private or public sector. The nature of bureaucracy is therefore important to understanding how effectively SIA techniques are used.

There are several common criticisms of bureaucracy. We have already mentioned that it tends to support the inherent conservation of social institutions. Another is that it often functions as a neither rational nor impartial means for implementing political decisions. Bureaucratic agenda of government agencies are characterized by a myriad of small decisions anchored in routine and prescribed rules rather than by official public service goals.

Kahn (1966) refers to this as a *tyranny of small decisions*, and it is especially pertinent for understanding the effect of bureaucratic decision making on development programs, and the problem of integrating new goals or definitions of development implied by social assessment procedures into bureaucracies having entrenched systems of beliefs and behavior. Ruttan (1984) notes, in his discussion of problems associated with the introduction of "green revolution" technologies, that they are essentially neutral with respect to farm size, but have been introduced into situations where economic, social and political, institutions are not. He cites a research finding that the nature of introduced technologies is less important than equity in the distribution of resources, including access of farmers to information from agricultural extension agencies and the financial support of government development agencies.

New agencies set up to conduct assessments of development (generally the ministry of the environment) often come into conflict with production-oriented agencies traditionally associated with economic growth programs. Indeed, these conflicts occur within the same agency or organization as it attempts to incorporate new goals and technologies associated with such planning procedures as social and environmental impact assessment. The ability of an organization to change and adopt SIA is impeded by a number of factors, including member loyalties to conventional economic goals, their skills and experience.

Friedland *et.al.* (1977) distinguishes agencies connected with economic growth from those responsible for evaluation. The latter typically deal with groups that may be excluded from the economic benefits of development or, more likely, experience some direct social or economic cost. Production-oriented agencies dominated by economists and engineers engage in technical planning, while other agencies must contend with political controversy related to issues such as poverty, regulation, and the unintended consequences of development. At present, production-oriented agencies have more power and influence in Third World countries than do evaluative or regulatory agencies. However, with increased public concern about the environment and quality of living, some balance in power between the two types of agency may emerge.

Conflict among local, state and federal governments is common and affects how social impact procedures are used. Public bureaucracies are inevitably part of the conflict, because they both possess information that is vital to assessment and employ professionals responsible for conducting impact assessments. Assessors may be recruited by agencies with the assumption that they will be sensitive to the agencies' political goals and act as advocates for decisions made before assessments were called for and conducted. Bureaucratic tendencies for secrecy and control of information are accentuated or encouraged by interested politicians. Social impact assessment is used in these situations, but seen primarily as a political weapon to defeat another level of government rather than as an aid to decision making or planning.

This situation was evident in one significant issue: the proposal by the Australian federal government to list a sizable segment of the State of Queensland's wet tropical rain forests on UNESCO's World Heritage Listing. According to Gibson *et.al.* (1988. p. ii).

> *Time constraints notwithstanding, the political environment was particularly volatile. For example, the social impact assessment team and others funded by DASETT, the responsible federal department, were refused access to relevant Queensland State Government Departments. Informally, the term used was "blacklisted." Opposition to the Federal Government's proposal was extensive in local areas, occasionally erupting in violent demonstrations. In some areas, the timber industry and local labor unions forbade their employees and members to speak with any members of the research team.*

Disciplinary Inertia and Integrated Impact Assessment

Inertia occurs when an individual, organization, or community cannot respond productively to change or opportunity. Disciplinary inertia is a situation in which professionals (e.g., engineers, biologists, sociologist, economists) are so narrowly specialized that they cannot effectively collaborate with each other. *Impacts* of development are never exclusively social, economic, or biophysical, so various disciplinary perspectives are needed in order to understand and anticipate potential impacts. Because there is no *interdisciplinary theory*, an integrated impact assessment therefore requires creating and sustaining interdisciplinary relationships among relevant professionals (Westman 1985).

There are several sources of potential tension and conflict in interdisciplinary teams (Burdge and Opryszek 1984). Disciplines have dissimilar and even contradictory assumptions about human behavior. How economically rational humans are, for example, distinguishes economists from sociologists. Ecologists discussing the complexities and fragility of biological communities often underestimate the complexity of human communities that are asked to adapt to policy changes designed to protect biological communities (Gibson *et al.* 1988). Professionals often have contrasting views on the role of the expert, ranging from acting as an independent investigator and local community advisor to working within a more authoritarian framework where it is assumed that professionals *know best*.

There are differences among professionals as to how they see the relationship between theory and action. An ideology of action and decision characterizes engineers in contrast with social science professionals who, by comparison, are more critical and reflective. Professionals are further divided by their dependence upon or loyalty to employers - such as government agencies, private consulting firms, business and industry, universities, and voluntary associations. The role that they ultimately adopt is related to where they work an the traditions and goals of that organization. Professionals in many organizations are under pressure to *integrate* their analyses with their employer's economic or political interests.

There are ways to overcome problems in interdisciplinary relationships. Burdge and Opryszek (1984), in one of the few articles on how to manage interdisciplinary teams, suggest innovations in the design of proposals, funding, data collection, and general administration of the team that obviate many problems that are routinely encountered. Their principal recommendation is that successful interdisciplinary research teams need... *a single organizational scheme, plenty of communication, and a strong but sensitive principal investigator.*

Rapid Change, Conflict, and Poverty

Social and environmental impact assessments are pragmatic aids to decision making, having the underlying assumption that project alternatives for development are studied and carefully selected in a rational and deliberate manner. However, human events and endemic conditions sometimes militate against adoption of such rational programs for analysis and decision making. Examples of these are rapid social and political changes, which produce effects beyond any consideration by social and economic planners — resulting in conflict, extreme poverty, and ignorance.

Rapid economic growth necessarily involves fundamental institutional changes affecting traditional leadership patterns, claims to traditional lands, and other values deeply embedded in sociocultural systems. Conflict over change is most likely to occur in circumstances where local people cannot adapt quickly to the impacts of rapid change. Although the official long-run objectives of economic growth programs are higher standards of living and increased opportunities for education and health care, rancorous conflict is often the immediate result.

Conflict is most likely in countries divided by deep-seated hostilities associated with social class differences and ethnic and religious identification. The conflicts are most intense when ethnic and religious identification correlates with socioeconomic status. In these circumstances, religious and ethnic conflicts are also economic and political. Rapid growth may accentuate perceived inequities and actual differences and, at the extreme end of the scale, create conflict situations comparable with Sarajevo and Belfast. Tension and conflict in these types of situations preclude the use of social impact assessment techniques except at a very general and technical level.

Impact assessment is often seen by decision makers as a means of resolving disputes. However, there is usually a certain degree of official disappointment when impact assessments produce data challenging cherished political values or interpretations by powerful politicians or entrenched professionals. Impatience with social and environmental impact assessment procedures emerges when new data and increased public involvement are perceived as delaying decision making and opportunities for rapid economic development. Politicians and professionals are under pressure to produce short-term results.

Authoritarian governments on either the political right or left are unlikely to enthusiastically embrace decision-making techniques having underlying presumptions that impact assessment is an educational, participatory, and scientific process and that data collected as part of impact assessments should be made public. A certain amount of conflict is inevitable when programs are proposed, implemented, and assessed, and knowledge of impacts motivates participation by diverse local, national and, sometimes international groups.

Many Third World countries are strongly committed to economic growth and as a result are changing quite rapidly because of internal pressure for change to deal with severe social welfare problems. They are also undergoing fundamental change as new technologies and economic development programs profoundly affect families and communities. Research by sociologists and anthropologists on the social impacts of urbanization and industrialization on indigenous people, small farmers, and the urban poor attest to the presence and impact of these changes.

Scarcities of skilled manpower and an overabundance of unskilled labor are also problems. The presence of a massive urban poor who are pessimistic about development improving their lot is a further complication. Having a concept of the future is hard for many having to live from day-to-day. According to Suprapto (1990) *... one must take into account the existence of a floating mass living well under the poverty line whose view about the future may be difficult to elicit, and may even have negative repercussions.*

In many Third World countries the level of comprehension of the less educated, poorer strata about development is so low that one of the main purposes of EIA/SIA is educational. If a peasant farmer is to have an informed attitude on, for instance, an oil refinery in the local village area or district, the first step is one of education. Failing that, NGOs (non-government organizations) have a major role in *fast tracking* the educational process by acting as agents and negotiators on behalf or disadvantaged groups. Even with education and effective NGOs, the role of the bureaucrat and political minister is much more powerful than in First World countries.

Conflict, poverty, and the necessity of rapid change are factors significantly affecting decision makers' evaluations of social impact methodologies. Rancorous conflict between groups in a society is a barrier to the use of social impact assessment methodologies as it is to any *rational* planning technique. Extreme poverty diminishes the response capacity of community members and increases the necessity of introducing rapid economic growth programs. Severe need may preclude careful and long-term planning and impact assessment. Professionals in these circumstances will be pressured to concern themselves more with economic development goals than the possible consequences of development.

Summary and Conclusions

There are several important institutional barriers and constraints to the adoption of SIA theory and methodology by decision makers. Among these are SIA assumptions about local participation and involvement and the role and authority of bureaucrats and professionals who are more compatible with Western political liberalism than with the ideology and culture of political systems in Third World countries. Adoption of SIA is itself a complex process, as it is common for it to be partially rather than fully accepted by decision makers. For example, rather than evaluating the impacts of alternative projects, decision makers may select a development project and then call for an assessment of its social and environmental impacts. Impact assessment can only be useful if done in initial stages of the planning process.

Although the politics of development has affected social impact assessment, there are movements by national governments and international donor agencies to integrate impact assessment, including SIA, more fully with the planning process. EIA/SIA is by itself a limited decision-making tool when development plans are required. What is needed is an approach that incorporates potential social impacts at the design/planning stage, so that the best plans can be found and promoted. It should be more than a simple assessment of the costs and benefits of a project and its micro-alternatives. It may have political value in this regard in pluralist countries where people are well informed and trying to cope with development, but people also want efficient ways of selecting and promoting the most desirable forms of development.

The trend in the general EIA field is to integrate impact assessment with the planning and decision-making process. Integrated impact assessment and integrated economic and environmental planning programs by the World Bank and the Australian International Development Assistant Branch are examples of this trend (Hundloe 1989). The implication for SIA is that it needs to assume a positive role in development planning, properly integrated with economic and natural environment considerations.

REFERENCES

Berger, T.R. 1983. Resources Development and Human Values. *Impact Assessment Bulletin* 2(2):129-147.

Burdge, R.J. and Opryszek, P. 1984. Interdisciplinary problems in doing impact assessment: The Case of Lake Shelbyville. *Technological Forecasting and Social Change* 25(1):29-36.

Burdge, R.J. 1987. The Social Impact Assessment Model and The Planning Process. *Environmental Impact Assessment Review* 7(2):141-150.

Burdge, R.J. 1990. The Benefits of Social Impact Assessment in Third World Development. *Environmental Impact Assessment Review* 10(1/2):123-134.

Burdge, R.J. and Robertson, R.A. 1990. Social Impact Assessment and The Public Involvement Process. *Environmental Impact Assessment Review* 10(1/2):81-90.

Corbett, J. 1985. The Policy Context of Social Impact Analysis. *In Social Impact Analysis and Development Planning in the Third World.* W. D. Derman and S. Whiteford (eds). Boulder, Colo.: Westview.

Daneke, G.A., M. W. Garcia and D. P. Priscoli, eds. 1983. *Public Involvement and Social Impact Assessment.* Boulder, Colo.: Westview.

Derman, W.D. and S. Whiteford, eds. 1985. *Social Impact Analysis and Development Planning in the Third World.* Boulder, Colo.: Westview.

Friedland, R., F. F. Piven and R. R. Alford. 1977. Political Conflict, Urban Structure, and The Fiscal Crisis. *International Journal of Urban and Regional Research* 1(3):447-471.

Gibson, D.M., R. E. Rickson and J. S. Western. 1988. World Heritage Listing of Queensland's Wet Tropical Rainforest: Assessment of Social Impact. Final Report (no number). Canberra, Australia: Australian Department of the Arts, Sport, Environment, Technology and Territories.

Henry, R.J. 1990. Implementing Social Impact Assessment in Developing Countries. A Comparative Approach to The Structural Problems. *Environmental Impact Assessment Review* 10(1/2):91-101.

Hundloe, T. 1989. Environmental Policy and The Australian Aid Programme. Unpublished report. Canberra, Australia: Australian Development of Foreign Affairs.

Kahn, A.E. 1966. The Tyranny of Small Decisions: Market Failures, Imperfections, and The Limits of Economics. *International Review for Social Science* 19(2):23-45.

Milbrath, L. and R. E. Rickson. 1989. Report to The Environment Protection Administration. Unpublished report. Taipei, Taiwan, Republic of China.

Ruttan, V.W. 1984. The Green Revolution: Seven Generalizations. *In Leading Issues in Economic Development*, G.M. Meier (ed). New York: Oxford. 4th ed.

Suprapto, R.A. 1990. Social Impact Assessment and Planning: The Indonesian Experience. *Impact Assessment Bulletin* 8 (1/2): 25-28.

Westman, W.E. 1985. *Ecology, Impact Assessment, and Environmental Planning.* New York: John Wiley.

Wisner, B. 1985. Social Impact, Socialism, and The Case of Mozambique. In *Social Impact Analysis and Development Planning in the Third World*. W.D. Derman and S. Whitford (eds). Boulder, Colo.: Westview, pp. 262-282.

Chapter 19

THE BENEFITS OF SOCIAL IMPACT ASSESSMENT IN THIRD WORLD DEVELOPMENT[1]

Rabel J. Burdge

INTRODUCTION

Development implies improvement in social conditions and the well-being of the population as well as an increase in Gross Domestic Product (GDP). As a component in planning for development, social impact assessment (SIA) provides a method for incorporating social factors through the identification of those features of the social environment that have the greatest potential to affect and be affected by a proposed project or policy change.

SIA originated in the U.S. in response to legal interpretations of the 1969 National Environmental Policy Act (NEPA) which required *impact statements* to be prepared whenever a project would bring about *significant environmental alteration*. Subsequent legal interpretations mandated that federal agencies and project proponents include *social effects analysis* in development decisions.

The considerable differences in national context between North America and less developed countries (referred to here as Third World countries), makes it probable that suggestions about the introduction of SIA will be met with the response *...its a nice idea but SIA won't transfer to my country because of differences in culture, government controls, regulatory procedures, the education level of the population*. Nevertheless, it is the basic premise of this chapter that the benefits from incorporating SIA into the planning process are such that it must be given careful consideration by Third World planners.

Potential Benefits

The benefits of SIA accrue both to the project proponent (whether private sector or governmental) and to human communities impacted by development.

Benefits to the Proponent: A Higher Rate of Project Success - Knowledge of the way in which physical elements of a project interact with indigenous social organization and culture provides proponents with the opportunity to ensure there is no 'mismatch' between project and people. Conflicts could inhibit the achievement of the desired economic and institutional objectives. As one development expert points out, the failure to appreciate the importance of social factors in the past has *...led to resistance to*

[1]Abridged from the original. Rabel J. Burdge. 1990. The Benefits of Social Impact Assessment in Third World Development. *Environmental Impact Assessment Review*, 10(1/2):123-134. Reproduced here with permission of the author and the publisher.

change, total loss of capital investment in big agricultural projects, and the failure of many technical assistance programs to make the initial breakthrough in recipient cultures Okediji (1965). Many government funded projects in Third World countries have joint goals of the social and economic development of a particular area. For example, large-scale reservoir and population relocation projects are frequently viewed by governments as an opportunity to alter the economic base of the population and provide new services (Scudder 1968 and Cernea 1985). The use of SIA would prove a useful tool in such cases, allowing evaluation of the likelihood of the target groups of such projects being effectively reached, decreasing the likelihood of unanticipated negative impacts occurring and, generally, resulting in higher rate of project success. Examples of schemes which have proven excessively costly or have failed altogether because of inadequate consideration of social factors are numerous. In a hydro-electric project in Columbia, a delay of 3 years and subsequent loss of at least $100 million (1980 dollars) was incurred when the 3,000 residents of Penol refused to be relocated because they were originally left out of crucial decisions affecting their lives (Scudder 1968). Those rural Colombians were eventually relocated to their satisfaction. However, the use of SIA would have alerted planners to this problem and might have eliminated it by identifying local concerns and needs in advance. In addition, local people could provide input and receive information about the project and resettlement opportunities.

Benefits to the Population Affected: Evaluation of Project-Induced Change - The use of SIA in the planning process has the considerable benefit of identifying impacts prior to project implementation, thereby allowing modification in project design or mitigation measures to eliminate or reduce negative impacts.

Social Impact Assessment and Third World Countries - What's Being Done?

During the late 70s and early 80s there was a growing recognition among the international donor agencies of the need to include social factors in the design and implementation of projects they funded. Increased emphasis was placed on ensuring that the benefits of development reached the poorest - a goal seldom reached in the past. Achieving this objective necessitated a greater knowledge of the characteristics of the *target group*, their relationship to dominant political and social groups and to the environment that sustained them.

As a donor country, the U.S. requires preparation of environmental impact statements as specified under NEPA, to include the assessment of impacts on human populations. Social soundness analysis (SSA) was developed by the U.S. Agency for International Development (USAID) in response to NEPA and the New Direction Legislation for Development Assistance established by Congress in 1973 (USAID, 1981). Although social soundness analysis was not developed by persons in the SIA network, the approach is similar. In 1981, a review of that agency's experience with SSA found that although the quality and usefulness of such analyses varied, they recommended it remain a required component of the project design phase (Ingersoll *et al.*, 1981). These evaluators found a steady improvement in the quality of SSAs and noted that at least 25 percent of the 48 social analysis in their sample, significantly influenced the design of proposed project. In the case of the Guinea Bissau Rice Production Project (1980), the authors noted *...social analysis, which identified* *potential implementation problems or constraints, as well as potential solutions to these problems, were significantly more useful in the design phase of the project process than those which did not utilize it.*

The World Bank appointed its first full-time sociologist in 1974 and social scientists are now routinely employed in agricultural and rural development projects. Michael Cernea, a rural sociologist with the World Bank comments . . . *the very concept of a 'target group' required World Bank staff to learn about social characteristics, to include social stratification, ethnic and kinship systems, community structure, land rights and tenure arrangements.* He goes on to cite the example of a project in Africa where infrastructure and off-farm employment were to be created but where the supply and availability of labor were not calculated. A subsequent social assessment revealed the potential for serious labor shortages during harvest periods. The project was successfully revised to account for the unavailability of labor (Cernea 1985).

The World Health Organization (WHO), in particular the Regional Offices for Europe, has become involved in a number of activities aimed at the promotion of EIA/SIA methodology. Their interest arises out of their broad definition of health as a *state of physical, mental and social well-being*, and a recognition that in the recent past, a number of projects in Third World countries (notably water impoundments) have had unexpected negative social, environmental and health consequences (Giroult 1983). WHO officials have pointed out that costs in submitting major proposals to social impact assessment was far less than the cost for correcting unforeseen negative impacts that occurred after implementation.

In addition to international donor agencies previously mentioned and the International Monetary Fund, the number of Third World countries doing some form of EIA/SIA has increased in recent years. The Philippines, Taiwan, Kenya, Mexico, the Dominican Republic, the Republic of Korea, Thailand, Malaysia, and several middle-east countries require EIA for some types of projects. EIA is also conducted on a less formal basis in Bangladesh, India, Pakistan, Indonesia, Singapore, Sri Lanka and the Cook Islands. However, the extent to which social and cultural factors are included in the broader term *environment* varies considerably.

The North American Experience with SIA - Has it any Relevance for Third World Countries?

Because environmental and social impact assessment requires trained investigators and additional money during the planning stages - does this mean they are a luxury that Third World countries simply cannot afford? While it is true that SIA developed in countries that have reached a high level of economic growth and industrialization, it does not follow that SIA has no benefits to countries with less governmental and financial resources. Indeed SIA can play a valuable role in the achievement of the goal for balanced development since it represents a methodology for ensuring that unanticipated negative impacts of social change are minimized. With appropriate exposure, many community development workers or agricultural extension workers could make a valuable input to the SIA process.

SIA Saves Money in the Long Run - Critics of both environmental and social impact assessment are quick to point out that additional analysis add costs to the project.

However, a recent study concluded; *although there may be costs involved in preparing social soundness analysis of proposed projects, the cost incurred if such analyses are not prepared, in terms of the less than optimal project performance, may be even greater* (Ingersoll *et al.* 1981). **The costs of such failures may be especially severe in Third World countries where they are borne by the public sector more often than the private**. Third World countries may look at the industrial countries of the west which achieved their high levels of economic growth and high living standards without any system of social accounting and conclude that they do not need SIA. However, when compared to the experience of the western industrialized countries, the social change occurring elsewhere is on such a scale and over such a short time period that some way of understanding the consequences is required. By projecting the distribution of costs and benefits of a project or policy, SIA has the potential of being a useful tool in ensuring social equity - given the political will and ability to act on the results of the SIA analysis.

Historic Parallels - The considerable differences in the economic, political and cultural contexts between most of North American and other parts of the world has meant that SIA has largely evolved to meet needs and use information sources that are not always available in Third World countries. Nevertheless, there are important parallels between the experience of social change in certain parts of North America and those facing developing countries. To cite a historical example, the coming of the coal industry to the southern Appalachia region of the U.S. in the early 1920s set in motion a type of social change that consistently happens in the Third World. First, a cash economy dependent upon wage labor was introduced by outsiders into an isolated area characterized by subsistence agriculture. Next, a series of *boom-bust* cycles created a region characterized by extreme poverty that continues into the 90s. If a population becomes dependent upon rural resource extraction industries (that characterize many Third World countries) they might lose their traditional relationship to the land and hence become dependent upon wages or the welfare system. If the resource extraction industry experiences decline or is made redundant, it is rare that the dependent population can, or is willing to return to subsistence agriculture.

Research findings from Water Impoundment Studies - Social impacts have been shown to be similar in both First and Third World settings where relocation involves people who have developed strong ties to their land and close neighbors (Cernea, 1985). For example, Scudder (1968) found that a background of stress and feelings of loss prior to readjustment characterized the relocation project studies in West and Central Africa. Jacomina de Regt, a World Bank sociologist working with involuntary relocatees from the Yacyreta hydro-electric project in Argentina and Paraguay (underway since the mid 1970s) reported similar findings, including a higher incidence of mental illness, alcoholism, family stress and loss of income. In the U.S., research has shown that similar impacts have occurred in rural areas when involuntary relocation of the population has been necessary (Burdge and Ludtke, 1973; Johnson and Burdge 1974). In addition, research in both areas has shown that the elderly are similarly affected. Some variables, however do not apply to the North American situation. For example, relocatees in Third World countries often experience severely reduced nutrition levels before adjusting their agricultural techniques to the new environment. The magnitude of impacts is often much greater in Third World countries since daily life is more closely linked to the physical surroundings than is the case for more developed countries. The point here is that the findings are similar regardless of the stage of the country in economic development.

SIA and Native North American Populations - The closest parallel in development experience between North American and Third World countries occurs when indigenous populations are confronted with resource development or government policies affecting traditional land-use. By native populations we mean those North American Indian and Inuit populations of Alaska and Northern Canada. Many SIAs have been prepared in the U.S. and Canada to fulfill the requirement that the impacts of project development on native North Americans be reported. These experiences will prove useful when doing SIA in other parts of the world.

The need to re-examine commonly used SIA methods when dealing with different populations and cultures is illustrated by the failure of a questionnaire designed to gauge the opinions of the Zuni Indian tribe toward a flood protection scheme (USDA 1981). Explanations for a meager two percent response rate include language barriers and also cultural differences in the way of resolving community issues. A number of other SIAs have been conducted on indigenous populations facing the sale of mining and/or water rights of their lands. The assessments vary in quality and effectiveness. One problem seems to be lack of effective communication between assessor and assessed. The tribal leaders of the Papago people, for example, completely rejected the finding of the EIA/SIA that had been prepared concerning the use of their water resources to supply another tribe (USDI 1981). Tribal leaders felt they had been inadequately consulted, their opinions ignored, and that they were losing resources essential to their future well-being.

The Role of the Social Impact Assessor

Canadian assessors, who have worked with northern Indian and Inuit people, make a convincing argument for using the qualitative approach rather than statistical analysis when reporting SIAs on indigenous cultures. (The diversity of cultures which exist in Canada makes that country's experience particularly relevant to Third World settings). Tester (1981) points out that *questionnaires and surveys characterized by the impersonal approach to respondents is simply not respected, understood or appreciated by native peoples*. Findings from assessments using such techniques may be met with local resistance. He goes on to say that there is often considerable need and desire on the part of local people for more information about the proposed project. Thus the assessor could play an important role in disseminating information on realistic estimates of likely social impacts (as opposed to the public relations type of information put out by the proponent).

The approach advocated by Tester and others is very similar to ethnographic methods used by anthropologists in that the emphasis is on informal, two-way communication between the assessor and the assessed. In order to understand the relationship between the population and their environment and thus predict impacts resulting from environmental alteration, the assessor assumes the role of *participant-observer*. Information gained through use of this method can also be very useful in planning for development since it involves assessment of the needs and goals of the community. Drawbacks to the participant observer method include the time it takes to do the study and need for highly skilled workers. Quantitative background data may be used to supplement the results obtained from close field observation.

The Berger Inquiry (Gamble 1978) into the building of the Mackenzie Valley pipeline in the Yukon Territory and Northeastern British Columbia, illustrated one approach for the social assessor that might be used on large scale projects. Public involvement, as a way of collecting information for assessment, was obtained through an extensive series of public meetings held in the towns and villages in which the native peoples lived. Recognizing the potential language barriers to effective assessment, translators were used so the views of non-english speaking tribal members could be included in the testimony. Another formidable barrier to successful representation of the views of indigenous populations is the imbalance between financial resources available to project proponent and supporters on the one hand, and tribal organizations and groups opposing the development on the other. To overcome this problem the Berger Inquiry made social impact assessment funds available to indigenous groups who could demonstrate that their views were important to the overall assessment.

In a recent article outlining the social soundness procedures utilized by USAID, Hansen (1985) points out that the social assessor must be a competent professional, have a working knowledge of the social organization and the culture in which the project is being conducted, and be both *applied* and *interdisciplinary* in orientation.

Suggestions for Implementing Social Impact Assessment in Third World Countries

Use Existing Organizational Resources Where Possible - The constraints of limited financial and trained manpower resources in Third World countries means that time consuming and overly complicated procedures should be avoided along with the creation of additional bureaucratic machinery within the donor or lending agency.

Flexibility in Choice of Methodology - Wholesale adoption of one methodology over another should be avoided. For example, it may not be a choice of the U.S. version of SIA (which is somewhat more quantitative and concentrates on large-scale demographic and economic related social changes) or the Canadian type of SIA (which relies more heavily on participant observation and active involvement of the assessor). Rather, elements of both may be used in combination to meet a particular country's needs. As Canter (1983) points out, methodologies are like tools which can be used to aid the impact assessor and thus there is no *right* one, rather they depend upon the particular development situation at hand.

Use of Nationals - SIA practitioners working in Third World countries must be recruited and trained from among the host country population. Not only will this make the process less expensive but it will also decrease the likelihood of a perceptual gap occurring between the researcher and the community under investigation. As Roper (1983) comments . . . *dissonance is most severe when the various parties involved differ in language, history and culture.* If this gap is present it may mean that the costs and benefits as perceived by the assessor may differ from the way they are perceived by those directly affected. USAID utilizes a mixture of host and donor country personnel in developing the project paper (PP) for each proposed project.

Use of Appropriate Methods and Concepts - Certain social indicators, public involvement techniques, and economic multipliers, for example, may not be suitable for local conditions or relevant to local concerns. Indicators of health and literacy will be more pertinent for the development concerns in Third World countries than they are in North America. The SIA process should be kept flexible and be subjected to frequent evaluation and revision if monitoring reveals the methods and indicators being used are not helpful in identifying and understanding social change.

Quantification - Quantification of social characteristics and impacts is desirable because policy makers and planners appreciate the simplicity of numbers. However, well documented qualitative indicators provide the context within which to evaluate social change.

Allowing Native Populations to Express Their Opinions - Methods for obtaining input from the impacted area will depend on such factors as the way people traditionally resolve community issues and the scale of the project and population affected. The example of the Mackenzie Pipeline Inquiry represents an approach that could be adopted for very large projects, but which might not be possible for smaller ones. Regardless of the setting, indigenous and impacted populations must be allowed to express their opinions in their own language.

Limitations of Ethnographic Techniques - Ethnographic techniques may prove useful in SIA to ascertain peoples beliefs concerning project impacts on their livelihoods, and whether they perceive these changes to be beneficial. It is important that all social groups in a region be included in assessment. However, because the ethnographic approach is lengthy, very descriptive, and requires highly trained observers, it must be supplemented with a variety of secondary data sources. Social assessors must consult the indepth anthropological literature that has accumulated about most Third World countries.

Selecting the SIA Variables - Choice of which social impact assessment variables to include should be make after a review of the findings on the impact of similar projects in the area under current investigation (Burdge 1987). **Scoping** should reveal the impacts that the proponent foresees as likely *benefits* of the project, e.g., more local jobs and higher per capita income. Scoping will also help to identify what the local population anticipates will be the negative impacts or *costs*, e.g., the loss of local autonomy or increased drunkenness, as well as their evaluation of the meaning of social change which will accompany the *benefits* of the project.

Avoiding Repetitive Data Collection - The financial and personnel constraints facing Third World countries make it necessary that repetitive data collection be avoided. Information from previous SIAs or SSAs must be widely shared. If a particular region is experiencing rapid growth through numerous developments and is somewhat culturally homogeneous, a case should be made for preparing a single, regional assessment and supplementing it with additional site specific data. Cochrane (1979) suggests that a national inventory drawn up through *social mapping*, might be useful in social and economic development planning. Such an inventory could be used when choosing appropriate sites for development projects or for designing projects that are compatible with local social and cultural characteristics.

SIA and the Planning Process - SIA should never, and in particular in Third World countries, be used as a justification for decisions already made. The assessment must be integrated into the planning process at an early stage and should be used in formulating and choosing among alternatives. For example, the alternatives to a particular site for a hospital should include not only other locations, but also other means for delivering health services. It may be that a number of mobile hospital units would be more effective in improving health delivery in a region rather than a centralized hospital, even though the latter may represent a monument to political patronage. In the rush to improve project efficiency, the imposition of the North American culture should be avoided.

SIA and Project Implementation - If possible, those conducting SIAs should include specific recommendations as to appropriate mitigation measures, as well as subsequent monitoring and ex-post facto analysis procedures. Also, if it is a development project that is under consideration, any potential implementation problems and methods for overcoming these problems for the indigenous population should be identified. If such is followed, SIA will become an indispensable form of information gathering for decision-makers. By better understanding the social changes resulting from development an appreciation of the benefits will be enhanced.

CONCLUSION

The expansion of social impact assessment into Third World countries will continue to be problematic and uneven. Very few of the legal and administrative frameworks have been created to define the responsibilities of the various governmental departments in the environmental and social assessment processes. The financial limitations and the shortage of skilled personnel mean that the assessment process will have to be adapted to available resources. Within each country, SIAs should not be developed in isolation from each other. By sharing information on actual impacts and successful methodologies, unnecessary duplication will be avoided. Methodologies and findings from North American assessments may prove useful since there are many parallels between the social change in some parts of the U.S. and Canada and that occurring in Third World countries. However, a social impact indicator may be valid for inclusion in North America, but not necessarily appropriate when applied elsewhere. Fortunately, the social assessors in Third World countries will reap the benefit of much of the *trial and error* that has been done on SIAs in North America.

The potential benefits of SIA outweigh its costs and the advantages accrue to both the project proponents and to the impacted populations. Proponents (almost always governments in Third World settings) would be alerted, through the use of SIA, to any local factors which may inhibit the economic and/or social goals of the project. Having SIA information prior to implementation will ensure there is no *mismatch* between project and population and thus increase the likelihood of success. The populations affected would gain both through the opportunity to provide input into decision making and in receiving information about projected changes to their environment. Based on social assessment findings, projects may be redesigned or mitigation measures introduced thereby reducing negative impacts. By identifying the social distribution of the 'costs' and 'benefits' of projects, SIA can play a role in issues of equity and in understanding the direction of social change.

As pointed out in chapter 20, project evaluation in Third World countries is largely determined by culture, religion and politics. I once had a student who dropped out of my SIA course because she felt politics dictated all decisions. She was more interested in controlling the political structure rather than understanding the social consequences of development. My response to her was that social impact assessment cuts down on the amount of politics in the decision process and allows the human considerations to receive more attention in the planning process.

REFERENCES

Burdge, R.J. 1987. The Social Impact Assessment Model and the Planning Process. *Environmental Impact Assessment Review*, 7(2): pp. 141-150.

Burdge, R.J. and R.L. Ludtke. 1973. Social Separation Among Displaced Rural Families: The Case of Flood Control Reservoirs. In *Social Behavior, Natural Resources and the Environment*. W. R. Burch *et al*. eds, New York: Harper and Row , pp 85-100.

Canter, L. 1983. *EIA Methods*. Presented at International Seminar on Environmental Impact Assessment, 17-19 July, University of Aberdeen, U.K.

Cernea, M. 1985. *Putting People First: Sociological Variables in Rural Development*. New York: Oxford University Press.

Cochrane, G. 1979. *The Cultural Appraisal of Development Projects*. New York: Praeger.

Gamble, D.J. 1978. The Berger Inquiry: An Impact Assessment Process. *Science*, 199 (3): 946-952.

Giroult, E. 1983. Keynote Address on Behalf of the World Health Organization, Presented at International Seminar on Environmental Impact Assessment, 17-19 July, University of Aberdeen, U.K.

Gold, Raymond L. 1985. *Ranching, Mining, and the Human Impact of Natural Resource Development*. New Brunswick, NJ: Transaction Books.

Hansen, David O. 1985. Social Soundness Analysis: An Institutionalized Role for Social Scientists in AID's Assistance Program. *The Rural Sociologist*, 5 (1): 37-42.

Ingersoll, J., M. Sullivan and B. Lenkerd. 1981. *Social Analysis of AID Projects: A Review of the Experience.* Washington, D.C.: Agency for International Development Report, prepared for AID/Bureau for Science and Technology.

Johnson, S. and R.J. Burdge. 1974. An Analysis of Community and Individual Reactions to Forced Migration due to Reservoir Construction, in *Water and Community Development.* D.R. Field *et al.* eds. Ann Arbor, MI: Ann Arbor Science Publishers, pp 169-188.

Okediji, O.O. 1965. The Socio-Cultural Problems in the Western Nigeria Land Settlement Scheme: A Case Study. *Nigerian Journal of Economic and Social Studies*, 7: 301-310.

Roper, R. 1983. Ethnography. In *Social Impact Assessment Methods.* K. Finsterbusch, L.G. Llewellyn and C.P. Wolf eds. Beverly Hills, CA: Sage Publications, pp. 95-107.

Scudder, T. 1968. Social Anthropology, Man-Made Lakes and Population Relocation in Africa. *Anthropological Quarterly*, 41: 168-176.

Tester, F.J. 1981. SIA-Approaching the Fourth World, in *Social Impact Assessment - Theory, Methods and Practice.* F. J. Tester and W. Mykes eds. Calgary, Alberta, Canada: Detselig Enterprises Limited.

U.S. Agency for International Development. 1981. Social Soundness Analysis. in *Aid Project Assistance Handbook 3*, Annex 4A. Washington, D.C.

U.S. Department of the Interior, Bureau of Indian Affairs. *Draft EIS Crow/Shell Coal Lease*, February, 1981.

U.S. Department of the Interior, Bureau of Indian Affairs. Final EIS-AK-Chin Water Supply Project, July 1981.

U.S. Department of the Interior, Bureau of Land Management. Draft EIS Bisti, De-na-zin and Ah-shi-sle-pah Proposed Wilderness Areas, 1982.

U.S. Department of the Interior, Water and Power Resources. A Social Impact Assessment of the Zuni Indian Reservation, (date not given).

Chapter 20

FUTURE PROSPECTS FOR INTEGRATING IMPACT ASSESSMENT INTO THE PLANNING PROCESS[1]

Roy E. Rickson, Rabel J. Burdge, and Audrey Armour

Impact assessment is most successful when fully integrated with planning at the appropriate jurisdiction level where project development occurs. When this integration is accomplished, environmental and socio-economic factors become central to planning decisions, rather than being treated as *external* or peripheral to the planning process. Achieving such integration, of course, requires a sound understanding of the nature of planning on the one hand, and how advances in knowledge about impact assessment and its many methodologies can fit into modern planning models on the other. Additionally, functional integration of the key components of the planning process, from project inception to post-development monitoring is an important goal of modern comprehensive planning. This kind of integration is essential because, as a dynamic process, planning requires data collection across time and ongoing revision of plans to ensure that planning goals are being met (Armour 1990). Similarly, impact assessment requires successful internal integration of all phases from scoping to monitoring, mitigation to mediation as well as continual and cumulative assessment of results.

Integrating Planning and Impact Assessment

Resistance to integrating impact assessment into the planning process diminishes the significance of planning rather than simply affecting impact assessment and its contribution to decision-making and planning. As an integral part of planning, impact assessment provides a theoretical framework, a body of research methodologies and political assumptions which are, on the surface at least, compatible with modern planning. These include initial investigation of conditions which would be affected by projects or policies, analyses and predictions of desired change through to mediation of conflicting interests and mitigation of undesirable consequences. Any dynamic planning model would necessarily include these dimensions.

There are two approaches to the incorporation of impact assessment into planning (Armour *et al.*, 1977). Integration, broadly speaking, involves changes in both administrative (legal-rational) and institutional processes. The first simply means that development law and policy are made to explicitly include statements specifying that impact assessments are necessary before development plans are accepted by legal authorities as legitimate. The second is more basic and refers to changes in attitude and *ways of doing business* such that social and environmental effects are incorporated into

---

[1]Abridged from the original. Roy E. Rickson, Rabel J. Burdge and Audrey Armour. 1990. Future Prospects for Integrating Impact Assessment Into The Planning Process. *Impact Assessment Bulletin*, 8(1/2): 347-357. Reproduced here with permission of the authors and the publisher.

all stages of development-related decision making, from the initiation of plans through their implementation.

In the first instance, the concern is with the structure of law and policy, what is written and what is required in order to make impact and/or assessment a legal and/or formal part of the process of planning and development. The second is more complex, reaching as it does to fundamental considerations of values and the social structures associated with development. Equity, the way in which we define *development*, and the roles that organizations (e.g., business and industry, government agencies, voluntary associations) and scientists and professionals play in the development process are all of concern. In this regard, the concept of *sustainable development* is a most appropriate one for modern planning, and impact assessment can be a major aid to achieving such a goal. **Sustainable development is progress that meets the needs of the present without compromising the ability of future generations to meet their own needs** (WCED, 1987:43). In such a framework, *temporal equity* (meeting the needs of present generations) is equated with *intergenerational equity* (where the goal is to "save the soil for our children" or "remember , we are borrowing this land from our children").

Comprehensive planning models that have emerged in the last two or three decades have incorporated social and environmental concerns in competition with economic goals in planning. Still, a considerable stumbling block has been that professional planners and the politicians that they serve are more responsive to short-run economic objectives and tax enhancing benefits than to social needs and long-run environmental goals.

Economic values are of course deeply institutionalized in modern societies due to obvious public concerns for economic well-being, government fiscal goals and those of powerful private industrial and business corporations. There are then strong and deeply rooted institutional constraints to full incorporation of impact assessment into the planning process. A desire for economic growth and the short-term benefits of economic security they bring is one set of constraints with a structural basis for resistance to be found in what Schnaiberg (1980) refers to as the *treadmill of the commons*. We seek individual enhancement to the determinant of long-run community stability.

Nonetheless, in recent years there has been a gradual move towards greater integration of economic environmental and social values. International and national government planning now (by the necessity of knowledge, political pressure, law, policy, public awareness and participation) incorporates economic development, environmental and sociological perspectives. Such changes have partly resulted from the publication of major reports that clearly demonstrate the seriousness of environmental pollution and its socioeconomic impacts (CEQ and U.S. Department of State 1982; Repetto 1985; Clark 1989; WCED 1987). In general, these reports have supported arguments for the necessity of integrating or balancing economic development goals with a concern for environmental quality.

Though some progress has been made, it is evident that basic structural change, in which international organizations and national governments fundamentally change how they plan, invest and use their resources is needed if environmental quality and social equity goals are to be fully integrated with development decisions. The Brundtland report (WCED 1987) makes an important point in this regard. It notes that a major institutional gap in planning for development must be closed. The *institutional gap is that* . . .

> *Those responsible for managing natural resources and protecting the environment are institutionally separated from those responsible for managing the economy. The real world of interlocked economic and ecological systems will not change; the policies and institutions concerned must (WCED p. 9).*

According to the Brundtland report (WCED 1987) there are two principal dimensions of integration which fundamentally affect our ability to undertake policies associated with sustainable development. One is based on changing public values, awareness of environmental problems and active citizen participation in expressing those views. Ultimately, private and public decision-making bodies are dependent on public legitimization of their goals and policies. People who manage such organizations and politicians who make laws will shift their overt values, attitudes and actions accordingly. A second point of integration (and one that is repeatedly emphasized in the EIA-SIA literature) is that the processes of economic, environmental and social planning and the process of impact assessment should be considered as integrally related and the structure of decision making altered accordingly.

Third World Countries

Numerous authors have referred to potential and present benefits of impact assessment theory and methodologies for facilitating Third World development (Henry 1990; and Burdge 1990). Progress has been made as many developing nations have enacted legislation and formed policies requiring impact assessments of development projects (Chuen 1990). These initiatives are reinforced by the policies of major international donor and aid agencies such as the World Bank, the Asian Development Bank and the United Nations agencies, particularly (UNEP) United Nations Environment Programme and (UNESCO) United Nations Educational, Scientific, and Cultural Organization and the World Health Organization which have accepted and promote the importance of *development without destruction* (UNEP 1988; Htun 1990; cf. Cernea 1988). Overcoming *institutional constraints* to full incorporation of impact assessment procedures into development planning remains, however, a considerable challenge. This is of course true in both the so-called developed and the developing world (Rickson *et al.* 1990). There is some evidence that integration of impact assessment (environmental and social) with economic planning and development is occurring. Nevertheless, there is considerable room for criticism and pessimism as to the rate of change (Armour 1990), and two writers suggest that, in the case of the World Bank, the change is more rhetorical than real (Hayter and Watson 1985). Henry (1990) is cautious about the potential success of SIA/EIA's contribution to development as the result of several structural factors: poverty and hunger, indebtedness, rural poverty, urban congestion, economic mismanagement, severe conditions of socioeconomic and political inequities. Fuggle (1990) argues that impact assessment procedures have been slow to affect decision making in Third World countries because EIA procedures have been perceived as causing expense and delay, cumbersome to implement and generally undesirable.

Incorporation of impact assessment into planning processes in developing nations clearly requires revisions of EIA/SIA models (Fuggle 1990) and recognition of the severe problems and cultural contexts to which a western oriented planning technique such as impact assessment must be adapted. Burdge (1990) underscores this in pointing to the lack of trained personnel, deficiencies in data collection and a cultural history which makes it difficult to incorporate impact assessment into traditional British Towne Planning procedures.

Newly Industrialized Countries

Evidence from most newly industrialized countries is that people now want a balance between economic growth, environmental quality and the general quality of life. Environmental quality is therefore on both the international and national political agendas. However, the concern is for more than quality of the human and physical environment *per se*. Equally important has been demands by local community members for the right to participate in decisions about development which impact upon their communities and individual lives. As a result, public opinion combined with active and political powerful environmental movement organizations substantially influence political decision-making. The political acceptability of environmental concerns has, to some extent, counterbalanced the personal and structural commitments to economic growth as a primary indicator of community, society and political success.

Almost any newly industrialized country could be used as an example of serious environmental problems and the contradictions present when economic development is the only goal. Taiwan is an excellent case of a newly emerged, highly sophisticated industrial society that is now struggling with the serious environmental and social impacts of it's *economic miracle*. Taiwan's overwhelming and successful commitment to economic growth culminated in extremely serious pollution problems and has lead to myriad serious social impacts (Rickson and Chu 1989). Hsiao's (1990) research in Taiwan has shown that citizens now rank environmental concerns as one of the most critical in their society. The same study by Hsiao also found that people overwhelmingly accept that environmental pollution will be the number one problem in years to come. The growing public awareness of environmental pollution as a social problem in Taiwan has mobilized the environmental movement and provided it with wide-spread political legitimacy. Health risks perceived by the public have been a major factor in mobilization of conservation and anti-pollution associations.

Recognition that the social and environmental impacts of its rapid economic development threaten the basis of its wealth and further economic development has forced Taiwan's political leaders to begin to address the balance between environmental concerns and economic development goals. It has an effective and influential federal government agency, the Environmental Protection Administration, sponsoring research and actively implementing law and policies associated with environmental management including, of course, social and environmental impact assessment. However, commitments to economic growth are deeply institutionalized in countries such as Taiwan and the proof of commitments will be the long-term willingness of the Taiwanese public and government to invest the large sums of money and human capital it will take to redress the damage done by the rapid, single focused and unrestrained economic growth.

Organization and Community Level

Most of the impact assessment literature has concentrated on incorporation of impact assessment procedures at the societal or government planning level in both First and Third World countries. Pollution from industrial waste, however, is still a serious problem and even though substantial progress has been made, company managers in all parts of the world continue to resist accepting industrial pollution as a cost of production and a social obligation (Rickson 1985; Clark 1989). First World multi-national corporations have shipped their wastes to selected Third World countries in attempts to avoid restrictive anti-pollution laws and policies in their own country.

The influence of industrial corporations in both First and Third World countries pose a considerable dilemma for integrating environmental management and impact assessment considerations into the decision-making process. Multi-national corporations are both politically powerful and a major source of toxic waste. Remembering that the environmental movement and associated environmental management techniques such as impact assessments emerged only in the past twenty-five years or so, progress has been made. However, deeply rooted institutional commitments by societies to economic growth and by industrial corporations to the maximization of profits, growth and efficiency, are fundamental constraints to incorporation of impact assessment techniques into plans for project development.

Successful implementation of impact assessment procedures requires that local communities incorporate EIA into their planning. Research on communities in every local conclusively demonstrate that public awareness about environmental pollution and its social impacts has increased dramatically. Community generated protests and the expansion of the environmental movement have and will continue to have substantial national and local impact. Community reactions to development are increasingly important because of their influence on regional and national politics.

There are considerable opportunities for making progress at the local level, but also serious constraints to integrating impact assessment into planning at that level. In most countries, local action is decisive in terms of the acceptance of planning programs initiated at the national level. Even though communities may have little actual political power at the national level, they often have de facto power through simple resistance and as a result of personnel or financial limitations by federal agencies in implementing environmental management or impact assessment policies. Local communities, however, often face a serious problem: impact assessment procedures are often perceived as having the potential to delay development projects to the detriment of the local citizens the projects are intended to serve. Community leaders often, therefore, have more difficulty balancing development with impact assessment and environmental management than do their counterparts at the state, provincial or federal level.

Impact Assessment as a Learning Process

In a recent book, Milbrath (1989) suggests that the solution to modern environmental problems and development of a *sustainable* society is *learning our way out*. Impact assessment is essentially a learning process, which when appropriately understood and applied, has the capacity to ensure that information about impacts of development (short and long-term social and environmental costs), shares equal billing with information about the possible economic benefits of development projects. Critiques of impact assessment procedures and recognition of powerful institutional constraints have pointed out the difficulty of achieving this critical goal (Schnaiberg 1980).

There are serious learning problems faced by societies. Knowledge production, scientific and technical work have been closely aligned with the economic goals of business and industry, and the general industrial system which Schnaiberg includes within the term *treadmill of production*. The critical question remains: how may industrial societies (both First and Third World) learn to deal with critical problems such as environmental pollution and socio-political inequity when solutions to these problems require change by powerful institutions committed to short-term maximization of economic growth? Part of the problem clearly is that scientists dedicated to research on development have often, in the past, overlooked some adverse consequences of technological change and rapid economic growth. Communication and cooperation between *impact* scientists and those committed to more conventional research goals is clearly needed. This, in turn, will require change by powerful educational and research institutions such as universities and research centres to incorporate environmental considerations and impact assessment into their teaching and research agendas.

It is clear that humans know much more about production than conservation. When we try to deal with critical problems such as environmental pollution, we typically find that: our knowledge is limited or undeveloped; we have great difficulty getting the type of information we need; and, social and political institutions are often resistant or incapable of incorporating such information into their decision-making and action frameworks (cf. Rickson, 1977). However, the materials included in this book and the accompanying volume, *A Community Guide to Social Impact Assessment*, show that progress has been made in the accumulated knowledge about new learning systems such as impact assessment and how the serious challenge of utilizing this information in the planning process remains.

REFERENCES

Armour, Audrey. 1990. Integrating Impact Assessment into the Planning Process. *Impact Assessment Bulletin*, 8(1/2): 3-14.

Armour, Audrey, Beate Bowron, Earl Miller and Michael Miloff. 1977. A Framework for Community Impact Assessment. In *Methodology of Social Impact Assessment*. K. Finsterbusch and C.P. Wolf, eds. Stroudsburg, PA: Dowden, Hutchinson and Ross, pp. 24-35.

Burdge, Rabel J. 1990. The Benefits of Social impact Assessment in the Third World. *Environmental Impact Assessment Review*, 10(1/2): 123-134.

Cernea, M.M. 1988. Involuntary Resettlement in Development Projects: Policy Guidelines. In *World Bank-Financed Projects*. The World Bank: Washington D.C., World Bank Technical Paper Number 80.

Chase, A. 1990. Anthropology and Impact Assessment: Development Pressures and Indigenous Interests in Australia. *Environmental Impact Assessment Review*, 10(1/2): 11-23.

Chuen, Ho Yueh. 1990. Legal and Institutional Arrangements for Environmental Impact Assessment in Malaysia. *Impact Assessment Bulletin*, 8(1/2): 309-318.

Clark, W.C. 1989. Managing Planet Earth. *Scientific American*, 261: 18-28.

Fuggle, Richard F. 1990. Integrated Environmental Management: An Appropriate Approach to Environmental Concerns in Developing Countries. *Impact Assessment Bulletin*, 8 (1/2): 31-45.

Giles, L.Y. 1986. Socio-economic Monitoring as a Planning Tool. In *Impact Assessment Today: Volume I*. H. A. Becker and A.L. Porter eds. State University of Utrecht: Utrecht, Netherlands, pp. 31-49.

Council on Environmental Quality (CEQ) and the U.S. Department of State. 1982. *The Global 2000 Report to the President*. Penguin, New York.

Hayter, T. and C. Watson. 1985. *AID Rhetoric and Reality*. Pluto Press, London.

Henry, Reg J. 1990. Implementing Social Impact Assessment in Developing Countries: A Comparative Approach to Structural Problems. *Environmental Impact Assessment Review*, 10(1/2): 91-101.

Hsiao, Hsin-Huang Michael. 1990. The Rise of Environmental Consciousness in Taiwan. *Impact Assessment Bulletin*, 8(1/2): 217-231.

Htun, Nay. 1990. EIA and Sustainable Development. *Impact Assessment Bulletin*, 8(1/2): 16-23.

Milbrath, Lester W. 1989. *Envisioning a Sustainable Society: Learning Our Way Out*. Albany: State University of New York Press.

Repetto, R. (ed). 1985. *The Global Possible*. A World Resources Institute Book, New Haven, CT: Yale University Press.

Rickson, R.E. and C. Chu. 1989. Economic miracles and environmental dilemmas: The case of Taiwan. *Society and Natural Resources*, 2(2): 143-150.

Rickson, R.E., R.J. Burdge, T. Hundloe, G.T. McDonald. 1990. Institutional Constraints to Adoption of Social Impact Assessment as a Decision-Making and Planning Tool. *Environmental Impact Assessment Review*, 10(1/2): 233-247.

Rickson, R.E. 1985. Comparative Bases of Industry Pollution Abatement and Commercial Innovation: Implications for Water Resource Management. *Water Resources Bulletin*, 21, 89-97.

Schnaiberg, Alan. 1980. *The Environment: From Surplus to Scarcity*. New York: Oxford University Press.

United Nations Environment Programme (UNEP). 1988. *Environmental Impact Assessment: Basic Procedures for Developing Countries*, Bangkok, Thailand, Regional Office for Asia and the Pacific.

World Commission on Environment and Development (WCED). 1987. *Our Common Future*. London and New York: Oxford Press.